THE RAMAYAN OF TULSIDAS

THE RAMAYAN OF TULSIDAS OR THE BIBLE OF NORTHERN INDIA

by
J. M. MACFIE

PILGRIMS PUBLISHING
◆Varanasi◆

THE RAMAYAN OF TULSIDAS
J. M. Macfie

Published by:
PILGRIMS PUBLISHING

An imprint of:
PILGRIMS BOOK HOUSE
(Distributors in India)
B 27/98 A-8, Nawabganj Road
Durga Kund, Varanasi-221010, India
Tel: 91-542-2314060
Fax: 91-542-2312456
E-mail: pilgrims@satyam.net.in
Website: www.pilgrimsbooks.com

First Published in 1908

Cover design by Sasya

ISBN: 81-7769-051-5

Printed in India at Pilgrim Press Pvt. Ltd. Lalpur Varanasi

INTRODUCTION TO THE NEW EDITION

Tulsi Das, the 16th century doyen of the Hindi literary world, as well as a prime mover and follower of the *Bhakti* movement, created the *Ramcharit Manas* (Ramayana), an epic of immense proportions, which even today carries great weight amongst the vast Hindu majority. Given the importance of his work especially in relation to the religious feelings of the majority of the Hindu population, it becomes necessary that a critical approach to his work should be made for those who truly wish to go to its depth and understand the implications therein.

Tulsi Das' leanings towards the *Sagun Bhakti* school (devotion to a personal god) led him to take up the task of relating the story of Lord Rama, the seventh incarnation of the God Vishnu. The story of Rama has become one of the most popular throughout India and has also spread to surrounding countries where it is presented in the form of a dance drama even today. The author has meticulously dealt with each chapter and given ample reference to the original text including lengthy passages translated from the *Ramcharit Manas* (Ramayana).

The author has shown a remarkably deep understanding of the subject, providing the student with a profound insight into this outstanding epic. The book provides a foundation from which one may then go back to and gain a better understanding of the original. As the author tells us this poem is in no way a simple translation of the Sanskrit written almost a millennium ago by Valmiki. We are told that he (Tulsi Das) was too great a poet to be a mere imitator. It appears from the text that Tulsi Das had wished to depict the character of Lord Rama after his own fashion. Notwithstanding the fact that he was an orthodox Hindu he was more progressive and wished to go beyond the earlier beliefs and practices of the Hindus.

Forming a cornerstone of religious beliefs and practices Tulsi Das' Ramayan stands almost at par with the Bhagavad-Gita in its importance to the Hindu community at large. In fact it is more popular with the masses as they are able to relate more easily to the characters of Rama, Laxman, Bharat and Satrughan. The stories of his valor and chivalry inspiring the masses to mould their lives on the same pattern as well as entertaining them during the long winter nights or hot summer evenings. These stories are re-enacted even today throughout South East Asia in the form of lavishly arranged dance dramas, which not only entertain the local people but also thousands of Western tourists. One of the most famous being the Lila found in Ramnagar near Varanasi, the seat of Hindu learning and orthodoxy, where for almost a month (sometime in October or Kuwar according to the Hindu calendar) the whole of the Ramayana is acted out by specially trained artists who claim to experience a divine intervention whilst the are acting.

The author's interest in the Hindu epics is reflected in his other publications, which include *Myths and Legends of Northern India, A Summary of the Mahabharat, The Ramayana of Valmiki, etc.*

Christopher N Burchett
June 2003
Varanasi

PREFACE

THE doctrine of *bhakti*, or devotion to God, runs like a thread of gold through the web of Hindu religious literature. The speculations of her philosophers could not satisfy the heart of India. The teaching of Monism, which declared that there existed but One Spirit, and that all else was an illusion—*maya*—" left no room for the exercise of love and piety."

The earliest exposition of bhakti is to be found in the *Bhagavadgita*, where, alongside of other teaching with which it fails to harmonise, it is definitely proclaimed that *devotion* to a personal God is a path by which a worshipper can most surely escape from the burden of re-birth. The warmth with which this belief was held depended on the individual temperament. Sometimes the devotion in which men indulged was more of the nature of contemplation than of love. Sometimes it expressed itself in forms that ignored all restraint. But nowhere has it reached a higher and purer level than in the writings of Tulsidas. Born four hundred years ago, his influence continues to this day over the whole of Northern India.

The following pages are an attempt to expound the teaching of his best-known poem. The choice of the sub-title is no exaggeration. The book is indeed the Bible of Northern India. Among the half-dozen volumes which a village may contain, this is sure to be one.

Writing in the vernacular which all could understand, proclaiming a gospel for low caste as well as high, bidding them give their love and worship to Rama, the purest manifestation of God which India knows, Tulsidas was loyal to the reforms which his great predecessor, Ramanand, had introduced. But the fact cannot be ignored that in other respects he remained an orthodox Hindu, combining his worship of Rama with a belief in all his country's gods.

This is no disadvantage to the student of Hinduism, because there is probably no book in existence which gives such a complete and vivid picture of what the average Hindu, at his best, believes as the Ramayan of Tulsidas.

J. M. MACFIE.

AJMER, RAJPUTANA.

"The religion of Monism did not satisfy my heart. . . . How can a soul in the grip of illusion (*maya*), detached and stupid, be the same as God ?" Uttar 170 (107) 185.

"Let others worship the quality-less Brahm, the invisible, of whom the Vedas sing. But my choice is the divine Rama, Koshal's king, endowed with qualities and real. May he receive me as his own servant, and give me devotion to himself." Lanka, 130 (109) 139.

"The Adorable (*bhagwan*) is one, passionless, formless, nameless, unborn ; He is existence, thought, joy ; the supreme abode. He pervades all things. He exists in all forms. He assumes a body and performs many deeds simply for the sake of those devoted to Him. He is supremely merciful and full of love to His servants, very affectionate to those who are His own, and in His compassion is not angry with them. He is the restorer of that which is past, the protector of the humble, the sincere and powerful Lord." Bal. 17 (17) 22.

"Knowing that everything in the universe, animate and inanimate, consists of Rama, I ever worship, with joined hands, the lotus feet of all things. I worship gods, demons, men, serpents, birds, ghosts, departed ancestors, gandharvas, kinnars and night walkers : may they all be merciful to me." Bal. 10 (10) 15.

"He who does not love Shiva's lotus feet cannot please Rama even in a dream." Bal. 113 (111) 127.

"Profound meditation, the repetition of prayers, the giving of gifts, the practice of asceticism, the various kinds of abstinence, sacrifice and vows do not secure Rama's compassion as love alone can do." Lanka, 138 (114) 148.

NOTE ON ABBREVIATIONS AND SPELLING

THE seven books of the poem with the corresponding abbreviations are: Bal Kand (Bal.); Ayodhya Kand (Ayodh.); Aranya Kand (Aranya); Kishkindha Kand (Kish.); Sundar Kand (Sundar); Lanka Kand (Lanka); Uttar Kand (Uttar).

The numbers are the numbers of the couplets or dohas and indicate that the passages quoted are in those dohas or the lines following. When three numbers are given, *e.g.* 166 (106) 181, the first refers to the Bombay text, the third to the Allahabad-Benares text, while the second within brackets refers to Growse's translation. In the Ayodhya book, the first and second and sometimes the third agree.

In Hindi the names of Rama, Shiva, Krishna, Indra (ending in *short* a), are sounded as Ram, Shiv, etc. But it has been thought best to give the spelling to which the English reader is more accustomed. In the case of Brahm, the name for the Supreme Spirit, it has been decided to spell the word as it sounds, to avoid confusion with the name for the Creator, Brahma. With regard to these and other names and words, with which the general reader is less familiar, it has not been considered necessary to mark the length of the vowels, or to insert diacritical signs. In the Index, however, these marks and signs have been supplied.

CONTENTS

INTRODUCTION:
THE POEM AND ITS AUTHOR

THE name of Tulsidas is a household word among the Hindi-speaking populations of Northern India. Born in the sixteenth century, he took the story of Rama, prince of Avadh, which he found in the Sanskrit poem of Valmiki completed more than a thousand years before, and retold it in the language of his own day. But though he used the material which the much earlier work contains, his own poem was in no sense a Hindi translation, nor even a version of the Sanskrit epic. He was too great a poet to be a mere imitator. And he had besides a quite independent outlook. He wished to interpret his hero after his own fashion. He was, it is true, an orthodox Hindu, professing a sincere belief in the scriptures of Hinduism. But he was a Hindu whose thoughts had travelled beyond the thoughts of earlier days. And there were in his own heart and in the hearts of others, religious aspirations which he sought to satisfy. This is particularly manifest in the wonderful wealth of glowing love and personal *devotion* which he showers on Rama, whom he identifies not only with Vishnu, one of the three great gods of Hinduism, but also with the Supreme Spirit. It is this remarkable quality, coupled to his unique gifts as a poet, which has made his work so popular, and which has done so much to nourish all that is best in modern Hinduism. Because he has helped to make God real. In the eyes of Tulsidas God is not a remote passionless Being, devoid of all attributes and impossible to define, but a God to whom men pray and who hears their prayers. He has appeared in human form as Rama. He is full of sympathy. He loves those who worship Him. And He is pictured as no other god has ever been pictured in Hinduism, as one who loves righteousness and mercy. Best of all, He is not only pure Himself, He demands purity in those who are *devoted* to Him.

In the pages that follow, it will be our task to show how that is the central theme of the poem. But it will also be necessary to explain how Tulsidas's effort to make God real has been weakened by those other elements in Hinduism, which are also present in his teaching. The poet may be an innovator, but he very seldom professes to discard any of the old "truths." He not only holds fast to the central dogmas of Hinduism, Karma and Transmigration, but with certain aspects of his mind he continues to be a polytheist. He has none of the iconoclastic zeal of his predecessor, Kabir. He does not seek to dethrone any of the other gods. Some of them he continues to worship. Of others he speaks with contempt, but he believes in their existence. His belief in them is rendered the more easy by the fact that he is also pantheistically inclined and can find room for all of them in his conception of the universe. This, however, requires to be set down, that whatever is written by way of criticism is written with feelings of sincere respect and admiration for the poet himself and the work he achieved for his country and his religion.

It has been said that this poem is more popular and more honoured by the people of the United Provinces than the Bible is by the corresponding classes in England.[1] It is never possible to substantiate such assertions. But the statement is worth repeating to show how the book's

[1] Griffith's "Introduction" to his translation of the *Ramayana of Valmiki*, p. viii.

popularity has impressed Western observers. Few books are more widely known or have exercised a greater influence. We might speak of it with truth as the Bible of Northern India. A copy of it is to be found in almost every village. And the man who owns it earns the gratitude of his illiterate neighbours when he consents to read aloud from its pages. The poet was wiser than he knew when he insisted on writing his book in the vernacular.[1] But he was rebuked for doing so. He was told that the only language worthy of such a theme was Sanskrit. Two of his replies are on record. To one who wrote erotic verse he said: "If you find a jewelled casket full of poison and an earthen cup full of nectar, which will you refuse and which accept?" To another he replied: "Whether in the vernacular or in Sanskrit, true love is needed. When a woollen blanket is necessary why buy a silken vest?"[2]

Valmiki's poem is called the *Ramayana*, which means Rama's *goings* or adventures. Tulsidas chose for his work another title, *Ramcharitmanas*, or the lake of the deeds of Ram. But in everyday use, this name is forgotten and it is called the *Ramayan* of Tulsidas. It has been subjected very naturally to a variety of interpolations, and additions have been made to it which are not the poet's own. One

[1] Kabir had set the example a hundred years before in the composition of his Bijak. There must have been others also who did the same, because Tulsidas, after mentioning the great poets of ancient days, writes in Bal Kand (18) 23 of very eminent Prakrit poets who had written the story of Rama in the vernacular nearer his own time.

[2] In the opening stanzas of the poem, Tulsidas refers time after time to the fact that he is writing in the vernacular. "My language is the language of common speech, and my intelligence is small. If in this there is matter for laughter, let them laugh: there is no harm." Bal. (12). See also Dohas (13) (13) (15) (18) (21), and opening invocation. (The corresponding numbers of Dohas in Allahabad text are 17, 18, 18, 20, 23, 31.) For his two replies, consult Grierson, *Indian Antiquary*, Oct. 1893. They appear in *Dohawali*, 351 and 572.

of the texts which have been employed is the Bombay edition of 1909, published by Hariprasad Bhagirathji, with a modern Hindi interlinear version. It gives the interpolations, specifying them as such, and adds an eighth book which critics reject as spurious. The second text employed is that prepared with great care by the Kashi Nagara pracharini Sabha (1903), with a commentary by Shyam Sundardas, and published by the Indian Press, Allahabad, 1922. The splendid English translation by F. C. Growse has also been used (the sixth edition, 1914, published by Ram Narayan, Allahabad). Another admirer of the poet whose studies in the *Indian Antiquary*, 1893, and in the *Indian Gazetteer* are of much value, is Sir George Grierson, who speaks of the *Ramcharitmanas* as worthy of the greatest poet of any age.

We are fortunate in having given to us the exact date when Tulsidas began to write his poem. In the Bal Kand, which deals with the hero's childhood, he says: "In the year 1631 Samvat, placing my head at the feet of Hari (Vishnu) I begin my story; on Tuesday, the ninth day of the month Chait, in the town of Avadh, the very day on which the books of revelation say that Rama was born." 44 (42) 54. This corresponds to 30th March, 1574 A.D.

The poem, however, was not completed in Avadh but in Benares. A dispute with one of the religious sects drove him to choose a new place of residence.[1] He had written the first three sections of his book when this transference took place. And one may note his change of abode in the fact that he begins the fourth section with a special outburst in praise of Benares.

"How is it possible not to render service to Kashi;

[1] Grierson says that the dispute was with the Vairagi Vaishnava sect, who ate together, seated in a row. The poet cooked his food and ate separately. He was himself a Smarta Vaishnava.

knowing that it is the birthplace of salvation, the mine of knowledge, the destroyer of sin, where Shiva and Bavani dwell? When the company of the gods were in distress, he drank the deadly poison. Why do you not worship him, oh foolish soul? Who is so merciful as Shiva?"

The *Ramcharitmanas* was the poet's first and greatest achievement. As he was born in 1532, that means he had reached his forty-third year when he began to write. He is credited with being the author of not less than twenty other poems, all relating to the worship of Rama or Sita. One of these, the *Satsai*, teaches greater devotion to the wife of Rama than Tulsidas manifests in his *Ramayan*, and it is therefore supposed unlikely that he wrote it. Another book, the *Dohawali*, mainly consists of verses extracted from his other works, and helps to cast some light on his career. The same is true of another book entitled *Binaypatrika*. He had, however, a long life still before him, as he did not die till 1623, at the age of ninety-one.

Any attempt to construct an authentic narrative of the poet's life is well-nigh impossible. Legend has been busy, and the brief references which he or other early writers make to certain incidents in his career, have been broadened out into expansive prose. Even the place of his birth is uncertain. Growse names a number of places, but declines to dogmatise. In one biography written by a Hindu,[1] it is said to have been the village of Rajapur in the district of Banda, south of the river Jumna. Sir George Grierson thinks that Tari in the Doab has the best claim. He belonged to the Brahmin or priestly caste. But mis-

[1] The author is Raghubansh Sharma Shastri, whose life of the poet (in Hindi) is given as a preface to the Bombay edition of the poem. Sir George Grierson's opinions appear in *Indian Antiquary*, 1893. Babu Shyam Sundardas is also in favour of Rajapur. See his biography of the poet in the Allahabad edition.

fortune shadowed his birth. The poet himself tells us in the *Binaypatrika*:

> "My father and mother brought me into life and then abandoned me. The Creator (*vidhi*) created me without good fortune and then forsook me."

This statement of the poet is said to mean that he was born at an unlucky hour: so unlucky that according to the views of the astrologers a child born then was sure some time or other to destroy his father. In obedience to this belief, the child had to be destroyed. But the parents, probably unable to take so extreme a step, preferred to abandon him. And the assumption is that some wandering sadhu picked up the Brahmin child and adopted him. He must have been fortunate in his foster-father, for he tells us in the *Ramcharitmanas* how, when he was still a child, his teacher took pains to relate to him, time after time, the story of Rama, until he was able to grasp it, so far as his limited intelligence allowed. Bal. 38 (40) 50.

It is sometimes said that the *Bhakt-mal*, which was written by a contemporary, Nabhaji, gives us information about the poet's career, but when we turn to the book itself we find that seven lines of verse only are allotted to Tulsidas. They are to the effect that Valmiki, the author of the Sanskrit Ramayana, has been born again as Tulsidas and, by means of his new Ramayan, has "supplied a boat for the easy passage of the boundless ocean of existence." In this, Tulsidas was repeating the service rendered by the earlier poet, a single letter of whose verse would save even the murderer of a Brahmin. "Now again, as a blessing to the faithful, he has taken birth and published the sportive actions of the god." [1]

[1] See the edition of the *Bhakt-mal*, published by Nawal Kishor Press, Lucknow, 1926, p. 762. Growse gives both the Hindi and an English translation in his Introduction, pp. v–ix, which I quote.

Here it will be seen there are no biographical facts at all. But in A.D. 1713, about one hundred years after the poet's death, a commentary on the *Bhakt-mal* was written by Priya Das. This commentary devotes eighty-eight lines of verse to Tulsidas. They mention seven separate events in the poet's life. The first refers to his wife. It is as follows :

"He had great love for his wife. Without asking his leave she went home to her father. He forgot all about himself and hastened there too. She was greatly ashamed and went away in anger, saying, 'Have you no love for Rama ? My body is but a framework of skin and bone.' When he heard these words, it was as it were the daybreak. He felt compunction and left her and sped to the city of Kashi (Benares). There he made his abode, worshipping the Lord publicly, making a rigid vow, and thirsting exceedingly for a vision."

What later days have done to clothe this somewhat bald utterance will be realised if we compare it with the interesting narrative by Raghuvansh Sharma Shastri in his life of the poet. He tells us how, after a son had been born to Tulsidas, his father-in-law more than once sent asking that his daughter might pay a visit to her father's house. The request was always refused. But it so happened that on one occasion her brothers came and took her away in her husband's absence. When the poet returned, he learned from the neighbours where she had gone. He naturally followed, probably with some feelings of indignation. When he proposed, however, that she should go back with him, she reproached him for his inordinate affection, saying that if he had been as devoted to Rama as he was to her unworthy body, he would have secured ere then supreme felicity. These reproaches made such an impression on Tulsidas, that he took her at her word, and went off. This was a response which was apparently more than she expected. Because she followed him, begging him to wait and take some food, and saying that when he had eaten she would return with him. But Tulsidas was not to be persuaded. He said she must remain where she was. He would go back alone.

From that day forward he seems to have lived the life of an ascetic. He and his wife never lived together again. It would appear that Avadh, the birthplace of Rama, was at first his principal haunt. Afterwards he lived in Benares. In addition, however, he made visits to the other holy places of Hindustan: Muttra, Brindaban, Kurukshetr and Prayag. As years passed, his devotion to Rama continued to grow. On one occasion his wife sent him a letter in which she said: "I do not fear that my heart will break. But I am afraid that your heart will be captured by some other woman." His answer was: "I am captured by Rama alone. That is the flavour of the love which I have tasted, taught by my own wife." There is very real pathos in the story that is told of how when Tulsidas was an old man he came one day in the course of his wanderings to his father-in-law's village, and to what had been his father-in-law's door. His wife, now also old, came to the door and asked him what he would eat. He replied that he would prepare his food with his own hands. She got ready an eating-place for him, and brought wood with some rice, vegetables and clarified butter. Something in his movements and gestures led the wife to realise that her husband was before her. But she said nothing. She offered him, however, the use of certain condiments such as pepper and camphor. To each offer he answered, "I have got it in my wallet." She also asked permission to bathe his feet. But he refused. During the night she lay awake, wondering how she could persuade him to let her go with him. "If he can carry about with him pepper and camphor, why may he not carry me ?" Next morning, when he was getting ready to start, she asked him to wait and eat. He refused. Then she said, "Do you not know who I am ?" He answered, "No." "Do you know whose house this is ? Do you know me ? I am your wife. Let me go with you." To each of these questions and appeals his reply was always No ! The old woman, thus rebuffed, showed that with the passing of the years she had not lost that pungency of speech which had bereft her of her husband so many years before, and she said, as is recorded in the *Dohawali* :

> "If there be in your wallet everything from chalk to camphor, you should not have left your wife. Either take me in your wallet or else abandon it and give yourself entirely to God."

As on the earlier occasion, his wife's reproaches drove him to a deeper renunciation. He left her where she stood, and gave all that he had left to Brahmins.[1]

One of the other events in the life of the poet, as recorded by Priya Das, is to the effect that through the intervention of Hanuman the monkey god, he obtains a vision of Rama, as he had so strongly desired. It is said that Rama and his brother Lakshman one day appeared before him, riding on horses and clad in green raiment. It was only when they had disappeared that he realised that he had seen his Lord. The god's great interest in his worshipper is shown by another of the seven incidents. One night some thieves came to rob the poet's house. But try as they might to enter, they were always met by a mysterious youth with a bow and arrows in his hand. They were so much perplexed that when morning came they went

[1] For this story of the poet's old age, we are indebted to the researches of Sir George Grierson. The life of the poet in the Allahabad edition should also be consulted.

to Tulsidas and asked who the lad was who stayed with him. "On hearing this question, he remained silent and wept; then gave away all he had, knowing that Rama himself had been the watchman." The thieves were greatly impressed. They became followers of Rama and abandoned their sinful practices.

The power of working miracles is also attributed to Tulsidas, and Priya Das says that he even raised a dead man to life. This miracle created so much interest that the poet was summoned to Delhi, and told by the Emperor to work a miracle. "It is noised throughout the world that you are master of everything." When Tulsidas refused and began to speak in praise of Rama, he was cast into prison. But the poet made appeal to Hanuman, who sent thousands of monkeys to his aid. They wrought so great havoc that the Emperor came and cast himself at the poet's feet and begged for mercy. His prayer was granted, but it was on one condition. The Emperor had to abandon Delhi and build for himself a new citadel. The reason given was that the ground on which the existing town stood was sacred to Rama. The frequency with which the site of Delhi was changed would lend itself to the growth of this legend.

The poet died at Benares. A couplet is all that we have to tell us where and when.

> "In the year 1680 Samvat, on the bank of the Ganges at the Asi-ghat, in the month Shravan, on the seventh day of the lunar fortnight, Tulsi abandoned his body."

His last words were to the effect that he had spoken of the glory of Rama's name, and the time for silence had come.

THE RAMAYAN OF TULSIDAS

I.

THE LIFE AND DEEDS OF RAMA.

A TEN-HEADED demon named Ravan, as the result of prolonged and amazing austerities, was told by Brahma, the Creator, to ask a boon. He replied, "May I never be conquered by either a god or a demon." In consequence of obtaining this boon, Ravan at once began to persecute both gods and Brahmins. The situation thus created by Brahma's gift at length became so unbearable that the celestials made appeal to Vishnu, the preserver god. In response to their appeal Vishnu promised to take human form on the earth in the persons of four brothers who would be born as sons of Dashrath, king of Koshal.[1] By appearing as a man, the god would be able to slay Ravan and at the same time do nothing to render the Creator's promise vain.

The scene changes to Avadh, Dashrath's capital. The king has reached old age, and as yet no son has been born to any of his three queens. But when he speaks to his family priest he is told that he need not be anxious. He will become the father of four sons, who will be famous throughout the three worlds and remove the earth's burdens. A sacrifice was at once begun, calculated to secure offspring. What the nature of the sacrifice was is not said. But Agni, the god of fire, very soon appeared

[1] Koshal is practically the modern province of Oudh. Its capital was Avadh; in Sanskrit, Ayodhya.

with the offering in his hand and told the king to divide it among his queens. To Kaushalya, apparently the senior queen, was given half; to Kaikeyi was given a quarter, and what remained was divided between them. But they each gave their share to Sumitra, the third queen. The result was that in due course all three became pregnant. Four boys were born. The son of Kaushalya was Rama; the son of Kaikeyi was Bharat; while Sumitra was the mother of twins, Lakshman and Shatrughn. Though all four shared in the divine nature of the god, Rama is the hero of the poem, and it is round him that the worship of men has gathered. This introductory chapter, however, will confine itself to recording the story of his earthly life, as free from the marvellous and supernatural as possible.

When Rama and Lakshman were in their sixteenth year, a holy man came and asked the king to allow the two boys to go with him to his hermitage and slay certain demons who were disturbing his prayers and sacrifices. Dashrath was very unwilling to let them go. He was especially reluctant to part with Rama. "What can a pretty little boy do against so fierce and terrible a demon?" But refusal to so great a saint was impossible. In any case, the king need not have been afraid. The demons were easily routed and their leaders slain. The poet wastes very little time in describing the engagement. He was more anxious to tell how the touch of Rama's feet restored to life the wife of an ascetic, who for her sins had been changed into stone. But, in particular, he was eager to relate how Rama, at the invitation of the saint, went to witness the ordeal of bending the bow of Shiva. This bow was in the possession of the king of Videha, a country to the east of Koshal. And its king had proclaimed that he would give his daughter Sita in marriage to the prince who could bend Shiva's bow. Many thousand kings were present at the ordeal. They all tried and failed. They could not even move it from the ground. It seemed as if Sita would die unwed. But when Rama made the effort, he not only lifted up the bow—he drew it so tight that it snapped in two. This wonderful feat caused so much excitement in heaven that the gods rained down flowers, and the nymphs of heaven began to dance and sing.

When Rama's father had been informed, and his presence in Videha secured, the marriage of Rama and Sita took place.[1] The other brothers also found brides there. With the return to Avadh of Rama and his young wife, the city was blessed with unprecedented happiness. The one desire of the people was that the king in his lifetime would make Rama regent. So indeed Dashrath himself planned, and when he told his purpose to his religious teacher, he found him equally anxious to have the installation carried through without delay. But though Rama was immediately informed and steps immediately taken, their plans were overthrown by the jealousy of heaven, because the gods could not see how Rama would ever have an opportunity of meeting and slaying their enemy Ravan, should he continue to live and reign in Avadh. It was necessary, in their opinion, that he should be driven to the forest. They accordingly applied to the wife of the Creator. Though the goddess knew that her brother deities were plotting wickedness, she agreed to carry out their wishes. The plan she chose was to make use of a serving-maid in the palace, a hunchback, whose mind she poisoned with envy and evil thoughts. When the hunchback saw the preparations for the installation of Rama, she went to Kaikeyi, the mother of Bharat, and tried to rouse her jealousy. At first she failed entirely. But gradually her words began to tell. And finally she persuaded the queen to demand that Rama should be sent into exile, and her own son made regent. Some years

[1] Sita was the incarnation of Lakshmi, the wife of Vishnu.

before Kaikeyi had rendered a great service to her husband, and been told to ask two boons—boons which to that moment she had never claimed. Tutored by the hunchback, however, she not only demanded that they be granted right away, but before saying what they were, she made the king pledge himself by a great oath that he would assuredly give her what she asked. No part of the poem is more powerfully told than that which describes the cunning plotting of the hunchback, and the grief of the king when he found himself bound by a promise which he could not break.

And so, before another day had dawned, Rama, to the unbounded sorrow of the citizens, had set out for the forest to live the life of a hermit for fourteen years. He was accompanied by his wife and his brother Lakshman, who refused to remain behind. Not long after their departure the old king died of a broken heart.

During these events, Bharat had been absent. But when he heard of what had happened, he followed his brother to the forest and did everything he could to persuade him to return to Avadh. But Rama was adamant, and he in turn found it a difficult task to persuade his unselfish and large-hearted brother to assume the government. In the end Bharat only consented to return on the understanding that he was to act as his brother's deputy ; in proof of which he took back to Avadh Rama's sandals and placed them on the vacant throne.

When Rama settled in the forest, the celestials came and built for themselves huts made of grass and the branches of trees. They appeared in the guise of the wild inhabitants of the jungle, and bowing before the prince declared that they had found their lord. Such feelings of adoration, however, did not lessen their fears when they heard that Bharat was following his brother to the forest, and once more they applied to the goddess who had helped them before. But she told them she was powerless to change the mind of Bharat. In their distress and selfishness they exercised their own powers of illusion (*maya*) and strove to create in the hearts of all concerned, feelings of sorrow, distress and fear. Indra, the king of the gods, in particular, employed all the craftiness for which he was noted. But they need not have been afraid. And when they saw their fears were groundless, their anxiety was changed into joy. In token of their divine approval, the drums of heaven began to beat, and flowers fell from the sky.

Very little is recorded of the life of the exiles in the forest. It was soon found necessary to change their dwelling-place because of the number of the people who came to see them, and they journeyed farther south. The little that is told is, for the most part, a record of their intercourse with various eminent sages, and of the opinions these holy men expressed, with reference to Rama. They identified him, not only with Vishnu, but with Brahm, the Supreme Spirit of the universe. In this fashion thirteen years passed away, and the last year of their exile was approaching, without any encounter between Rama and the demon he was destined to destroy. But one day a female demon, a sister of Ravan, came to their neighbourhood. As soon as she saw Rama she fell deeply in love. Changing herself into a very beautiful woman, she made overtures to the prince. But Rama, looking at Sita who was standing near, said, " My younger brother is the person you should seek." When Lakshman finally rejected her with scorn, the demoness assumed her real and ugly form. The sudden and horrid change filled Sita with alarm, and out of regard for his wife, Rama told Lakshman to mutilate the fiend and cut off her nose and ears. The maltreatment of this woman was the beginning of the end, because she went at once to two of her brothers and cried for vengeance. Assembling their demon hosts they attacked the hermitage. In obedience to his brother's command, Lakshman took Sita to a cave for safety, and remained with her there on guard. The prince thus faced his assailants alone. The demons numbered fourteen thousand. They were of immense size and power. But Rama slew them all. In the hour of death, because they uttered his sacred name, every one of them attained *nirvana.* This victory afforded great relief to the gods, who were very anxious lest their champion should be slain, and to express their satisfaction the drums of heaven sounded, and flowers fell from the sky.

Ravan's sister, however, escaped the slaughter, and at once hastened to the presence of her other and much greater brother. When Ravan heard of the destruction of his followers and the death of his brothers, he was overwhelmed with fury and promised full revenge. But, strange to say, he had another thought in his mind. Among gods and men, demons and serpents, he said there was no one the equal of his brothers who had been slain. The person who had killed them must be God himself (*bhagwan*). If God (*jagdish*) had become incarnate (*avatar*) he would go and fight against him. In losing his life at the hand of the Lord (*prabhu*) he would escape the burden of rebirth and cross the ocean of the world. But should it prove that Rama was a man and nothing more, then he would kill both brothers and carry off Sita.

Rama, fully conscious of what was to happen, told Sita that he was about to act a part, after the manner and fashion of men. And it was his wish that she should be absorbed in fire, until he had destroyed the demons. In obedience to her lord's desire, Sita pressed his feet to her heart and entered into fire. But she left behind an exact image of herself, both in form and disposition. Lakshman, who was not present at the time this wonderful incident took place, was ignorant of the transformation.

In carrying out his plans, Ravan sought the help of another demon, called Marich. This demon at first urged Ravan not to offend Rama further, but when he saw that his master would take no refusal, he changed himself into a beautiful deer and approached the hermitage. When Sita saw it she asked her husband to kill the deer and bring her the skin. Rama at once took up his bow and arrows and went in pursuit. He was not ignorant of the deception which the demon in his folly tried to practise on him. But he knew that the time had come when he must carry out the wishes of the gods. The chase led both hunter and hunted far from the hermitage, until the demon fell, pierced to the heart with one of the prince's arrows. With his latest breath he called out, and in a loud voice, "Lakshman! Lakshman!" Far off in the hermitage, Sita and Lakshman heard the cry. And thinking that her husband was in peril, Sita appealed to her brother-in-law to go to the rescue. Lakshman at first refused. He had two reasons for doing so: he did not believe that any harm could come to Rama, and he had been straitly charged by him not to leave Sita's side. When Sita, however, continued to taunt and reproach him, he reluctantly obeyed her. The princess was thus left alone. Ravan's opportunity had come. Approaching Sita in the guise of an ascetic, he spoke to her in language that suited his disguise. But soon changing his tone to words of endearment, he roused the anger and alarm of the pure-minded princess. The demon, finding himself repulsed, assumed his real form, laid rude hands upon her, and, placing her in his car, rose up into the air. Reproaching herself for the folly which had driven first Rama and then Lakshman from her side, Sita raised piteous cries for help. Her cry was heard by the king of the vultures, who made a brave effort to arrest the demon. The bird succeeded in tearing Ravan out of his aeroplane and hurling him to the ground. For a time it seemed as if the bird would be victorious, but eventually Ravan was able to cut off the vulture's wings. When he had rendered his opponent helpless, Ravan once more placed Sita in his car and resumed his flight. It so happened, as they journeyed south, that Sita saw some monkeys sitting on a rock. She called out Rama's name and dropped a garment. The demon carried her to his palace in the island of Lanka. There she was confined in a garden to which Ravan came time after time, endeavouring to bend her to his will. But all his efforts were in vain. Mourning for her absent lord, her soul was possessed by one desire, and her courage sustained by thinking of his virtues and repeating his name.

When Rama, having killed the demon, was returning to the hermitage, he met his brother on the way to help him. At once his heart was smitten with a sudden fear, and he asked, "Why have you left Sita alone, contrary to my commands, exposed to the dangers of the forest?" And when he arrived and found the hermitage empty, the grief to which he yielded was, as the poet says, the grief of an ordinary man. He begged the birds and beasts, the trees and flowers, to tell him where she was. Searching on every side, he at last came to where the vulture was lying. The bird was able to tell him that it was Ravan who had carried off Sita, and after uttering a hymn in praise of Rama, passed to heaven. When the two brothers had duly performed the funeral rites of their departed friend, they resumed their search. After a variety of adventures they arrived at a mountain where Sugriv, the monkey king, lived. When he saw them approaching, Sugriv became anxious and sent his friend Hanuman, the son of Vayu, the wind god, to ask them who they were.

When Vishnu undertook to appear on earth in the person of the four sons of Dashrath, the Creator told the other deities that they must go down to earth in the form of monkeys, and assist Vishnu in his undertaking. Nothing is said at this stage that these monkeys were incarnations of the gods. But as the story proceeds, we shall see to what extent they, and Hanuman in particular, aided Rama in the overthrow of the demons. As soon as Rama had declared his name and origin, Hanuman fell at his feet in adoration. The subsequent meeting with the monkey king led to pledges of mutual friendship, Rama undertaking to help Sugriv in a quarrel he had with his brother, Bali, and the monkeys to assist in the recovery of Sita. Fresh light on the rape of Sita was secured by the fact that Sugriv and his ministers proved to be the monkeys whom Sita had seen seated on a rock. They had heard her pathetic cries, and they had recovered the garment she had dropped. When Rama saw the garment, he pressed it to his bosom and gave way to a fresh outburst of grief.

Rama almost immediately performed his part of the alliance by slaying Sugriv's brother, Bali. It is said that the two monkeys engaged in single combat, Rama concealing himself behind a tree. When he saw his friend losing ground, he put an end to the battle by driving an arrow into Bali's heart. As for the enterprise against Ravan, the approach of the monsoon made it necessary to wait till the rains were over—a period of waiting very trying to the heartbroken husband. Ignorant of where she was, not knowing whether she was alive or dead, he declared he would get news of her, even if he had to fight with the gods of the lower world. And when the rains did cease, it seemed as if the monkeys had forgotten their pledge. Incited to action, however, by Lakshman and Hanuman, the monkey king sent out great numbers of his followers to search the world in every direction for news of Sita. Rama entrusted Hanuman with a ring and told him that when he found the princess he was to assure her of speedy and certain deliverance. In course of time, Hanuman and his companions reached the shores of southern India. There they encountered a huge vulture, who was possessed of marvellous powers of vision. This vulture was the brother of the bird which had befriended Sita and, as he stood by the shores of the sea, was able to look right across the intervening waters to Ravan's palace in Ceylon. And there he said he could see Sita quite plainly, a prisoner in the garden where the demon had placed her. The difficulty was how to get across. The vulture reminded Hanuman of the fact that by repeating Rama's name, those who had faith in him were able to cross the ocean of existence, and it should therefore be no difficult task to overleap a much narrower sea. And so it fell to Hanuman to make the effort. Swelling out his body till it became as big as a mountain, he made the leap and landed safely on the other side. Arrived in Lanka, he contracted himself to much less than his usual size, and, after a number of adventures, reached the grove where Sita was kept a prisoner. Shortly before she had been visited by Ravan in one of his many attempts to break down her resolve; and in a passion of grief she was appealing, when Hanuman reached the garden, to one of her female guardians, to bring wood and fire, that she might attest her loyalty to Rama by a voluntary death.

Even as she made this appeal, Hanuman, by this time concealed in the branches of a tree above her head, threw down the ring which he had received from Rama. When he saw that the princess recognised the ring, he whispered that he had come as Rama's messenger and told her not to be afraid. His presence was soon discovered, and after a long battle, in which he slew great numbers of demons, the monkey allowed himself to be overpowered. Brought into the presence of Ravan he was asked how he had dared to kill so many demons. But Hanuman in reply asked

Ravan how he had dared to carry off Sita. Did he not realise that it was by virtue of Rama's power that Brahma had created the world, that Vishnu preserved it, and Shiva would destroy it? Did Ravan imagine that any one of these three great gods would be able to protect him in face of Rama's opposition? Ravan's answer to these observations was to order his followers to tie rags dipped in oil to Hanuman's tail, set them on fire and let him go. This was done on the theory that a monkey is prouder of his tail than of any other part of his body. It was, in any case, a very foolish thing to do, because when Hanuman was set free, he enlarged himself to an enormous size and, using his burning tail as a torch, he leaped from house to house, and set their roofs on fire. Very soon the whole capital was in a blaze. Not a house escaped destruction. Having achieved his object, the monkey dipped his tail in the sea, paid another visit to Sita, once more leaped across the straits, and hastened to Rama with his news.

Immediate preparations for the invasion of Lanka were begun. Millions of monkeys and bears, of all sizes and colours, gathered from all quarters, and directed their course to the south. It was not possible for many of them to imitate Hanuman's method of transit. And arrangements were made for spanning the distance with a bridge composed of mountains and trees. Some of the monkeys were so huge that they could handle hills as easily as others handle pebbles. The work was speedily accomplished, and Rama showed his gratification by fashioning and setting up a phallic emblem of the god Shiva, which he reverently worshipped. Great and wonderful as the bridge was, it was no easy task for so many millions to get across, and not a few were compelled to fly over, while others made use of sea monsters which had left their ocean depths and come to gaze on Rama's face.

Ever since his encounter with Hanuman, many of

Ravan's friends had urged him to restore Sita. But the infatuated demon refused to listen. He boasted how, in former days, he had fought with and overthrown a great variety of gods, and he was not afraid of men and monkeys. He also claimed to be a special devotee of Shiva, whom he had worshipped, not with an offering of flowers, as was the common practice, but with his ten heads, which he had cut off time after time, and cast into a fire, as Shiva himself was well aware.

War was inevitable; and it is described at great length. Large numbers of demons were slain, but the mere fact that they uttered Rama's name, though in the accents of hate and with no thought of devotion, was sufficient to secure their entrance to heaven. The most exciting moment in the fight was when Lakshman was struck on the breast with such terrible force that he became unconscious. Rama was in great distress, and asked why he had imperilled the life of his brother for the sake of a woman. A physician who was brought from Lanka to see the patient, prescribed the use of herbs which grew on a certain mountain in the north of India. Hanuman was sent to bring them. He found the mountain but he could not recognise the herbs. He therefore tore the mountain from its base and placing it on his shoulder set out on his return journey. As he passed over Avadh, Bharat saw what he thought was a great demon flying through the air, and discharging an arrow brought Hanuman and the mountain crashing to the ground. As he fell he called out, "Oh, Rama! Rama!" These words wrought an immediate change in Bharat's breast, and rushing forward he begged to be forgiven. It did not take long for the monkey to recover, and when he had told Bharat of the situation of affairs at Lanka, he once more addressed himself to his journey. Time was very precious. Hanuman therefore seated himself on Bharat's arrow; or, as we read in the text, "Mount my arrow along with the mountain, and I will send you to the All-merciful."

The herbs effected the desired result. Lakshman's life, which had been despaired of, was saved.

Despite this, and other equally marvellous deeds, it was discovered that Ravan's son had begun a sacrifice which, if he had been able to complete it, would have made it impossible for any one to destroy him. The gods therefore appealed to Rama not to trifle with Ravan any longer. He had afflicted all of them quite enough already, and Sita was in great distress. Thus appealed to, Rama went forth to battle. It is a gruesome picture which the poet draws of the terrible slaughter. Rivers of blood, rivers on whose banks vultures sat, tearing at the entrails of the slain, as intent on their sport as any fisherman. So many of his followers were destroyed that Ravan felt he was left alone. But he still fought on. When the two principal combatants were at last face to face, the demon discharged thousands of arrows and discs and spears. But Rama turned them all aside. The prince's arrows, on the other hand, were so impatient to get to work that they could not remain in the quiver. The stringing of his bow filled the universe with dread ; the sea, the great tortoise, and the earth itself trembled. The elephants which support the world squealed with fright. But the gods laughed, well content. Rama smote Ravan's ten heads with ten arrows. He also cut off his twenty arms. But no sooner were they off than they grew on again. This continued till the very sky was full of heads and arms ; indeed there was no room for them in either earth or heaven. It was a source of great amusement to Rama to go on cutting off the demon's heads and arms. But such ignominious treatment naturally made Ravan very angry, and he discharged so many arrows that Rama and his chariot were completely hidden. The heads and arms too, as they went flying through the air, began to cry, "Victory! Victory! Where is Rama? Where is Lakshman?" These shouts made the monkeys and gods afraid. They began to think that both brothers had been overthrown. Indeed we are told that Rama did swoon, when struck by the most powerful weapon which Ravan had. But the swoon was not real. It was only a pretence on the hero's part. In any case, this incident caused great alarm, and the lesser gods became so frightened that they ran away and, declaring that all was over, hid themselves in some caves which were near at hand. Brahma and Shiva and a few very wise saints alone were undeceived, and remained looking on. It was not to be wondered at that the gods should have become alarmed, because by his powers of magic and illusion Ravan multiplied himself into millions of Ravans, and every bear and monkey saw before himself a fear-inspiring Ravan. The terror, however, did not last long. By the exercise of still greater power and with a single arrow, Rama scattered the illusion, and there was only one Ravan as before. When the gods saw how they had been deceived, they came back to the scene of conflict, only to scatter screaming once more when Ravan sprang into their midst. The poet dwells at length on this wonderful scene. He tells us that the hero would have brought the combat to an end much sooner had it not been that he could not smite Ravan on the heart because Sita's image was imprinted there, and Rama could not strike that part of the demon's body until the fear of death had driven from it all thought of Sita. Another explanation, however, is given for this delay in killing Ravan. It was put forward by the demon's brother, who had deserted to Rama's side. He said that in Ravan's navel there was a certain quantity of amrit, the liquor which confers immortality, and until that amrit was dried up, Ravan could not die. Rama, with a smile, acted on this information.

He struck the demon on the place indicated with an arrow. This seems to have dried up the amrit. With other arrows he then struck off the heads and arms. And for the first time since the fight began, no fresh heads and arms took their place. Ravan was dead at last. His headless, armless trunk fell lifeless to the ground. The arrows which Rama had discharged returned to their quiver. The gods, with Brahma and Shiva at their head, began a hymn of praise.

Sita had been delivered at last. She was overwhelmed with joy when Hanuman brought her word of Ravan's death, and escorted her to her husband's presence. But her joy was changed into sorrow when Rama declared that she must submit to the ordeal of fire before he could receive her back as his wife. Fire alone could test her purity, and prove that she was unstained. This apparently harsh act on the part of Rama caused great amazement. Sita, however, submitted without fear. She knew that she had never been disloyal to him in thought, word or deed. And the fire did her no harm. "It was as cool as sandal wood." The image of Sita which had been substituted for the real Sita, and the stain of Ravan's touch, alone were reduced to ashes. The real Sita emerged from the flames more beautiful than before. She came escorted by Agni, the fire god, in person.

Before returning to his own country, Rama requested Indra, the king of heaven, to restore to life the large number of bears and monkeys who had been killed in the course of the conflict. This Indra did by sending a shower of amrit over the field of battle. But it had no effect on the demons, because, as has been said, at the hour of death the image of Rama was in their hearts and they had already achieved absorption in Brahm. The monkeys and bears were incarnations of the gods, and were restored to life because it was Rama's will. Ravan's aeroplane was used to convey the two princes and Sita back to Avadh. It was large enough to carry an immense number of the bears and monkeys also. As they journeyed north, Rama showed to Sita the bridge that they had built, and the phallus of Shiva which he had fashioned and worshipped. He showed her the places they had stayed at together; he pointed out the spots where he and Lakshman had lived after she was carried away. When they reached the Ganges, and especially when they saw Avadh, they bowed their heads in worship.

One day remained of the appointed years of exile. Rama could not return till the full period had expired. He therefore sent Hanuman on in advance and himself waited in the forest until Bharat could be informed. The monkey found Bharat in deep distress. He thought Rama must be dead. Great was the joy of the citizens when they heard that Rama was near at hand. The women thronged the roofs of their houses to watch for the aeroplane in the sky. And when they did come, no words can describe the emotion that filled every heart. Rama looked at each of the citizens, both men and women, with eyes of affection, and by assuming countless forms was able to embrace every one of them at the same moment—a mystery, says the poet, which no one can understand.

During the years of Rama's reign, the days of the Golden Age returned. There was no sickness, no sorrow, no strife, no sin. Every one adhered to the religion of his own caste and stage in life. Rama ruled over the whole earth, with its seven encircling seas. He offered millions of horse sacrifices and gave untold wealth to Brahmins. Sita was in every respect an ideal wife and daughter. Though she had servants without number, she attended to the needs of her husband and mothers-in-law with her own hands. She became the mother of two sons. Their names were Lav and Kush.

II.

THE LESSER GODS.

TULSIDAS makes frequent reference to the Vedas and their teaching. He tells us over and over again that "it is thus that the Vedas sing." But, as Growse remarks, he had not the faintest idea of their contents, and the gulf that divides him from these ancient scriptures is nowhere more profound than in what they each believed about the heavenly powers. The gods with whose praises the *Rig-Veda*, the oldest collection of the Aryan hymns, is concerned, were for the most part nature deities, the heaven and the earth, the sun, the wind, fire, rain and tempests. They were gods not difficult to appease, and their worshippers asked them for health and happiness, for children and cattle, for long life and the forgiveness of sins. If precedence is to be judged by the number of hymns addressed to them, Indra, the god of the firmament, and Agni, the god of fire, held the foremost place; while Prajapati, to whom at least one creation hymn belongs (*Rig-Veda*, x. 121), is definitely spoken of in the *Brahmanas* as the creator, and his work described.

As the centuries passed, however, a great change took place. And by the time we reach the Epics of Hinduism, the *Ramayana* and the *Mahabharata*, we find ourselves in a new world, where new gods are worshipped. Some of them, it is true, continue to bear the names of the ancient gods, and some of them fulfil more or less their old functions. But though they are still accepted and believed in, they have had to stand aside and make way for three new gods round whom the thoughts of men, very different from the old thoughts, had come to gather. So far back as the days before the Christian era, what we call Hinduism, in contrast to what is spoken of as Vedic Religion, had already begun to take shape, and the great gods of Hinduism are Brahma, Vishnu and Shiva. Brahma is the creator, the successor of Prajapati already referred to. Vishnu's name appears in the *Rig-Veda* as a very secondary deity, and Shiva is reckoned as the Rudra of the earlier period; but in those days they were nature gods, associated with the sun and the tempests.

These three gods also gradually came to be spoken of together. Vishnu, the preserver god, and Shiva, the destroyer, are linked with Brahma, the creator, in what is called the Hindu Triad. But they in turn are reckoned in the later speculations of Hinduism as the manifestations of the Supreme Spirit, the Eternal Brahm. What the relation of these three gods to one another is, Tulsidas very seldom attempts to define, though he makes frequent reference to them in this linked relationship. As we shall see, his chief concern is to show that Rama, the hero of his poem, is not merely one of the many incarnations of the god Vishnu, but, far more than that, the embodiment of the eternal and absolute God.

But though Brahma, Vishnu and Shiva have taken rank as the chief gods, and Rama is identified with the Supreme, the others, who may be spoken of as the lesser gods, are very much a reality, and have also their parts to play.[1] There are certain of them to whom the poet makes frequent appeal for help in the composition of his poem—the goddess of wisdom, for instance, generally supposed to be the wife

[1] Though a thousand years separate Tulsidas from the time when the *Ramayana* of Valmiki was finally redacted, it is the Hinduism of that poem on which his own work is, to a large extent, based.

of Brahma, and Ganesh, the elephant-headed god, who is a son of Shiva. From time to time also, in the course of the narrative, different individuals are spoken of as bowing their heads and addressing prayers to their own favourite gods, or to the gods in general without specifying whose particular assistance is invited. Thus, confining ourselves to the first book of the poem, the Bal Kand, we read of the kings who tried in vain to bend the bow of Shiva, that "they bowed their heads to their own special gods." 253 (259) 282. But when Rama addressed himself to the same task, the people in their desire to see him succeed entreated the gods by their own past good deeds. 263 (269) 292. In a somewhat earlier passage the people make a similar appeal; but they addressed themselves not only to the gods but to the spirits of their ancestors (*pitri*) and Ganesh. "Worshipping their ancestors and the gods, and remembering their past good actions, they said, 'If our merit is of any use, may Ganesh grant that Rama will break Shiva's bow as if it were a lotus stalk.'" 258 (264) 287.

At the marriage of Rama and Sita we are told 322 (328) 355, that "The gurus caused the Brahmins to worship Gauri and Ganesh," the wife and son of Shiva, and that these two deities appeared, accepted the worship and blessed them. Later on, in connection with the same ceremony, it is said that the gods were worshipped and that on the offering of the sacrifice the god of fire appeared in bodily form to receive it. The function was brought to a conclusion by the bride's father, who, when he had offered a large number of gifts, bowed his head before the gods (*dev*) and entreated them with joined hands, saying, "The gods (*sur*) and the saints desire a good disposition. Can you satisfy the Ocean by offering it a few drops of water?" But we feel the reality of these lesser gods perhaps even more in the numerous pictures we receive of their meetings together for pleasure or business. They have become an organised society, with wives and children. They have their own palaces and gardens, sometimes their own particular heavens. They have their own special vehicles; Indra has an elephant, the others travel in chariots and aeroplanes. But Brahma is their president, and we come across the phrase, "Brahma and the gods," over and over again. And in particular, Brahma is their court of appeal; it is to him they flock when they are in any difficulty. It is he who expresses their feelings when they have anything to say. When mortals have done what pleases them, they rain down flowers and cause the drums of heaven to beat. They are easily moved by both joy and sorrow. When the news of Shiva's second marriage reached them, it was not Brahma only whose joy overflowed. Bal. 101 (99) 114. The whole community of heaven got ready the cars in which they were accustomed to travel. "Vishnu, Brahma and all the gods got into their chariots and went to the wedding." Bal. 102 (101) 116. In similar fashion they came down to earth to be present at Rama's wedding with Sita. They had been attracted by the magnificence of the preparations, and as they looked on from afar, said that they had lived to no purpose, and when they reached the capital of the bridegroom's father, they declared that heaven was a poor place in comparison. Brahma, in particular, was amazed to find that, though he was the Creator, "he saw nothing like it in his own handiwork." Bal. 313 (319) 346. The beauty of the bride and bridegroom was equally astounding. Brahma was sorry that he had only eight eyes to gaze with. Kartikeya, the god of war and Shiva's own son, boasted that he was better off than the Creator, because he had no less than twelve eyes. But Indra was particularly proud, for he had no less than a thousand, and he thought that the curse, which had inflicted him with so many, had proved a blessing in the end. At the wedding, Vishnu and his wife were also present, looking with love at Rama and Sita, their own incarnations. In the account given of the meeting of the newly wedded pair, it would seem as if for the moment the celestials were looking down from heaven ; but we are told later that Brahma, Vishnu and Shiva, with the other celestials, took part in the marriage festivities. They assumed the guise of learned Brahmins, and were escorted to seats of honour by the bride's father. The celestials were so delighted with all they saw and heard that they asked Brahma to allow them to be born in Avadh.

To understand more clearly Tulsidas's general conception of the gods, let us take another illustration. The power of demons was a great source of worry to the celestials. There was one demon in particular who conquered the lords of all the worlds, and made the gods miserable. Spoken of as the ageless and undying, he had defeated them times without number. At last they went to the Creator, and asked for his assistance. When he saw their distress, he promised them relief, saying that a son would be born to Shiva, who would overcome their oppressor. Bal. 94 (92) 106. Their greatest enemy, however, was the demon Ravan. How he came to possess so great strength will be explained in a later chapter. Here it is enough to note that he also had subdued the whole universe, and caused an infinite amount of sorrow to gods and men. And here again we find gods and saints crowding round the Creator's throne, and begging him to do something for their relief ; and though Brahma admits that he himself is helpless to do anything, he says that a deliverer is at hand. Vishnu will come to their assistance. 190 (196) 214. And before they had separated, as the result of a prayer addressed to him by the Creator, the voice of Vishnu was heard from heaven telling Indra and the saints and sages not to be afraid, because for their sakes he would appear in human form and bring them deliverance. After Vishnu had spoken, Brahma told the celestials that they must assume the form of monkeys and render service to their deliverer. This instruction was at once obeyed, and we find that in his subsequent war with Ravan, Vishnu in his incarnation as Rama was greatly helped by innumerable hosts of monkeys.

Despite this transformation, the celestials were able to be present at all stages of Rama's human career. They were present, as we have seen, at his marriage. They were also present at his birth, filling the very heavens with their chariots, singing his praises and raining down flowers. Indeed, when Rama and his brothers did anything unusually remarkable, the gods were sure to be at hand, giving manifest expression to their pleasure and admiration. On the occasion, for example, of Rama breaking the bow of Shiva, the noise of it filled the universe, and made such a fearful sound that the horses yoked to the Sun's chariot left their course; the four elephants who uphold the earth, groaned; the earth itself shook, while gods, demons and saints had to put their hands to their ears. But when they recovered from the shock, the celestials were able to join with Brahma in singing Rama's praise and to rain down flowers.

In view of such strong feelings of gratitude and admiration on the part of the celestials, in view of the fact that they appear later as Rama's allies, and in the guise of monkeys, in his fight with Ravan and his demon followers, it is strange to find the gods—at least the lesser gods—actuated by feelings of jealousy and envy towards him. This is specially true of Indra. In the Vedas, where he appears as god of the firmament, Indra occupies a foremost place. More hymns are addressed to him than to any of the other gods. In the days of the Epics he had been pushed aside by Brahma, Vishnu and Shiva. Nevertheless he was not very far behind them, and he is spoken of as king of *swarga* or heaven, where the celestials lived. It may have been that his character was against him, and certainly he was involved in a number of scandalous intrigues. In particular, Tulsidas does more than hint at the curse uttered against him by an outraged husband, for his body was covered by a thousand stains, emblematic of his sin, and afterwards changed into eyes. Manifestly the poet had no respect for this deity, and with a healthy freedom he tells us over and over again what he thinks of him.

"The king of the gods is the limit for deceitfulness and evil conduct. Another's loss and his own gain is what he delights in. His ways are the ways of a crow. Cunning, and of unclean mind, he puts his trust in nobody." Ayodh. 289 (289) 301. And Rama himself is made to add, "The conduct of Indra is like that of a dog." Time after time the selfishness of the gods is emphasised, and when they thought they had any reason to fear that Rama would not adhere to his purpose of slaying Ravan, the bad side of their natures showed itself. Indeed no sooner was Rama's wedding over than they began to exercise a malign influence. It was necessary that Rama and Sita should be driven into exile. Otherwise the demon king would not carry off Sita, and provoke the wrath of her husband. If this did not happen they could not see how their enemy would be slain. And so they resolved to plot and plan to effect their purpose. It looked as if Rama were so happy that the promise Vishnu made would never be fulfilled.

"The evil-minded gods hoped that some obstacles would intervene. To them the rejoicings of Avadh afforded no pleasure. They liked it as little as a thief likes a moonlight night." Ayodh. 11. They therefore begged Saraswati to come to their help. The goddess agreed, and did as they asked. But she did not conceal her opinion of their characters. "The desires of the gods are vile. Their dwelling-place is lofty, their acts are low. They cannot bear to see the prosperity of another." Ayodh. 12.

On a later occasion, when Rama had gone into exile, and his unselfish brother was seeking to persuade him to return and claim his rights, the gods once more appealed to the goddess to render Bharat's efforts vain. She said they were "both selfish and stupid."

> "The illusive power (*maya*) of Brahma, Vishnu and Shiva is very great, nevertheless it cannot comprehend the understanding of Bharat. Why then do you tell me to make it of no effect? Is the moonlight able to rob the moon?" Ayodh. 283 (283) 295.

It is indeed a humiliating picture which the poet draws of the lesser gods. So long as Rama is doing what they wish, they are delighted. But even when he is face to face with their great enemy, they have not the courage to fight. The very sight of the demon makes them take to their heels in consternation and with loud cries. In extenuation of such cowardice it is fair to add that they had good cause to be afraid, because "only the Creator, Shiva and learned saints who were acquainted with Rama's power refused to run away." Lanka, 111 (92) 120.

In concluding this study of the lesser gods we shall refer to their reception of Rama when he had rescued Sita and put Ravan to death. "Among others the gods, selfish as they always were, came and spoke, as if they were in pursuit of the highest good." Lanka, 127 (106) 136.

When they had addressed Rama as the Supreme Spirit, the Eternal, the all-pervading Brahm, who had appeared on earth in seven different incarnations,[1] they confessed,

[1] As the fish, the tortoise, the boar, the man-lion, the dwarf; as Parashuram, and now as Rama. The poet does not refer to Buddha. The Krishna incarnation was later, and Kalki is still to come.

"We gods possess the highest rank, but in our selfishness we have forgotten to worship thee." Lanka, 127 (106) 135.

Thereafter Brahma broke into a long hymn of praise, in the course of which he said:

> "A curse on the life we gods possess: without devotion to thee existence goes astray." Lanka, 128 (107) 137.

Best of all, Indra is made to appear and confess his sin.

> "I was very proud. I thought there was no one equal to me. But now that I have seen the Lord's lotus feet, my grief-causing pride has ceased."

And then he adds what is one of the finest passages in the poem:

> "Let others worship the invisible, the quality-less Brahm, of whom the Vedas sing. But my choice is Koshal's king, the divine Rama, endowed with qualities and real. . . . May he receive me as his own servant and give me devotion." Lanka, 130 (109) 139.

It is sometimes suggested that such detailed reference to the lesser gods does not mean that our author believed in them. Some would seek to compare them and the demons to the angels and devils in whom many Christians believe. Others would argue that they are merely introduced as a foil to the greater power and dignity of the greater God, or gods of the poem. But it is quite impossible to accept any of these suggestions. The Hindu mind, in matters of religion, consists of a series of compartments, and the contents of one do not require to be reconciled with the contents of the others. The Hindu never claims to be a monotheist. He is at best a henotheist: that is, he worships one god at a time. When a Hindu becomes a monotheist, he ceases to be a Hindu, and finds refuge in religious societies like the Brahma Samaj or the

Prarthna Samaj of recent days. More frequently he turns for satisfaction to Christianity or Islam.

But when he does not go that length, he can claim that he is not quite so inconsistent as superficial observers might suppose. For, after all, what does the orthodox Hindu believe? He believes in a Supreme Spirit, all-pervading and devoid of qualities, but who finds expression in three forms, Brahma, Vishnu and Shiva. His cosmogony also is able to account for the existence of gods and demons, men and beasts, by saying that Brahma, the Creator, had mind-born sons through whom the three worlds became inhabited. If he is more pantheistically inclined, he can offer what seems, to him at least, a more thorough-going explanation of all apparent inconsistency, by saying that everything, from Brahma to a stone, is but a manifestation of Brahm or, as we have it given to us even more drastically in the words of a speaker in the *Vishnu Purana*, "I am all things; all things are in me. Brahm is my name" (I. 19).

We get an excellent illustration of the poet's own attitude in the opening stanzas of the poem. There is, perhaps, no more beautiful expression of his faith in God and in Rama as the incarnation of God, than in the following statement:

> "The Adorable (*bhagwan*) is one, passionless, formless, nameless, unborn, existence, thought, joy (*sachchidanand*), the supreme abode. He pervades all things. He exists in all forms. He assumes a body and performs many deeds simply for the sake of those devoted to Him. He is supremely merciful and full of love to His servants, very affectionate to those who are His own, and in His compassion is not angry with them. He is the restorer of that which is past, the protector of the humble, the sincere and powerful lord." Bal. 17 (17) 22.

And yet a few pages earlier we read :

> "Knowing that everything in the universe, animate and inanimate, consists of Rama, I ever worship with joined hands the lotus feet of all, gods, demons, men, serpents, birds, ghosts, departed ancestors, Gandharvs. I worship kinnars and night-walkers. May they all be merciful to me. The 84 lakhs of births are of four kinds. They live in water, on dry land and in the sky. Knowing that the whole universe consists of Sita and Rama, I worship it with joined hands." Bal. 10 (10) 15.

III.

BRAHMA, THE CREATOR.

As has been mentioned, Prajapati the lord of creatures became, in course of time, Brahma, the Creator. There was indeed a day prior to the age of the Epics when Brahma was the highest god. This was his position, for example, in the *Laws of Manu*, where Vishnu and Shiva are only once mentioned, while Brahma or Prajapati is referred to over and over again, always in subordination of course to the impersonal quality-less Soul of the Universe, Brahm.

In the more ancient part of the Epics it would appear as if Brahma were continuing to hold his own. But in the later sections of those poems we can see that Vishnu and Shiva are pushing him aside, and claiming, more and more, the worship of men. How that process worked is shown very clearly in the following illustration. The first three *avataras* or descents of Vishnu, those of the fish, the tortoise and the boar, were originally attributed to Brahma. But the followers of Vishnu somehow managed to appropriate them to their own favourite deity. It has been suggested that the Creator had no strong Brahma sect to push his claims as Shiva and Vishnu had to push theirs, and certainly not a few passages could be quoted from the impartial pages of the *Mahabharata* and from the sectarian Puranas, in which the followers of these two younger gods make the most extravagant claims for their own special object of worship, asserting that he is the Supreme Spirit, and as such includes within himself every other god.

But there is another and deeper reason than the assertiveness of the sects for the gradual weakening of Brahma's power and influence. The assertiveness of the sects may have been responsible to some extent. But why were the followers of Vishnu and Shiva so confident and eager ? It was because they believed their gods could do something that the Creator could not do. Brahma's work of creation, so far as the existing universe is concerned, is finished. His work, such as it is, good or bad, was completed long ago, and he can do nothing to alter it. A process was set in motion and actions have taken place, which must bear their inevitable fruit. What has been, has been, and what will be, will be. He is Pitamaha, the grandfather. He has retired from active work. No great purpose is gained by worshipping him. Why should men erect temples in his honour ? [1] There are gods more potent—a god who may be appeased, or a god who will be gracious. If Brahma created this world, that was an event which took place in the distant past. But it is Vishnu who preserves the world, and Shiva who destroys it. Is it not better to gain favour of the one and to placate the other ? This indeed may be called the motive of the whole poem, to show that there is a God who can save. However great Brahma's work of creation may have been, despite the fact that gods and men make constant appeal for his assistance, Brahma's own creation is often beyond his control. This is set forth very clearly in the opening pages of the poem. It is a very remarkable utterance, because it attributes everything that exists to the Creator ; even the Supreme Spirit and Maya are included. But other forces have since begun to operate and deprived Brahma of at least much of his power.

[1] In the *Mahabharata* we read, "Men worship Shiva the destroyer because they fear him, Vishnu the preserver because they hope from him ; but who worship Brahma, the creator ? His work is done." Quoted by Hopkins, *India, Old and New*, p. 113.

"The good and the bad, Vidhi created both; the Vedas declare their many virtues and defects. The Vedas, histories and Puranas say that what Vidhi has created is a mingling of good and evil. Pain and pleasure, sin and religious merit, day and night, the religious and the wicked, good caste and low caste, demon and god; high and low, nectar and life, poison and death; Maya and Brahm, the individual soul and the lord of the world (*jagdish*); the seen and the unseen, the beggar and the king; Kashi and Magadh; the Ganges and the Karmnasha; the land of death (*Marwar*) and Malwa; [1] Brahmin and outcaste; heaven and hell, sensual desire and asceticism; Veda and Tantra; a distribution of good and evil; sensate or insensate, whether full of virtue or defect, the Creator has made all things. Good men are like the swan, they keep the milk of goodness and reject the water of evil. When Vidhata gives such powers of discrimination to them, they abandon what is wrong, and the mind falls in love with virtue. But Time, their natural dispositions (*svabhav*) and the fruit of what they did in their former lives (*karma*) exercise violence upon them, and even a good man, in the grip of things as they are, makes mistakes." Bal. (6) 11.

The Creator then has made all that is. He even gives to his creatures the power to discern between good and evil. But the influence of Time, their natural dispositions and the fruit of their past actions cause them to err. Time, Svabhav and Karma are more powerful than the Creator. As the poem advances, the poet has many opportunities of enlarging on this theme. But that does not mean that the world has been utterly forsaken. Vishnu comes to its

[1] Magadh was the home of Buddhism in contrast to Kashi, a centre of Hinduism; the Ganges washes away every sin; the Karmnasha, a river between Kashi and Behar, destroys all merit. Marwar is in the desert of Rajputana; Malwa is famous for its fruitfulness.

relief. "Hari takes those who put their trust in him and corrects their wanderings, removing their sorrows and their sins." Bal. (7) 12.

And Brahma himself is conscious of the fact that there are grave limits to his power. In the face of an evil for which he himself was responsible, he frankly admits, "There is nothing I can do." Bal. 190 (196) 216. Brahma had conferred on the demon Ravan the invincibility which proved so great a scourge to both gods and men. What he had conferred he could not, however, withdraw. But there was one who was more than equal to the situation, and so the Creator says to his brother celestials who had invited him to interfere : "Keep courage in your hearts. I cannot help you. But Vishnu can help both you and me. He knows about our sufferings. The Lord (*prabhu*) will remove our bitter afflictions." Bal. 190 (196) 214.

And yet, despite all that has been written on the comparative position of the three great gods of Hinduism, one is struck, not by the subordinate position which one would expect Brahma to occupy, especially in a poem so definitely devoted to the portrayal of Rama as the incarnation both of Vishnu and the Supreme Spirit, but by the prominence he continues to secure. The same contradiction exists in India to-day. It is true that there are very few temples to Brahma, in contrast to the many thousands and hundreds of thousands in honour of Vishnu and Shiva.[1] Nevertheless the fact remains that in the speech of every day, when men speak of life and the deeper things of life, they speak of Parameshwar, and when they do so, they probably think neither of Vishnu nor of Shiva, but of God their Creator.

[1] Monier Williams has given currency to the belief that there are only two temples to Brahma in all India—one at Pushkar near Ajmer, Rajputana, and one in Idar state on the frontier of the same province. But Pandit Gauri Shankar of the Ajmer Museum has visited three other temples in the native states of Rajputana where the image of Brahma is still worshipped.

This is a matter so important that it needs to be examined in detail. It would appear, despite the progress of these other gods, and the development of their worship, that the human heart, by some ineradicable instinct, turns, in moments of joy and sorrow, instinctively to its Maker in either praise or blame.

In the seven books of his poem Tulsidas refers to Brahma under one name or another more than 350 times. On at least 240 occasions the names used are Vidhi, Viranchi, Vidhata or Kartar—all words that specifically denote his function as maker or fashioner of the universe. He is referred to as Brahma about fifty times, while in reference to the mythological stories connected with Brahma, he is sometimes called "*the four-faced*," or "*he who was born from the lotus*."

When the name Brahma is used it is as a rule in association with other gods: "Brahma and the others." Bal. 77 (75) 89. "Brahma and the other gods." Bal. 264 (270) 293. "Shiva, Brahma and the others" Bal. 313 (319) 346, or we read of Brahma's weapons and Brahma's dwelling-place. Occasionally we read of something Brahma said or did. "Brahma said, 'The desire of Hari is very powerful.'" Kish. 11 (7) 9. "Shiva, Brahma and the other gods reverence Rama." Lanka, 130 (109) 139.

Other names are also used. Aj, which means the *unborn*, is the most interesting, and is used at least seventeen times; also, as a rule, in association with the other gods, most frequently with either Shiva or both Shiva and Vishnu. Ish, or Ishwar, which means either lord or god, appears at least eighteen times, but it is to be noted that when Shiva is referred to in association with Brahma and Vishnu, or with Brahma alone, he also is frequently called Ish. Another name, Daiv, meaning peculiar to, or belonging to, the gods, and derived from *dev*, a common name for the lesser gods, is also used.

The point on which one wishes to lay emphasis, however, is that Tulsidas has the first member of the Hindu Triad very often in his thoughts, and in the large majority of cases when he refers to him it is by names which directly signify his proper function—not Brahma, not Ishwar, not Jagdish, not even Aj, but the words Vidhi, Viranchi and Vidhata, all of which by their derivation and meaning show that he is the arranger, disposer and maker of the universe.[1]

In illustration let us take first a few references to Brahma's work as creator.[2]

"From the time Viranchi made the world, we have seen and heard of many marriages." Bal. 319 (325) 352.

"In all that Vidhi has made, I have not heard of or seen any one like Bharat." Ayodh. 221 (221) 231.

"Mingling the milk of goodness with the water of evil, even so has Vidhata fashioned the world." Ayodh. 222 (222) 232.

"Viranchi has created for the forest Kol and Kirat women who know nothing of the luxuries of life." Ayodh. 58 (58) 60.

"When Viranchi made and adorned Sita, he made her after consideration for the dark-coloured bridegroom." Bal. 228 (234) 255.

"What was the purpose of Viranchi when he made women ?" Bal. 333 (339) 366.

[1] Vidhi occurs at least 160 times, Viranchi 50, Vidhata about 30 times and Kartar thrice. Daiv occurs 16 times.

Brahma himself uses *Ishwar* when he tells his brother deities to appeal to Vishnu :

"Devise a plan by which Ishwar will come and help." Bal. 94 (92) 106.

[2] There are a number of passages where the poet, to enhance the grandeur of some human contrivance, speaks slightingly of the Creator :

"The cleverness of Viranchi appeared contemptible." Bal. 103 (101) 117.

"Their splendour caused dismay to Vidhi." Ayodh. 206 (206) 215.

The elaborate passage which makes the Creator primarily responsible for everything, whatever its nature or character, has been already quoted. Bal. (6) 11. Elsewhere we have the same idea, though in fewer words:

"The king's love and the queen's cruelty—Vidhi made them both, the limit." Ayodh. (36) 37.

"The mandate of God (*ish*) is on all our heads, in creation, preservation and destruction; whether it be poison or amrit."

"The manifestations of Vidhi are thus immovable and without beginning." Ayodh. (280) 282.

Attention should also be called to the recurrence of the very primitive idea regarding creation in the statement:

"By the power of penance Vidhata created all things." Bal. 84 (82) 96.

What is of more importance is the Creator's relation to the inhabitants of the universe. We have seen how the gods made frequent appeals for his help. He was sometimes also brought into very close relations with the demons. Brahma had a most unfortunate facility for granting boons. It is true that he was not as a rule his own master. If saints or demons only practised asceticism long enough and vigorously enough, they could extract from the Creator almost any favour they liked, and Vishnu's incarnation as Rama was rendered necessary by a boon which Brahma had conferred on Ravan. That evil creature had practised penance so long and so earnestly that the Creator just had to come and say, "My son, I am pleased, ask a boon"; and the demon, bending before Brahma and clasping his feet, said to the lord of the world, "Grant that I may not die except by the hand of a man or a monkey." Bal. 182 (180) 206. And the answer he received was: "Be it so; you have performed a great penance."

Ravan, as a result of this promise, could not be killed by either gods or demons. In his pride he had not thought it possible that man or beast could slay him. To overreach him it was therefore necessary for Vishnu to be born as a man, and for the gods to become monkeys. Bal. 192 (198) 218.

What Brahma could grant to demons, perhaps against his will, it was believed that in more natural fashion he would give men and women, and so, time after time, we find appeals addressed to him, sometimes more or less in the form of an oath, thus :

> "Oh, Vidhi! What is going to happen?" Ayodh. (68) 70.
>
> "Oh, Vidhi! quickly remove the foolishness of Janak." Bal. 252 (258) 281.

But much more generally we read that prayers were addressed to him, or hopes expressed that he would hear his suppliants.

> "Rama, practise every continence to-day that Vidhi may give to our affairs a happy settlement." Ayodh. 10.
>
> "If Vidhi give me another birth, may he do me this kindness, that Rama will be my son and Sita my daughter-in-law." Ayodh. 17.
>
> "There is one plan, I may mention, which you can adopt if God (*daiv*) grant his assistance." Bal. 80 (78) 92.
>
> "In his heart, he was appealing to Vidhi that Rama would not go to the forest." Ayodh. (43) 44.
>
> "Day and night they continued to pray to Vidhi, desiring devotion for Rama's feet." Uttar, 46 (25) 47.
>
> "In whatever births we may wander, in bondage to our former births, may God (*ish*) grant us this." Ayodh. 24.

The Creator's interest and readiness to help are manifest :

"Seeing them, Vidhi was pleased in his mind." Ayodh. (271) 283.

"God (*ish*) is our shield and the king of Mithila is our helper." Ayodh. (273) 282.

"By God's grace (*ish*) and with your blessing, my sons and daughters are pure like Ganges water." Ayodh. (271) 283.

"When Ish is favourable every kind of benefit in the world is obtained by men." Bal. 349 (346) 374.

But he can also be angry and show his power, while anxiety is manifested as to his real intentions and character.

"If Vidhata is hostile to any one, then a grain of dust is equal to Mount Meru, a feather is like the King of Death, and a rope becomes a snake." Bal. 181 (179) 205.

"What Vidhi has written on the forehead, god (*dev*), demon, man, serpent, saint, no one is able to wipe out." Bal. 80 (78) 92.

"If Vidhata is good and gives to all appropriate rewards, then the bridegroom for Janaki has been found. This is not a matter for doubt. If by the control of Vidhi the wedding is thus arranged, then every one will be pleased." Bal. 227 (233) 254.

"Whom God (*daiv*) creates to be under the control of an enemy, he will not desire to live : death is better." Ayodh. 21.

"Vidhi made me deformed in body, and made me a slave." Ayodh. 16.

Indeed the poem shows that however willing people may be to credit Brahma with good intentions, they often find it impossible to do so, and when they don't get what they would like, they grumble, and that very vigorously, against God. The poet himself may not be specially perplexed by the problems of sin and suffering, because his object is to show that he has found an answer to men's perplexities in Rama, the incarnation of the Supreme Spirit. But he is true to life and human experience when he makes his characters, the men and women of Avadh, cry out against their sufferings. They feel as if some lesser god had made the world. The Creator cannot finish the task he undertook, or if he meddles, things are only made worse.[1]

"Vidhi interfered and spoiled the matter when it was half done." Ayodh. (153) 160.

"Vidhi arranged everything well, and has (now) spoiled it." Bal. 271 (277) 293.

"What is Vidhi after now ?" Bal. 268 (274) 299.

"When Vidhi is opposed, every one is opposed." Ayodh. (174) 182.

"The ways of Vidhi are all crooked. He is utterly beyond control, cruel and without pity. He made the moon pale, the tree of Indra's heaven into a common piece of wood, and the sea salt." Ayodh. (114) 119.

"Vidhi's understanding is crooked. He uses a thunderbolt to break a milk bubble. We hear of amrit and see poison ; all his doings are hard. On every hand there are crows, owls and cranes ; the auspicious swan is only to be found in Manas lake (and can't be reached). . . . The ways of Vidhi are very contradictory and wonderful. He creates, he nourishes, and again destroys. It is like children at play. Vidhi's methods are those of a fool." Ayodh. (269) 281.

[1] Occasionally people realise that the fruit of their former lives is the cause of their sufferings :

"All this is the result of my sin. I can do nothing, Vidhi is against me." Ayodh. (35) 36.

Just as, conversely, a ferryman tells Rama that he has got compensation for all his past sorrow, in the sight of Rama's face :

"To-day Vidhi has paid me all my wages." Ayodh. (98) 102.

> "What a wicked thing Kartar has done!" Ayodh. (236) 246.
>
> "The love I bore for Rama, Vidhi was not able to endure, and played this low trick by means of my mother." Ayodh. (250) 261.
>
> "My bad luck, my mother's wickedness, the incomprehensible action of Vidhi, and the cruelty of Time, have all combined to obstruct and destroy me." Ayodh. (256) 267.

In concluding this series of quotations, an observation made by Ravan may well be added. The penance which ultimately compelled Brahma to grant him a boon, was the throwing of his ten heads, one after the other, into a sacrificial fire. On one of these skulls, as it was burning, the demon read, written by the Creator, words to the effect that he would die at the hands of a man. But as he told the story, he merely laughed, not believing that the words of the Creator could be true.

> "I considered there was no cause for fear: Viranchi wrote it when he was old and his intelligence feeble." Lanka, 38 (28) 43.

The reference to what was written on the skull of Ravan naturally leads to another matter in connection with the Creator—the suggestion made over and over again that people are not personally responsible when they do wrong. Such an assertion is all the more remarkable in view of the very vigorous and penetrating fashion in which Tulsidas exposes and condemns human frailty and sin. Thus we find Bharat saying that Vidhata had made him to be a disgrace to his family, and lamenting that his mother had brought ruin to Rama; but he is told not to worry.

> "Rama loves you, you love Rama. Your mother is not to blame; the blame rests with the Creator (*vidhi*), who is adverse." Ayodh. (193) 201.

Rama also speaks in similar fashion. In one of those many passages where his magnanimity is so beautifully revealed he goes out of his way to show kindness to his foolish stepmother, whose jealousy had procured his exile :

> "Falling at her feet, he spoke words of comfort, placing the guilt on the head of Time, Karma (the fruit of actions) and the Creator (*vidhi*)." Ayodh. (234) 244.

The language he uses to his brother in extenuation of the same offender, is even stronger :

> "Do not be depressed. Know that man's life is in the control of God (*ish*). The people who blame your mother are fools, who have never served in the schools of the philosophers and the saints." Ayodh. (252) 263.

IV.

KAL, KARMA, VIDHI—TIME, THE FRUIT OF ACTIONS AND THE CREATOR.

THERE is often a very real temptation to translate the various words for Creator by our English terms, Destiny and Fate. The Creator seems so helpless in his own universe. He seems to be nothing more than an impersonal force, which cannot be moved. This temptation is specially strong with phrases like *Vidhi-bash*—" in the grasp of the Creator "—which Growse sometimes, but not always, translates as, " in the grasp of Fate " ; and in such statements as :

> " You can do nothing against the acts of Vidhi." Ayodh. (197) 206 ;
>
> " You cannot wipe out the writings of Vidhi." Bal. 107 (104) 120 ;

or when we come across two separate words for God in the same sentence, to translate at least one of them by Fate.

> " They blamed Daiv, saying to each other, the doings of Vidhi are all crooked." Ayodh. (114) 119.
>
> " What a wicked thing Kartar has done. Looking at her they were greatly distressed at all the things Daiv had caused her to suffer." Ayodh. (236) 246.

The inclination to use Destiny and Fate in our translations is even greater in relation to two other words which appear with great frequency throughout the poem. I refer to the words *Karma* and *Bhavi.* Nevertheless, if we ever speak of Fate or Destiny in reference to Hindu thought,[1] it cannot be said too often that we are importing into our discussions ideas which are foreign to Hinduism. Even when Tulsidas speaks of the handwriting of the Creator on Ravan's skull, or elsewhere—a phrase he may have borrowed from Mohammedanism—he is not thinking of anything being predestined or foreordained by God irrespective of what a man has been or has done in his former lives. But he is thinking—indeed he is obsessed by the thought—of how the soul is born time after time in age after age, and that in those endless births the soul is accumulating a mass of actions (*karma*) which cling to it all through its career. That is what the Indian calls Karma, and, according to Tulsidas, Karma is more powerful than anything else.

And the same is true of the other word which Tulsidas uses, and which is frequently rendered as *fate* ; I refer to Bhavi. Tulsidas often says of some one or other, " He is in the grasp of Bhavi," just as he says, " He is in the grasp of Vidhi." But this word Bhavi means that which is in process of becoming ; that which is bound to happen ; the inevitable.

Now, when Tulsidas tells us that Karma is supreme, or says men are in the grasp of the inevitable, he is thinking of what is the governing idea of Indian thought. It is not Brahma or Vishnu or Shiva who is the ruler of the universe. It is Karma or Bhavi, who is the real god of Hinduism. As we shall find, Tulsidas has reasons to give us for believing that both must bend before the all-conquering might of Rama, and that there is hope for both gods and men if they take refuge in him. Nevertheless, here is the central thought of Hinduism : the inevitableness of Karma—not a something that has been appointed in any arbitrary fashion by some one outside ourselves,

[1] *Necessity* would be a better word than either of them. It takes things as they are and apportions no blame.

God or another, but a something for which we are ourselves responsible. Because it is the accumulated total of our own past actions and character in previous existences, and which stands to our credit or to our debit, a blessing or a snare. " The dread of continued rebirth is the one haunting thought which colours the whole texture of Indian philosophy," says Monier Williams, and it is the burden of the common man as well. Unfortunately, as we have seen, it tends to sap a man's moral strength also, for it makes it very easy to find an excuse for our sins by blaming a past of which we have no recollection. Is a man happy, his Karma explains his happiness. Is a man unfortunate, then his Karma is to blame even more completely and thoroughly than the Creator can be—an idea very well brought out in the following passage : " Is not Vidhi hostile to us ? They speak truly who say that Karma is supreme." Ayodh. (88) 91. The Creator may or may not be hostile : there may be two minds on that matter. But there is no doubt about the other : Karma is supreme.

How that thought permeates the poem let us now proceed to examine. It will enable us to realise how the Creator came to be so helpless in his own universe.

Take these illustrations of how the Creator and Karma are jointly involved ?

> " You cannot escape from what Vidhata has fashioned. It is written in my Karma that I should marry a madman. Then why blame any one ? People like you can't wipe out the writing of Vidhi." Bal. 106 (104) 120.
>
> " Bhavi is overwhelming : loss and gain, life and death, honour and dishonour are in the hands of Vidhi." Ayodh. (165) 172.

Or less certainly, as we cannot tell who the fashioner is :

> " Oh, fashioner of that which has to be ! what is

going to happen, and who will save us ? " Bal. 95 (93) 107.

We have the two ideas, battling even more confusedly, when Rama's mother says :

> " Sorrow and joy, loss and gain, Karma is beyond our control. Blame no one, the ways of Karma are obscure. Vidhi knows. He is the giver of the fruit of good and bad Karma. The mandate of God (*ish*) is on all our heads. . . . The manifestations of Vidhi are thus immovable and without beginning." Ayodh. 270 (270) 282.

This was in reply to another queen who had said that the methods of Vidhi were those of a fool, and that he acted with the fickleness of children at play. Probably there is no passage in the whole poem which gives us more clearly the working of these two forces, the Creator and Karma, as they appeal to the poet's mind. Rama's mother is shocked at the language of her sister queen ; she thinks no one is to blame, not even the Creator. She claims for him a dignity and an authority which we have seen many others would deny to him. But after all is said, is not Karma greater than God ? because at best it is our Karma, not God, which is responsible for our present, and will account for our future.

It is true that some passages speak of God giving people their Karma, or awarding the fruit of their Karma, as in the two following utterances, both made by Bharat :

> " Their fathers and mothers are the source of the birth of all ; their good and bad Karma, Vidhata gave." Ayodh. (244) 255.
>
> " After due consideration, God (*ish*) awards the fruit in accordance with our good or bad Karma. According to the Karma we do, so do we find the fruit. That is

what the Vedas, moral systems, and everybody says." Ayodh. (74) 77.

But it will be noted that even here the Creator, despite his prominence, is an arbiter and nothing more. He merely awards the verdict in accordance with what we ourselves have done.

There are at least fifty references to Karma or Bhavi, and in view of their importance it is desirable to give a few examples. It will be noted that the phrases applied to the Creator are frequently used. Karma is spoken of as cruel, and the purposes of Bhavi are immovable ; just as Vidhi was cruel, and nothing could be done to change what he had decreed.

"Do not think of your loss and vexation. The course of Time and Karma cannot be altered. Do not blame any one. Vidhata is in every way hostile to me." Ayodh. (158) 165.

"Bhavi is strong. Loss and gain, life and death, honour and dishonour are in the hands of Vidhi." Ayodh. (165) 172.

"It is Hari's wish, and Bhavi is strong." Bal. 67 (65) 78.

"Shiva admonished her in various ways, but Uma being under the control of Bhavi, would not understand." Bal. 73 (71) 85.

"The king, being in the power of Bhavi, thought it was one of Love's diversions." Ayodh. (25) 25.

"Karma is cruel. I am not to blame." Ayodh. (57) 69.

"The ways of Karma are cruel, nothing can be done." Ayodh. (99) 96.

"The king's minister was like some high-born dame, virtuous and wise, who in thought, word and deed looks upon her husband as a god, nevertheless deserts him because she is in the grip of Karma." Ayodh. (139) 145.

" Her mind turned round, as Bhavi willed it." Ayodh. 17.

" Although you have done no wrong, Bhavi cannot be wiped out." Bal. 180 (178) 204.

This is the unmistakable teaching of the earlier parts of the poem. Bhavi cannot be wiped out, every one is in the grasp of Karma. And yet we are not allowed altogether to forget that if Karma is supreme, it is by Rama's appointment.[1]

" Rama has made Karma lord of all things, and as we act, so must we taste the fruit. Nevertheless he plays at odds and evens, according as hearts are devoted or not devoted to him." Ayodh. 210 (210) 219.

As the work proceeds we shall find that by Rama's grace, and through the devotion which men are able to show for him, the power of Karma is either weakened or destroyed.

There are also a number of references to the belief in transmigration, and the quality and character of these varying births are ascribed to Karma.

" In whatever births we may wander, in the grip of Karma, may God (*ish*) give us this, to be worshippers of Rama." Ayodh. 24 (24) 24.

The same thought is expressed in Kish. 13 (9) 11, but the prayer is addressed to Rama, and naturally there is no reference to the Creator.

[1] Observe, however, the reference to Shiva : " If your daughter will practise penance, Tripurari is able to wipe out Bhavi." Bal. 81 (79) 92. This is a stronger statement than anything we read at this stage about Rama. It is in agreement with the clear fact that Rama and others are invariably represented as praying to Shiva as the chief object of their worship.

In the sequel, or *Uttar Kand,* again, an inspired crow tells us :

> "In my different births I did different kinds of Karma ; but though I remember them all, and they were very many, I was never so happy as in my present birth." 137 (93) 150.

The most interesting passages, however, are those in which we do not read of Karma alone, but associated with Time. It is not to be wondered at that the Hindu should speak with an awed whisper when he refers to Time. There are few matters in which his imagination has more expanded itself. There are eighty-four lakhs of lives through which each living creature has to pass, it may be as a god or a demon, it may be as a man or as a beast. Between these 8,400,000 lives, the *Mahabharata* and Puranas have placed long periods to be spent in either heaven or hell. No wonder the most searching appeal of the Hindu is to devise some method by which he will escape this endless process of rebirth. And so just as he is impressed by the thought of Karma and all it means to him, so is he impressed by the thought of Time, the field in which these actions are working out to their inevitable end.

And as he thinks of these twin forces and meditates on their power, the Creator, of whom his less sophisticated fathers once thought so much, and reckoned the greatest of the gods, seems to be in the grasp of forces greater than he can control—Time and Karma, Rebirth and the fruit of our own past deeds.

> "Life and death, all that we suffer and all that we enjoy, loss and gain, the society of friends and separation from them, are all in the grasp of Time and Karma, in alien grasp, just like day and night. Fools rejoice in happiness and lament in sorrow. A resolute man treats both alike. Be brave and exercise judgement.

Give up your grief. You are the well-wisher of all." Ayodh. (144) 150.

Farther on we read :

"The ways of Time and Karma cannot be altered, as you know. Do not blame any one. It is Vidhata who in every way is hostile to me." Ayodh. (158) 165.

There are other passages again which refer, not only to these two potent forces, Time and Karma, but also to what they have produced, viz., our natural dispositions and qualities (*swabhav gun*), thus making us what we are. And the wonderful power of Rama to help and save is shown by the fact that during his long and glorious reign, all the creatures in the world suffered nothing from the deeds caused by Time (*kal*), Karma, natural dispositions and qualities. Uttar, 43 (22) 44. A later passage says that the same four—Kal, Karma, Svabhav and Gun—were ill at ease. The night of ignorance passed away, and Sin, like an owl, disappeared. 52 (31) 53.

Once he gets hold of a new phrase, the poet likes to use it, and a few stanzas farther on he speaks of how men have to live through the eighty-four lakhs of rebirths, ever under the control of Illusion (*maya*) and surrounded by Time, Karma, Natural Dispositions and Qualities.

In a passage already quoted, we have seen how Rama, wishing to set his stepmother at ease, told her that she was not to blame for driving him into exile :

"Time, Karma and the Creator, the guilt rests on their heads." Ayodh. (235) 245.[1]

In direct opposition to such a dangerous statement, however, we find Rama giving expression to a very different opinion in the last book of the poem. It was after his return from exile and the rescue of Sita. Speaking of

[1] See also Ayodh. (198) 207, where a sage tells Bharat not to blame his mother.

those who by their foolishness and sin spoil their chances in the next world, he adds :

> " The sacred books say it is great good fortune to be born in the form of a man, a condition which the gods find it difficult to reach. It is in that condition one can realise oneself. It is the gateway to salvation. And yet when they don't secure salvation and go to the other world and there suffer torment, beating their heads and repenting, men falsely lay the blame on Time, Karma and God (*ishwar*)." Uttar, 64 (43) 65.

This is a remarkable utterance. It cannot be reconciled with Rama's words to his stepmother. And it is difficult to understand why Tulsidas should put into the mouth of his hero two statements which contradict one another so completely. But the second of the two may be reckoned with confidence as his more considered utterance. Indeed, it is the only logical position. Tulsidas may grumble at Karma, as he grumbled at the Creator. He may feel at times the mystery of life and its frequent unreasonableness. But if we believe in Karma and Transmigration, believe that we are what we are in character and disposition in this present life, because of what we were and what we did in our previous lives, we cannot possibly blame God for being what we have made ourselves. Nor can we blame our Karma, for our Karma is just ourselves, the accumulated actions, the inevitable fruit of our own doings. Its other name, as we have seen, is Bhavi, that which inevitably happens, and has gone on happening in the spacious fields of Time. I have said that Karma is the real god of the Hindu, the god whom he fears. It might be called an idol more than a god, for it is the work of his own hands. It was he who fashioned it and gave it shape—he who gave to it all that makes it what it is.

V.

SHIVA, THE DESTROYER GOD.

It has been already said that Shiva, the third member of the Hindu Triad, occupies a very prominent position in the poem. And were Tulsidas a common sectarian poet like the character he pictures towards the close of his poem, one might be inclined to think that he dwells on the greatness of Shiva's power and wisdom as a foil to the still greater power and wisdom of Rama. But all such imaginings are erroneous. Tulsidas is an orthodox Hindu, who is able to find room in his heart for more than one god. It is true that we are told :

"The glory of Rama's name cannot be measured. The Eternal Shiva, Shiva the Adorable, the very essence of wisdom and goodness, is always repeating it." Bal. 58 (56) 67.

On the other hand, it has to be remembered that in quite a number of passages we have Vishnu, in his original form, speaking as follows :

"Go and repeat Shiva's hundred names and your mind will at once secure comfort. There is no one so dear to me as Shiva. Never allow yourself by foolishness to forsake this truth. The person on whom Shiva does not take pity, will never achieve devotion to me." Bal. 146 (144) 165.

And this statement is confirmed by one of the great sages.

"The man who does not love Shiva's lotus feet can

not please Rama even in a dream. A love free from guile for the feet of the lord of all things is the one token that you are a devotee of Rama. Who is there so faithful to Rama as Shiva is? And who is so dear to Rama as Shiva?" Bal. 113 (111) 127.

Nor is there any doubt as to the prevalence of Shiva's worship in Avadh. All classes of the people, including Rama and his parents, made constant appeal to him. Indeed, apart from the devotion specially centred in Rama himself, it is Shiva who is worshipped in a more real and genuine fashion than any of the other gods. We read of the other gods receiving a general worship, and we have seen how Brahma is regarded. But it is in relation to Shiva that we get the most of the illustrations of real prayer and worship, and see how those who sought his help addressed him. And this is conspicuously true of both Rama and Sita, in reference not only to Shiva, but also to his wife, under the name of Gauri, and their elephant-headed son, Ganesh.

Thus we find the people, in their desire to see Rama chosen heir-apparent, begging Shiva's favour. Ayodh. 2. At a later period they are shown as worshipping Ganesh, Gauri, Shiva and the Sun, and then addressing this special prayer to Vishnu.[1]

"Sprinkle our hearts with this bliss-conferring ambrosia (*amrit*), oh God (*dev*), give to the world its life's desire." Ayodh. (262) 273.

Rama's father is also referred to as praying to Shiva,

[1] As a Smarta, Tulsidas himself would worship these five. Shiva and his wife worshipped their own son Ganesh!

"Shambhu and Bhavani worshipped Ganesh. Let no one who hears this entertain doubts, but understand that they are all eternal gods." Bal. 110 (108) 124.

Gauri and Ganesh. Bal. 302 (308) 334. But it is to Shiva alone he says :

> " Hear my prayer, undying Shiva ; thou art quickly pleased and a generous giver. Remove the affliction of your humble suppliant." Ayodh. (44) 45.

Sita also addresses a very definite appeal to Shiva, with his wife and son. It was when she was anxious that Rama should be her husband. We are not told what she said to Shiva and Ganesh, but as she stood before the shrine of the goddess she said :

> " There is no beginning, nor middle nor end of thee. Thy glory is boundless. The Veda comprehends it not. Thou art the cause of the existence, the continuance and the disappearance of all things. You know well my heart's desire, because you dwell for ever in all hearts. There is no need that I should say that aloud to thee." Bal. 240 (246) 267.

In reply, the image smiled and dropped a garland. But more than that, we are told that the goddess herself appeared, and said with a smile :

> " Listen, Sita, my blessing is certain. The desire of your heart will be realised. The bridegroom you wish will be got." Bal. 241 (247) 268.

Sita again sought the help of the same three at the time Rama was called on to bend the bow of Shiva :

> " Be pleased, oh great god (*mahesh*) and Bhavani (Gauri). Make fruitful my worship of you. Be favourable to me and make the bow light. Oh lord of hosts (Ganesh), the god who gives boons, I beg you to make the weight of the bow very small." Bal. 268 (266) 289.

As for Rama and his brother, when they were boys, it is said that " they lived in Shiva's heart." Bal. 249 (255) 277. When Rama was married, the queen mothers gave rich presents to the Brahmins and worshipped Ganesh and

Shiva. Bal. 344 (350) 378. When the bridegroom returned to Avadh, he entered the city remembering Shiva, Gauri and Ganesh. Bal. 345 (351) 379. When any one, Rama as well as others, wished to confirm a statement with an oath, they said : "Be Shiva my witness."

When Rama went into exile he bowed in reverence before the feet of his religious teacher, and called on Ganesh, Gauri and Shiva, and it is added that they gave him their blessing. Ayodh. (78) 81. When the exiles reached the Ganges, Sita uttered a short prayer to that sacred river, praying that they might be granted a happy return ; but of Rama it is said that he gave adoration to Shiva. Ayodh. (99) 103. Having reached the farther shore of the river, Rama once more turned his thoughts to Ganesh and Shiva. At the junction of the Ganges and the Jumna, the exiles bathed at that specially sacred spot, and in addition to the local deity, the god of the place of pilgrimage, he worshipped Shiva. Ayodh. (102) 106.

One of the most genuine prayers in the poem is addressed to Shiva by Rama's father :

> "Remembering Mahesh, he addressed him humbly : 'Hear my entreaty, eternal Shiva. You are quickly pleased, compassionate to the lowly, and bountiful. Knowing me to be a man in need, put away my pain. You control all hearts. Give, then, to Rama such understanding that he will ignore my words and remain at home, forgetting his natural disposition and love. May I be disgraced : may my good name perish from the earth : may I fall into hell rather than go to heaven. May I suffer every kind of insufferable pain. But let not Rama be hidden from my eyes.' " Ayodh. 43 (43) 44.

When Bharat also was burdened by bad omens, and before he heard of his brother's exile, it was to Shiva that he addressed his prayers. This passage is of particular interest, because it almost certainly refers to the worship of the phallus :

> "Bharat fed Brahmins daily and gave them gifts. With various rites he poured water over Shiva. In his mind he besought Mahesh for the happiness of his father and mother, his relatives and brothers." Ayodh. 150 (150) 157.

Of Rama himself we read, that when the exiles reached the banks of the Ganges :

> "The lord of the house of Raghu bathed and worshipped a clay image of Shiva (*parthiv*), bowing his head." Ayodh. 99 (99) 103.

There are two other passages, both associated with Rama, in which the *linga* or phallus is definitely spoken of. When the monkeys were helping Rama to construct the bridge across to Ceylon, he said :

> "Here I shall set up a Shiva. My heart desires it greatly. Having set up the linga according to the proper rites, he worshipped it, saying, There is no other I love like Shiva. If any one be called my devotee and do violence to Shiva, that man even in a dream cannot be loved by me. If any one hostile to Shiva desire to be my devotee, that man is a fool with very little sense, and hell is his portion. The devotee of Shiva who does violence to me, the devotee of mine who does violence to Shiva, will both dwell in a deep hell for the period of a Kalpa." Lanka, 2 (2) 4.

Again, on his return to Avadh after the rescue of Sita, Rama pointed out the various places of interest, as they travelled through the air in Kuver's aeroplane. And when they saw the beautiful bridge that the monkeys had built, Rama said :

> "'Here is the place where I set up a Shiva, the abode

of joy'; and as he spoke, he who is the abode of mercy and Sita bowed their heads in worship." Lanka, 143 (116) 153.[1]

When Tulsidas makes it so very clear that not only the people of all classes, but Rama himself, the incarnation of the Supreme Spirit, gave such preference to the worship of Shiva, he is giving expression to his own feelings also, because he repeatedly appeals to Shiva and Ganesh for help in the composition of his poem, and says that if any man or woman will listen to the glories of Rama, Shiva will cause all his hopes to be fulfilled. Kish. 35 (30) 33.

But, best of all, we have another passage which is a real confession of the poet's own faith, not only in Shiva and his consort but in the saving power of Benares, one of Shiva's special haunts.

> "Why should we not worship Benares (Kashi), where Shiva and Bhavani (Gauri) dwell, knowing it to be the birthplace of salvation, the treasury of knowledge, the destroyer of sin. When all the gods were in perplexity he drank up the deadly poison. Why should you not worship him—you stupid person; who is merciful like Shiva?" Kish. 1.

Indeed the exhortation to worship Shiva is repeated over and over again in all parts of the poem. It is said that the Vedas declare him to be the religious teacher of the three worlds (Bal. 120 (118) 134); that saints, ascetics, gods and sages and persons of piety, worship him as the source of happiness (Bal. 115 (113) 129); that he is an ocean of mercy, a granter of boons, the remover of the distress of those who seek his protection, and yet, if he is

[1] There is only one reference to the linga of Shiva in Valmiki's *Ramayana*. Ravan was its worshipper. See my *Summary of Valmiki's Ramayana*, p. 342.

not appeased, no one will attain his purpose apart from Shiva, though he perform millions of penances and austerities. Bal. 82 (79) 93.

This enthusiasm for Shiva, in a poem devoted, as is often supposed, to the almost exclusive praise of Rama, is carried still farther, and in the Sanskrit invocation to the Ayodhya book Shiva is spoken of as "the chief of divinities, the eternal lord of all, the complete, the omnipresent," while it is to be noted that the god's consort, it may be in a mood of wifely exaggeration, declares her husband to be: "the universal spirit; the great god; the father of the world, the friend of all." Bal. 75 (73) 81. But the poet himself goes further when he asserts that Shiva is *pure intelligence and bliss*, the abode of joy, entirely free from delusion, frenzy and lust. Bal. 87 (85) 99. And in saying so, especially when he uses the words *pure intelligence and bliss*,[1] he is using at least parts of a phrase, *sat chit anand*, that can only be applied to the Supreme Spirit. Such, indeed, is the position assigned to him in the last book of the poem, by one who was a servant of Shiva, but who also worshipped Rama. We are told that "Shiva and Brahma worship Rama." Uttar, 154 (102) 168. Nevertheless, in a prayer addressed to him, Shiva is called "the omnipresent all-pervading Brahm, Supreme Spirit; the unborn, the unembodied; the unconditioned," and a great deal more, which reminds us, as has been said already, of the *Mahabharata*, which with wonderful impartiality devotes itself to praising at one time Vishnu and at another time Shiva, in language which would seem to exclude or to dethrone every other god in the universe. The prayer ends with the assertion that for those who fail to propitiate Shiva, there will be, neither in this world nor in the next, any hope of happiness or any end to their

[1] See Bal. 150 (148) 171, where "*intelligence and bliss* (chidanand)" are applied to Brahm.

pain. Tulsidas seals the prayer with his approval by saying:

> "The man who repeats this prayer, upon him Shiva will show favour." Uttar, 157–8 (104–5) 172–3.

Shiva's wife, again, is held in almost equally high honour. She is the mother of the world, the unborn, the faultless. And reference is made to the belief that along with Shiva their male and female energies are united. This is a recognition and acceptance by the poet of one of the most unattractive aspects of Hindu religion, the worship of the *linga* and *yoni*, the reproductive organs of the two sexes. Bal. 107 (105) 115. No true understanding of the poet's theological and religious outlook can be secured without a careful study of those portions of the poem which are devoted to Shiva. To secure that, let us examine them with some detail. To begin with, consider what Tulsidas has to tell us of Shiva's wife, and her self-immolation in the burning fire. It was done out of devotion to her husband. She was the first to perform the rite of Sati, giving, as is supposed, her name and example to a cruel practice, which only the British Government was able to suppress. The story of the goddess's devotion is one of the oldest in Hindu literature. But it is told in a new fashion, that it may link together the fortunes of Shiva and Rama. One day as Shiva and his wife, at this stage in her career called Sati, were wandering in the forests of Central India, they saw Rama. It was soon after he had lost his wife, carried off by the demon Ravan, and the distracted husband was searching for her everywhere. When Shiva saw Rama he did not greet him. He merely passed on, giving utterance to his devotion in the words, "Hail, Sachchidanand, Purifier of the world." This word, *Sachchidanand*, is always applied to the Supreme Spirit, Brahm, of whom, according to orthodox

Hinduism, the Triad, Brahma, Vishnu and Shiva, are manifestations. It means existence, thought and joy (*sat chit anand*). Sati recognised the import of such language, and her mind was filled with wonder and doubt, and she said to herself, "My husband is the lord of the world, and the whole world worships him. Gods, men and saints all bow their heads before him. And yet he has made obeisance to this king's son and called him the supreme abode of existence, intelligence and joy." Bal. 63 (60). If Rama is really the Supreme God, why should he lose his wife, and even more especially, if he is all wise and knows everything, why should he not be able to find her?" Shiva saw his wife's perplexity, and bade her go and stand in Rama's path, disguised as Sita. She did so, but as Rama drew near, he was not deceived for a moment. He smiled when he saw her, and, hailing her by her own name, said, "Where is Shiva, and what is your reason for wandering alone in the forest?" Bal. 64 (62) 75. The goddess was overwhelmed with confusion. But Rama was very gracious, for he revealed part of his divine glory; and in this wonderful manifestation she saw not only Rama, but his lost wife and also his brother, repeated over and over again, surrounded by saints and sages. But most wonderful of all, she saw in presence of each of the reduplicated Ramas, a Brahma, a Vishnu and a Shiva, each of them endowed with surpassing glory, but each of them bowing at Rama's feet and worshipping him. She also saw the wives of those three gods in their divine forms, which means that she saw herself, and in addition she saw also the rest of the gods, accompanied by their wives, indeed the whole universe, both what moves and what cannot move.

But however well intentioned Sati's action may have been, it had disastrous results. Shiva realised that having once taken the form of Sita, it was impossible for him to recognise her any longer as his wife. He therefore gave himself up to meditation and passed into a trance which lasted for 87,000 years. Sati was heart-broken, but she prayed to Rama in her perplexity. When the trance came to an end, Shiva found his wife seated at his side. He was as kind to her as before, but realised it would be a sin to touch her. Now it so happened that just at that time Sati's father, Daksh, had resolved to celebrate a great sacrifice. A large number of gods and their wives were invited. But much to Sati's indignation, owing to an old quarrel between the god and his father-in-law, Shiva had not received an invitation. Indeed, the first news Sati had of the approaching function was seeing the sky filled with the air chariots of celestials and their wives, hastening to the ceremony. As she listened to the music of the heavenly nymphs, enough to make a saint forget his vows, Sati declared that, invited or not, she was determined to be there also. Her husband advised her strongly not to go. "You will get," he said, "the welcome given to the uninvited." Daksh had asked all his other daughters to be there, and she had been purposely ignored. But Sati would not listen. And so she went. Every one was afraid to speak to her. Her father looked at her with anger, though her mother and sisters ventured to smile. Sati boldly approached the sacrifice. She wished to see if her father had really dared to insult her husband and set apart nothing for him. When she saw that her fears were realised, her anger burst forth.

> "Listen," she said to the assembled multitudes, "you have all heard and talked about this insult to Shiva, and very soon you will reap the fruit of it in many ways. My father will repent it. . . . The universal Spirit (*jagat atma*), the great god, the father of the world, the friend

of all, it is he whom my fool of a father has reviled." Bal. 75 (73) 87.

And so, scorning to retain a body which owed its life to such an unworthy sire, she cast herself into a sacrificial fire. When he heard of his wife's death, Shiva in his anger came and scattered the sacrifice. He also gave to the gods the punishment they deserved.[1]

In her next birth Sati was born as the daughter of the mountain king, Himalaya. Her name was now Parvati. Her parents were shocked when a rishi told them that their daughter was destined to marry a person who had nothing to recommend him, a jogi with matted hair, a recluse caring for nobody, naked and hideously adorned.[2] Bal. 79 (77) 90. As Parvati listened to this description of her future husband, she was delighted. With her dying breath she had prayed that she might be devoted to Shiva in all her future lives. And the rishi was manifestly setting forth the characteristics of Shiva. And so it proved to be, because when the horrified parents asked the saint what they were to do in such a distressing situation, they were told they could do nothing. But for their consolation, he added :

> " If God (*daiv*) will help you, there is one scheme you may adopt. All the faults I have mentioned are to be found in Shiva. If a marriage can be arranged with him, every one will say that his vices are virtues." Bal. 70 (78) 92.

[1] Tulsidas says: "This story all the world knows, and so I have only told it in brief." The story of Daksh's sacrifice seems to have made a profound impression. It appears in both the Epics. See my *Myths and Legends of India*, p. 83.

[2] There is one reference to Shiva's consort under her more terrifying form as Kali, in Lanka, 109 (89) 117. " As though the goddess Kali, with a rosary of skulls in her hand and accompanied by all her attendants, had bathed in the river Blood and come to worship at the shrine of Battle." Growse's translation.

It was accordingly resolved that Parvati should begin to practise penance as the best means to approach Shiva. These penances eventually lasted for many thousand years. For 10,000 years her food consisted of dry leaves. At a later stage she ate nothing at all. Such rigid penance brought Brahma to her side, saying :

"Listen, oh daughter of the mountain king, your efforts will bear fruit. Abandon your intolerable pains. You will secure Shiva for a husband." Bal. 86 (84) 98.

All this time, Shiva continued to live the life of an ascetic, meditating upon Vishnu. Eventually Vishnu appeared and told him that he was to marry Parvati. Shiva reluctantly consented to act on this advice. But before taking any definite action, he sent the seven sages to make trial of Parvati's love. In the testing which they applied, the sages asked the maiden to tell them what she wanted. She frankly replied that she wished to marry Shiva. At which the sages laughed and said :

"You wish to marry a husband who is nothing but a homeless wanderer, a worthless, shameless, ragged wretch, a wearer of skulls and snakes, without kindred and without a home. Tell us what pleasure can you find in such a bridegroom. It was on the advice of others he married Sati, and afterwards left her and caused her death." Bal 90 (88) 102.

They told her she would be much better off if she married Vishnu, but she would not listen. She admitted that Vishnu was faultless, and that Shiva had a great many defects ; however, her mind was made up and it was too late to change. When they saw their arguments were of no avail, the rishis departed, saying as they went :

"Victory, Victory, Victory to Bhavani, the mother of the world. You who are Maya (illusion) and Shiva the adorable are the father and mother of the whole universe." Bal. 93 (91) 105.

Later on, the maiden's parents are told that their daughter is the mother of the world, the unborn, without beginning, the indestructible *Shakti*, the everlasting abode of Shambhu. They add that she is the creator, the preserver and the destroyer of the world and assumes what forms it pleases her. Bal. 107 (105) 121.

Despite the intervention of Vishnu and the report of the rishis, further persuasion was required to get Shiva to yield. In response to a deputation of the gods to the Creator, the god of Love was sent to wound Shiva with his darts. As the result of driving five arrows into Shiva's heart, he awoke. Opening one of his three eyes, he gazed at his assailant, with the immediate result that the god of love was reduced to ashes. Once more the gods assembled, with Vishnu and Brahma at their head, and went to Shiva, singing his praises one by one. When asked to speak, Brahma said : " It is manifest that you are in love, and we wish to see your marriage with our own eyes " (Bal. 99 (97) 112), and with Parvati, of course, who had indulged in so long a penance to secure that end. When Shiva finally yielded to their persuasion, Brahma sent the seven sages to tell Parvati's father. Himalaya was delighted, and after fixing an auspicious planet, day and hour, he wrote a letter to the Creator with the necessary information.

" When the Creator got the letter and read it, he could not contain himself for joy." Bal. 101 (99) 114.

The poet next described the preparations for the marriage:

" The followers of Shiva adorned their lord, with his hair matted together on the top of his head as a crown, and a serpent for his chaplet. They put serpents in his ears for ear-rings, and serpents for bracelets on his wrists. His body they covered with the ashes of cow dung. A tiger's skin was his garment. The moon was on his brow, the Ganges on his head; he had three eyes; a serpent was his Brahminical cord; his throat was black with poison; on his breast hung a rosary made of dead men's skulls. In such inauspicious fashion Shiva the merciful was arrayed. He carried a trident and was seated on a bull. . . . Vishnu and the Creator, with all the other gods, mounted each their carriages and set off for the wedding." Bal. 102 (100) 115.

As he watched the procession, Vishnu observed with a smile: "The celestials look well in every way, but the guests are not worthy of the bridegroom."

He therefore proposed by way of a joke that each god should go separately, attended by his own particular retinue. The result was that Shiva's own followers fell into line and, marching by themselves, were appreciated at their full value.

"Some of them had no heads; some had very big heads; some had neither feet nor hands; the feet and hands of some were very large; some had very big eyes, some had none at all; some were very thin, others were very fat. But whether stout or thin, whether they were clean or dirty; in their hands they carried skulls full of blood. They had the faces of dogs, asses and pigs, an innumerable host that could not be numbered, ghosts, evil spirits, witches of all kinds, dancing and singing, twisting about in an amazing fashion."

It is needless to enter into the details of the marriage ceremony, to describe the amazement of the inhabitants of Himalaya's capital, or the horror of the queen when she saw the bridegroom and his followers. Eventually the minds of the parents were set at rest by the double assurance that the bridegroom was the great god Shiva, and their daughter the eternal mother of the world. This description of Shiva and his followers may seem very fantastic and very wonderful, but it is a description that can be found over and over again in the literature of Hinduism. And if we did not record it, we would be shutting the door on one of the many compartments which compose the poet's mind.

And yet as we read the text of the poem we feel that Tulsidas is somewhat perturbed. As we have already seen, the ideal he sets before us in Rama is very high indeed, and the moral teaching of the poem is also worthy of admiration. When he deals with the lives and characters of the lesser gods, he is frankness itself. Consequently when he writes of Shiva, he cannot help feeling that there is something wrong. The reader will remember the passage already quoted, when the rishi assured Parvati's parents that once their daughter was married to Shiva, his vices would be reckoned as virtues. He thereafter proceeded to develop the dangerous but common apology employed for the gods: "No blame attaches to the powerful; they are like the Sun, like fire and the Ganges." And then he adds the very necessary but somewhat illogical warning: "But the fool who says that a man can do what a god does, will fall into hell, and remain there for many millions of years." Bal. 80 (78) 92.

In offering this apology Tulsidas is practically repeating the claim made by the author of the *Bhagavata Purana* (x. 33) on behalf of Krishna, that the gods are to be judged by a standard different from that applied to men. "Revere the actions of Krishna, but do not give your mind to the doing of them."

When the wedding was over the newly married pair returned to Kailas, where Shiva had his peculiar home. And there Parvati, recalling the foolishness of which she had been guilty many thousands of years before, in her previous existence, but with her mind not yet set at rest, once more asked her husband to explain the mystery of Rama :

> " If he was a king's son and in distress for the loss of his wife, how could he be the Supreme God, Brahm ? Bal. 118 (116) 132.

Shiva thereupon set himself to tell the whole story of Rama. And we are to understand that the rest of the poem is the narrative of the god—a conceit, however, which Tulsidas sometimes forgets as he warms to his theme.

VI.

VISHNU, THE PRESERVER GOD.

VISHNU, one of the aspects under which the Sun was worshipped in the days of the *Rig-Veda*, had come to be reckoned as one of the prominent gods by the time the *Shatapatha Brahmana* was put together. In that book (i. 25) we are told how the gods and demons, both sprung from Prajapati (Brahma), engaged in war. At first the demons were successful and boasted that the world was theirs. They resolved to divide it among themselves. But the gods, when they heard of what was about to happen, "placing at their head Vishnu the sacrifice," went and claimed a share. To this demand the demons replied: "We give you as much as this Vishnu can lie upon. Now Vishnu was a dwarf." The result was that when the prostrate Vishnu had been surrounded by sacred texts and by fire, the gods gained possession of the whole earth.[1] Here we have one of the earliest stories which bring Vishnu to the front as the god who in a pre-eminent fashion comes to the help of his brother celestials and rescues them in their troubles. And by the time the *Ramayana* and *Mahabharata* were compiled, he ranks with Brahma and Shiva as one of the three great gods of Hinduism. He is essentially the preserver god, the god for whom men are able to entertain feelings of confidence and affection. And in particular he makes descents (*avatara*) to the world, and renders it a service. These descents are usually

[1] See Muir's *Original Sanskrit Texts*, vol. iv. p. 123.

reckoned as ten in number. Vishnu's incarnation as Rama was the seventh of these descents, and accordingly we find the gods saying to him :

"When the gods were in trouble, oh Lord, you assumed various forms, as a fish, a tortoise, a boar, as a man-lion, a dwarf, as Parashuram, and destroyed what troubled them." Lanka, 127 (106) 135.

Tulsidas himself refers to these incarnations throughout the poem, though never in detail. But the reason he gives for such action on the part of Vishnu is put more worthily :

"When religion suffers, and demons in their pride do wicked things which cannot be borne, to the injury of Brahmins, cows, gods and the earth, then the Lord (*prabhu*) assumes various forms of body in his compassion and removes the sufferings of the good." Bal. 129 (127) 144.

For Vishnu's appearance in the person of Rama, the poet gives three separate reasons which have no connection with one another.

The first reason is associated with a rishi of the name of Narad, who, according to the literature of India, was always travelling between earth and heaven. It was he who negotiated Shiva's second marriage. He was a devoted worshipper of Vishnu. His piety and asceticism, however, had become so powerful that Indra, the god of heaven, feared that the holy man would rob him of his throne. The god of love and a number of celestial nymphs were therefore sent to try and tempt him from the paths of virtue. Their efforts were unsuccessful, and Narad was very proud of himself for so completely resisting the assaults of love ; he even went to Shiva and boasted of his victory. Shiva listened, but advised him never to speak of his experiences to Vishnu. This advice, however, was unwelcome, and the saint, after paying a visit to Brahma's heaven, went off to the Sea of Milk to tell the object of his special worship how successful he had been. When Vishnu saw him approach,

> " he rose with joy to meet him and caused the rishi to sit down beside him. The lord of all that moves and does not move, smiled and said : ' It is a long time, holy one, since you conferred such mercy upon me.' " Bal. 136 (134) 155.

When the god had heard Narad's story, he decided it was necessary to humble his votary's pride. He therefore created by the power of illusion (*maya*), a wonderful city more beautiful than anything in heaven, with a king to rule over it whose daughter's charms surpassed those of Lakshmi, Vishnu's own spouse. In accordance with the custom of ancient days, this princess was to choose a husband for herself. Kings and princes came from all parts of the world to win her favour. Curiosity brought Narad to be a witness of so wonderful a gathering. But when he saw the incomparable princess, all his vows of chastity were forgotten, and when the day of the maiden's choice arrived, the man who had resisted all the efforts of Indra, was seated among the candidates. Before doing so he had asked Vishnu to endow him with the gift of beauty. The god gave him an ambiguous answer. He said he would do what was best for Narad—a reply which the saint chose to interpret as the realisation of his own desires. In any case he was convinced that Vishnu had made him beautiful —a delusion which was confirmed by two of Shiva's impish followers. In the guise of Brahmins, and seating themselves beside Narad, they passed the time of waiting by telling one another that they had never seen any one so handsome ; they were confident that the princess would choose the saint for her husband. But when the princess came in front of Narad, what she saw was a horrid, ugly, deformed old man with a face like a monkey's. While the maiden was moving here and there among the candidates, Vishnu himself appeared, and without further hesitation she placed the garland round his neck. Narad was very much distressed.. But his distress was changed to anger when Shiva's two followers told him to look at himself. When the saint saw what he was really like, his wrath could not be controlled, and he cursed Shiva's followers to be born again as demons. He then went forth in search of Vishnu, saying :

> " 'Shall I curse him or shall I kill myself ? He has made me a laughing-stock to the world.' On the way he met the enemy of the demons (Vishnu) with Lakshmi and the princess. (The god) addressed him with a smile and in gentle words. 'Where is the holy man going like one distracted ?' As he heard these words, great wrath sprang up in Narad's soul, and being in the power of Maya, he lost all control of himself and said, 'You cannot endure to see another's prosperity. Your envy and deceit are well known. At the churning of the ocean you made Rudra mad : you incited the gods and made them to drink poison. The demons' share was intoxicating liquor ; Shankar's share was poison ; your share was Lakshmi and the beautiful jewel.[1] You are always selfish, cunning and deceitful. Always doing what you like, with no one over you, you do whatever comes into your mind. You make the good bad and the bad good. . . . Now you will reap the fruit of what you have done (to me). You have given me a body born from the womb. You also shall have such a body. This is my curse. You have made me like a monkey ;

[1] Rudra and Shankar are other names for Shiva. The reference is to the churning of the ocean, when Vishnu appeared as the *tortoise avatar*.

monkeys will be your helpers. You did me a grievous wrong ; you will be distressed by the loss of your wife.' " Bal. 144 (142) 163.

" The Lord accepted the curse with joy, thus achieving the purpose of the gods. He who is the *Treasury of Compassion* recalled the power of his Maya. When Hari had withdrawn his Maya, both Lakshmi and the princess disappeared." Bal. 146 (144) 165.

The recall of Vishnu's delusive power at once wrought a great change in Narad's mind. Falling at Hari's feet, he begged that his curse might be annulled. Vishnu, however, said that such was not his will. It was then that Narad, when asking how his great sin could be removed, was told to go and repeat Shankar's hundred names and he would find comfort.

With such words of consolation Narad set out for heaven, singing Rama's praises as he went. He was met in the way by the followers of Shiva, whom he had cursed to be born again as demons. Their hope was that Narad would recall his words. But the saint declined to do so. Indeed, he promised them great profit would ultimately accrue to both. They would be born as demons of very great power.

" When by the strength of your arms you will conquer all things, Vishnu will assume a body. You will die by the hand of Hari in battle. Thus you will obtain salvation and not be born again." Bal. 147 (145) 166.

In the description of Narad's curse and what it entailed, it is plain that Tulsidas is thinking of the second member of the Triad, and not attempting to identify him with the Supreme God. This fact is brought out even more clearly when we examine the names employed for Vishnu in the Hindi text. It is true that the term Vishnu only appears thrice, but Hari, its equivalent, appears at least eight times. And though Prabhu (lord) and Bhagwan (adorable) might be applied to the Supreme, they can equally well be used for lesser deities by their worshippers. What is most noteworthy, however, is the way in which the god is, time after time, called the husband of Lakshmi, or the husband of Shri, or the husband of Rama, or the husband of Kamala —all names of Vishnu's consort. And this is rendered still more emphatic by Narad's reference to the belief that Lakshmi was one of the products which Vishnu secured at the churning of the Ocean. It is also worth noting that in this particular narrative, the poet projects himself into the future, and speaks of Vishnu as Rama or as Raghupati and Raghunath,[1] thus closely identifying the god with the life he was eventually to live on earth.

All this is specially remarkable because, when we turn to examine the second reason for Vishnu's incarnation, we find that the poet is almost entirely thinking of Rama as a manifestation of the Supreme Spirit. It is true that at the outset he calls him now Prabhu, then Hari, and finally Vasudev—a name associated with the worship of Krishna, a later incarnation of Vishnu. But in contrast to that, read what Shiva is made to say to Parvati before he has begun to tell his story at all :

> " Hear another reason, oh daughter of the mountain king, why the uncreated, the quality-less, the incomparable Brahm became king of Koshal." Bal. 148 (146) 167.

It is associated with Manu, the survivor of the flood, and his wife. The whole narrative is so remarkable that it requires to be told with some detail. Though Manu had kept the commands of the Lord in every way, it was only in his old age that he realised his life had been spent without devotion (*bhakti*) to Hari. He and his wife

[1] Rama was a member of the family of Raghu ; he was thus the *nath* or *pati* (the lord) of Raghu.

therefore resolved to surrender their kingdom and retire to the forest.

"Repeating with fervour the twelve-lettered charm,[1] husband and wife turned their thoughts to the lotus feet of Vasudev. They lived on leaves, fruits and roots, remembering Brahm, Sachchidanand. Again, for the sake of Hari, they did penance. Abandoning roots and fruits, water was their only nourishment. The endless desire of their hearts was : May we see with our own eyes the chief object of love : Him who is devoid of qualities and parts, without beginning and without end : whom those who speak of the supreme object of life contemplate ; Him whom the Vedas call Neti, Neti, intelligence and bliss (*chidanand*), without form, without attributes, the incomparable one, from whom Shambhu, Viranchi and Vishnu in various forms arise." Bal. 150 (148) 171.

Manu and his wife spent at least a hundred thousand years in this fashion, and the Triad finally intervened :

"Vidhi, Hari, Hara, seeing their amazing penance, came near Manu many times and tempted him, saying, 'Ask a boon.' But he was steadfast. They could do nothing." Bal. 151 (149) 172.

Eventually a voice was heard. It was the voice of the omniscient Lord telling Manu to ask a boon. Falling on his knees, Manu said :

"Listen, Oh Thou, the dust of whose feet Vidhi, Hari and Hara worship. If you are pleased, grant me this boon. May we see the form which dwells in Shiva's heart . . . the total of all qualities and the negation of all qualities which revelation declares."

When the form was at last revealed, it was more like

[1] Om Namo Bhagavate Vasudevaya.

that of Vishnu than of the Supreme Spirit. Because, with much else, we read of red lips, shining teeth, eyes like the lotus, the sectarial marks on the forehead, and the Srivatsa jewel on his breast. He had a waist like a lion, and arms as long as an elephant's trunk. He had a quiver at his side, and a bow and arrow in his hands. One feels that this manifestation does not correspond with what the devotees had desired. But the text goes on to tell us that on the left side of the god was seated,

> "the primal energy (*param shakti*), the treasury of beauty, the mother of the world, from whose parts arise innumerable Umas, Lakshmis and Sarasvatis." Bal. 154 (152) 175.

These are the wives of Shiva, Vishnu and Brahma, and then looking into the future, the poet adds :

> "Even thus was Sita seated at Rama's side."

With a fresh access of gratitude the devotees clasped the god's feet. The Lord was very gracious and, placing his hand on their heads, he raised them up, saying once more, "Ask a boon." And Manu said, "Oh, gracious lord, treasury of mercy, giver of beautiful gifts, I wish a son like you." When the wife was asked what she wanted, she said, "That also is my desire," and then she added :

> "You are the father of Brahma and the other gods, the lord of the world, you are Brahm, who knows the secrets of all hearts."

The devotees received a gracious response. They were told to go and live in Indra's heaven.

> "Enjoy yourselves there ; after some time has elapsed you will be born king of Avadh, and I shall be your son. Assuming a form of my own accord, I shall be manifest in your house, and, assuming a body with all my parts, shall perform deeds affording joy to those devoted to

me . . . and this my Maya, the primal energy by whom the world is created, will also descend." Bal. 157 (155) 179.[1]

The third reason given by Shiva for Vishnu's incarnation as Rama is the reason given by Valmiki in his *Ramayana*, and is practically the only reason which Tulsidas thinks of in the rest of his poem. The language used in reference to Vishnu is very varied. He is called Hari, and he is called Prabhu. He is also spoken of as the beloved of Ocean's daughter. But in a hymn of praise addressed to him, Brahma says he is Sachchidanand, and is the sole cause of creation. The voice that gave an answer to this prayer is called *Brahm-bani*—the voice of Brahm.

The story is as follows : A very pious and powerful king was, by the cunning stratagem of one of his enemies, made to offend grievously a vast company of Brahmins whom he had invited to a great feast. Not less than one hundred thousand of these holy men were present. In one of the dishes this enemy had been able to place, along with other kinds of meat, some pieces of Brahmin's flesh. But just as they were about to eat, a voice from heaven was heard telling the Brahmins to refrain, or they would be eating a Brahmin's flesh. The guests got up in great dismay, but not unnaturally they were very angry and they cursed the king to be born a demon with all the members of his house. Again, however, the heavenly voice was heard, saying the king was not to blame. And when inquiry was made, the wickedness of the king's enemy was laid bare. But it was too late to do anything, because a Brahmin's curse, once it is uttered, cannot be recalled.

[1] Here Maya is called *adi shakti*. In Bal. 192 (198) 218, Rama says he will descend with his *param shakti*. Sita is thus identified not only with Rama's *shakti*, but with Maya. See also Bal. 154 (152) 175. *With all my parts*, indicates a full incarnation. The *Vishnu Purana* says Krishna was a part of a part of the Supreme Spirit.

In due time the monarch, and all the members of his family, were born as demons; the king himself was the mighty Ravan with ten heads and twenty arms. The monarch and his brothers, though in the guise of demons, were as remarkable for piety as they had been in their previous existence. Their acts of penance were so compelling—Ravan, for example, cast his ten heads one after the other into a sacrificial fire—that the Creator had to come and tell him to ask a boon.

The ten-headed clasped the feet of the god and said:

> "Hear, oh lord of the world, may I not be slain except by a monkey or a man." Bal. 182 (180) 206.

At this point Shiva, who tells the story, interjects the observation, "I and Brahma jointly conferred the boon, saying, 'So be it, you have done great penance.'"

From the time they were born as demons the sons and servants of Ravan practised every kind of wickedness. But it was only after he had obtained this boon from Brahma [1] that Ravan in his pride decided to interfere with religious ceremonies of all kinds; the feeding of Brahmins, sacrifice, offerings and funeral rites. By so doing he hoped to make the gods hungry and weak. For fear of Ravan they had to hide in the caves of Mount Meru. They fled before his approach. His very footsteps shook the earth, and at the sound of his voice the wives of the gods were seized with the pains of labour before their time. In the greatness of their terror, the celestials could neither sleep by night nor eat by day. If the demon by any chance caught a wandering god or Brahmin he held him to ransom.

[1] Ravan had two other brothers, who also secured boons: *Vibhishan* asked for a perfect devotion to the feet of Bhagwan. *Kumbhkarn* was so huge and terrible, that when Brahma saw him, he said: "If this low creature is always eating he will lay the world waste." He therefore caused Sarasvati to pervert his mind, and he asked as a boon that he might sleep for six months at a time.

"By the power of his arm he had brought everything under his control. No one had any kind of independence. Ravan ruled the world in accordance with his own will." Bal. 189 (195) 213.

At last the Earth, in the form of a cow, went to the gods and asked them to come to her relief. They said they could do nothing. But they took the suppliant with them to the Creator. Brahma said he was equally helpless. He added, however, that there was one who could deliver them :

"Take courage, oh Earth, and remember Vishnu's feet. The Lord knows the sufferings of his people. He will break these grievous afflictions." Bal. 190 (196) 214.

"But where can we find him ?" one of the gods asked. "We must go to his heaven" : "We must go to the Sea of Milk," said others in reply. "I was present in the company," said Shiva, "and seizing the opportunity, I observed, Hari is present everywhere and always the same. I know he reveals himself by love (*prem*). Tell me in what country, time or place he is not."

When Shiva had thus spoken, Brahma, crying out, "That is true," began a hymn of praise addressed to Vishnu. It was in a voice from heaven that the fear of the gods was removed :

"Don't be afraid, oh sages, saints and Indra. For your sake I am about to descend in human form, with all my parts, in the glorious solar race. Kashyap and Aditi did a great penance, and I formerly promised them a boon.[1] They will appear as Dashrath and Kaushalya in the town of Koshal. In their house I shall descend four brothers, the crown of the family of Raghu. I shall make true all that Narad said. I shall descend with my

[1] Tulsidas here identifies Manu and his wife with Kashyap and Aditi.

supreme energy and will remove the whole of the earth's burdens." Bal. 192 (198) 218.

These promises Brahma helped still further to fulfil by telling his brother deities to go down to the earth and in the form of monkeys worship Vishnu's feet.

It is to be observed in connection with this important passage that Vishnu declared that he would be accompanied by his supreme energy (*param shakti*). This refers to the idea so common in Hinduism where the energy or active power of a god is personified as his wife. We have already seen how Lakshmi is spoken of as the consort of Vishnu, just as Sarasvati is the wife of Brahma, and Parvati is the wife of Shiva. The poet, however, shows no sympathy with the unhealthy conceptions which such speculations often involved.

A later chapter will describe what was the manner of Vishnu's appearing when he was born in the house of the king of Avadh. For the rest of the poem he is naturally merged in Rama, though it is worth noticing that both he and Lakshmi were present at the wedding of Rama and Sita, who were their own incarnations.

VII.

THE HINDU TRIAD—BRAHMA, VISHNU AND SHIVA.

WE have now to give some consideration to what Tulsidas says of the three great gods of Hinduism in their relationship to one another. But before dealing with those passages which bring them all together, let us take the references where we find any two of them.

Brahma and Vishnu are thus combined with regard to one matter only; that was when, in association with the lesser gods, they persuaded Shiva to marry, and later on took a prominent part in the marriage festivities. What they did and said in connection therewith has been described already in the chapter dealing with Shiva. Here it is enough to note that the words used are *Vishnu and Viranchi*.

Vishnu and Shiva are spoken of together on ten occasions, and, strange to say, in nine of these their names are always the same, not Vishnu and Shiva, but *Hari* and *Hara*. When the poet so consistently writes of them under these names one feels that he is recalling a form of worship in which these two gods were thus associated in the minds of worshippers, probably to the exclusion of Brahma; it may be before any formal conception of the Hindu Triad was thought of. In any case, we know that there has been such a more or less exclusive worship of *Hari-Hara* in India, and images erected in which they were physically conjoined. Illustration has already been given of how Shiva speaks in the highest terms of Vishnu or of his incarnation in Rama. And it is equally true that Vishnu has the same lofty conception of Shiva, saying, as he does, that unless they are worshipped together no blessing can accrue. It will be remembered how Vishnu told the penitent Narad, a fervent devotee of his own, to go and repeat Shiva's hundred names and his mind would at once secure comfort.

> "There is no one so dear to me as Shiva ; never allow yourself by foolishness to forsake this truth. The person on whom Shiva does not take pity will never achieve devotion to me." Bal. 146 (144) 165.

One feels that this language is more than an echo of what Vishnu says of Shiva in the *Mahabharata*, xii. 342.

> "I am the soul of all the worlds, of all the universe. Rudra again is my soul. It is for this that I always worship him. If I did not worship the auspicious and boon-giving Shiva, no one would worship myself. . . . He who knows Rudra knows me, and he who knows me, knows Rudra. He who follows Rudra follows me. Rudra is Narayana (Vishnu). Both are one ; and one is shown in two different forms." [1]

The references to *Hari-Hara* are none of them specially remarkable. But most of them do have a suggestion of the exclusive worship in which they have shared. They are worth recording. In Bal. (4) 9, among the sins of which wicked people are guilty, it is said they seek to eclipse the glories of *Hari-Hara*. In Bal. (12) 17 it is said that those who love the feet of *Hari-Hara* will find the story of Rama to be sweet as honey. Again, it is recorded of Narad, that he was as dear to *Hari-Hara* as Hari (Vishnu or Rama) is to the world. Bal. (29) 41. In a long statement in praise of the attractiveness of the story of Rama, it is said it is like *Hari-Hara*, easy of approach and gracious

[1] See M. N. Dutt's translation of *Mahabharata*, vol. ii. p. 556 of the Shanti Parva.

to their servants. Bal. (39) 51. The same book says that no enemy of *Hari-Hara* can reach Kailas, the heaven of Shiva, even in a dream. Bal. (113) 129. And as a proof of the great courtesy with which he received certain nobles, it is recorded that Rama acted towards them as if they were *Hari* and *Hara*. Ayodh. (306) 319. While the enormity of killing a cow is brought home to us by the statement that those who listen to blasphemous words against *Hari-Hara* are as guilty as if they had killed that animal. Lanka, 41 (31) 46.

The two remaining passages occur close together and in the Ayodha Kand. Bharat is the speaker on both occasions. Anxious to clear himself of any complicity in the plot to secure his brother's exile, he says :

> " May the Creator (Vidhi) give to me the lot he gives to those who forsake the feet of *Hari-Hara*, and worship horrible demons, if I knew of this plan." Ayodh. (161) 168.

And again in similar language he asks, not the Creator, but Shiva, to treat him in the same way.

> " Those wretches who do not love the society of the good, who turn away their faces from the supreme object of life, who do not worship Hari (Vishnu) in his incarnations and find no joy in the glories of *Hari-Hara*, who abandon the ways of the books of revelation and go a contrary road, may Shiva give to me their lot if I knew of this plan." Ayodh. (161) 168.

So far as noticed, there is only one occasion where the poet links these same gods together by any other name than Hari and Hara, and it is in the Bal Kand 75 (73) 87. There it is said that when any one speaks blasphemy against the saints and against *Shambhu* (Shiva) and *Sri-Pati* (the lord of Lakshmi) his tongue ought to be cut out ;

but if that is not possible, those who hear should close their ears and go away.

When we come to deal with passages referring to *Brahma and Shiva*, we find that there are a large number of them. This is only natural in view of the fact that their colleague in the Triad has left the heavenly sphere and become incarnate in Rama. Their first appearance together was when Shiva made himself jointly responsible with Brahma in granting the boon to Ravan, a boon whose consequences rendered necessary Vishnu's incarnation. "I and Brahma," he told his wife, "jointly conferred the boon." Bal. 182 (180) 206. And the asceticism which secured this boon would seem to have been specially directed to these two deities, for we find Hanuman saying to Ravan that it was by worshipping *Viranchi and Shiva* in every way he had achieved his purpose. Lanka, 23 (19) 28. These two gods were also present with the other celestials at Rama's marriage with Sita, setting out from heaven in their respective vehicles, and sitting at the feast in the guise of Brahmins. Bal. 313 (319) 346.

But what concerns us chiefly is the very frequent reference to the fact that Brahma and Shiva were constantly worshipping Rama, or discovering that their power was as nothing compared with his. The language is more or less stereotyped. We are told that *Viranchi and Shankar*, or *Shiva and Aj*, worship Rama's lotus feet; or that they adore him, either alone or in association with the sages and other gods.

Rama's brother, Bharat, it will be remembered, is also an incarnation of Vishnu. And of him it is said in Ayodh. (276) 288, that *Vidhi and Shiva*, as well as other celestials, could not say enough of his virtues, while it is asserted that *Aj and Shiva* are constantly seeking his favour. Aranya (2) 7.

Again we are made to realise Rama's greatness by such

statements as these. Ravan is told that *Shambhu and Aj* could not help him unless he surrendered Sita. Sundar (35) 35. And in the next book, Ravan is similarly assured that should he continue to oppose Rama, *Brahma and Rudra* would not be able to protect him. Lanka, 36 (26) 41. While Rama himself declared that Bali would not escape, even though he took refuge with *Brahma and Rudra*. Kish. 8 (6) 8.

Similar to these quotations, but in language that is even stronger in its effect, we read that the delusive power —*Maya* or *moh*—of Rama subdues *Shiva*, *Viranchi* and all others, both great and small (Lanka, 64 (50) 72), that it fascinates them (Uttar, 85 (63) 87), that it blinds them (Uttar, 96 (69) 99), that they see it and are afraid (Uttar, 98 (70) 100).

There should also be noted the curious attempt to describe Rama in the terminology of the Sankhya philosophy, where it is said that Shiva is his consciousness (*ahankar*) and Aj his intelligence (*buddhi*). Lanka, 19 (16) 21.

In all the quotations given so far it may be reasonably supposed that Brahma and Shiva are being made to sing the praises, or to acknowledge the power of the god whom they persuaded to become incarnate. But alongside of these utterances, there are others where we find Brahma and Shiva recognising that Rama is something more than one of the many incarnations of Vishnu. Indeed they recognise and acclaim him as the Supreme Spirit. Thus in the opening pages of the poem we are told :

> " Sarasvati, the serpent king, *Shiva and the Creator*, the Vedas and the Puranas, are constantly singing Rama's praises, saying, ' Neti, Neti.' " Bal. (17) 22.

These two words, " *Neti, Neti*," " Not thus ! not thus ! " are the words used in the Upanishads with reference to the Supreme Spirit, to show that any attempt to define him must fail. And naturally in the next stanza, as in many other parts of the poem, Tulsidas goes on to tell us that Rama is the unborn, the all-pervading, the passionless; that he is *Sachchidanand* (existence, intelligence, bliss) who has become incarnate. When the poet entertained such thoughts of Rama, it was not unnatural that he should describe how even as a child he revealed his divine form to his mother.

> "He manifested before her his marvellous undivided form, in every hair of which there were a million worlds, with suns and moons, *Shivas and Brahmas* without number." Bal. 207 (213) 233.

The same thought is expressed in a less attractive way in the Uttar Kand, where the inspired crow tells how he jumped down Rama's throat when he was laughing, and in Rama's belly he saw, in addition to numberless worlds, with mountains, rivers, oceans and forests, gods and saints and men, millions of *Brahmas and Shivas*. Uttar, 114 (79) 118.

In concluding this series of extracts there remains to be added, though it has no reference to Rama, the statement that without the assistance of a religious teacher it is not possible for any one to cross the ocean of existence, even were he the equal of *Viranchi and Shankar*. Uttar, 133 (90) 142.

It now remains to review the passages where *Brahma*, *Vishnu* and *Shiva* are spoken of together. There are close on thirty such references. A selection only is possible. To begin with, let us take those which place the gods together in a general way. It will be noticed how frequently the names Hari and Hara for Vishnu and Shiva appear.

"*Vidhi*, *Hari*, *Hara*, the poet Valmiki, Brihaspati and

Sarasvati, in speaking of the glory of a saint are ashamed." Bal. 2.

"With the exception of *Vishnu*, *Viranchi* and *Mahesh*, all the gods got ready their chariots and went (to the sacrifice of Daksh)." Bal. 72 (70) 84.

"If you can bring Brahmins under your control, then *Vidhi*, *Vishnu* and *Mahesh* will be in your power." Bal. 170 (168) 194.

"A charm is a very little thing, but *Vidhi*, *Hari*, *Hara* and all the gods are in its power, just as a little goad controls a great and furious elephant." Bal. 260 (266) 289.

"*Vidhi*, *Hari*, *Hara*, the guardians of the eight quarters of the world and the god of day who knew the greatness of Rama, having assumed the guise of Brahmins, gazed at the festivities with delight." Bal. 320 (326) 358.

"*Vidhi*, *Hari*, *Hara*, Indra and the guardians of the world, all sing the praises of Dashrath, the father of Rama." Ayodh. (166) 173.

"Were Bharat to acquire the rank of *Vidhi*, *Hari* and *Hara*, he would not feel the intoxication of kingly power." Ayodh. (222) 232.

"The boundless love that Bharat and Rama had for one another is more than the understanding of *Vidhi*, *Hari* and *Hara* can fathom." Ayodh. (231) 241.

"The Maya of *Vidhi*, *Hari* and *Hara* is very powerful, but it cannot comprehend the mind of Bharat." Ayodh. (283) 295.

"The man (says Rama) who abandons hypocrisy and serves Brahmins in thought, deed and word, brings *Me*, *Viranchi*, *Shiva* and all the gods into his power." Aranya, 56 (28) 42.

"As for *Vishnu* with his four arms, *Vidhi* with his four heads, and *Purari* (Shiva) with his strange attire and his five faces, and all the other gods, there is not one of them whose beauty can be compared to theirs." Bal. 225 (231) 252.

"If Rama is against you, you cannot escape, though you took refuge with *Vishnu*, *Aj* and *Ish* (Shiva)" Sundar, 59 (56) 158.

It has been already stated that when the crow jumped into Rama's mouth, he saw there millions of worlds and millions of Brahmas and Shivas, but somehow that statement did not satisfy him; and after declaring how he stayed a hundred years in each of the many worlds, he said:

"Each of these worlds had its own *Vidhata*, its own *Vishnu* and *Shiva*." Uttar, 117 (80) 120.

In the two last quotations Rama is recognised as being not merely an incarnation of Vishnu; he possesses more power than any of the Triad; he is also identified with the Supreme Spirit of the universe. A later chapter will show how that claim is made in every section of the poem. Here we shall merely give those passages where this claim is made in reference to the Triad itself. Tulsidas himself tells us:

"I adore the name of Rama, the source of Agni, the sun and the moon, the substance of *Vidhi*, *Hari* and *Hara*." Bal. 24 (22) 34.

Again, when Rama revealed his divine form to Sati:

"She saw many *Shivas*, *Vidhis* and *Vishnus*, each excelling the other in glory, bowing and worshipping at the feet of the Lord. She saw all the gods in their diverse forms." Bal. 65 (63) 76.

In this vision she also saw herself as well as the wives of Brahma and Vishnu repeated without number. Bal. 66 (64) 77.

Mention has already been made of the penance of Manu and his wife.

"Their ceaseless desire was to see Him who is without attributes and without parts, without beginning and without end, whom the Vedas say cannot be defined, from whom *Shambhu*, *Viranchi* and *Vishnu* arise in various forms." Bal. 150 (148) 171.

When after a hundred thousand years, Brahma, Vishnu and Shiva approached them and told them to ask a boon, the devotees paid no attention. It was the Supreme God they were resolved to see.

"*Vidhi*, *Hari* and *Hara* seeing their amazing penance came near Manu many times and tempted him, saying, 'Ask a boon.' But he was steadfast. They could do nothing." Bal. 151 (149) 172.

At long last, when the Supreme Spirit did show Himself and promised that He would become incarnate as Rama, Manu in a hymn of praise, says, "*Vidhi*, *Hari* and *Hara* worship the dust of Thy feet." The completeness of the identification of Rama, not with Vishnu but with the Supreme God, is made even more emphatic by the statement that when the God revealed himself,

"On his left side shone the primal energy, the treasury of beauty, the mother of the world, from whose parts, a very mine of qualities, spring countless Umas, Lakshmis and Sarasvatis . . . even thus was Sita seated at the left side of Rama." Bal. 154 (152) 175.

Again when Rama arrived at the hermitage of Valmiki the sage, addressing him as the Supreme God, said :

"You are the guardian of the bridge of revelation ; the lord of the universe (*jagdish*), and Sita is Maya (illusion) who in accordance with your gracious will creates, preserves and destroys the world. . . The world is a drama, and you are looking on. You make *Vidhi, Hari* and *Hara* to dance. Even they do not comprehend your mystery. Who then can know you ?" Ayodh. (121) 127.

To which there follows a claim equally lofty, uttered by another of the great sages :

" *Vidhi, Hari, Hara,* the sun, the moon, the guardians of the spheres, Illusion (*maya*), Life, Karma . . . are all obedient to Rama." Ayodh. (243) 254.

It now remains to give the four passages which refer to the work of the Triad, as Creator, Preserver and Destroyer of the worlds. In two out of the four it will be noted how the poet seeks to enhance the superiority of Rama.

" Rama is as skilful in creation as 100 millions of Vidhis, as able to save as 100 millions of Vishnus, as able to destroy as 100 millions of Rudras." Uttar, 131 (89) 140.

" It is by his power that Viranchi, Hari and Isha (Shiva) preserve, destroy and create the worlds." Sundar, 20.

The other two refer to the power oi penance and occur in the Bal Kand, 84 (82) 96, and 169 (167) 192.

" By the power of penance *Vidhata* creates the world ; by the power of penance *Vishnu* preserves it ; by the power of penance *Shambhu* destroys it." [1]

[1] There are also a variety of passages which ascribe the creation, preservation and destruction of the world to Rama, as in Lanka (7) 9. " Worship him who is the creator, preserver and destroyer."

VIII.

BRAHM, THE SUPREME SPIRIT.

However numerous the gods whom India has worshipped, she has always recognised the One behind the many. This Supreme Spirit is called Brahm. It is Brahm who is the theme of the Upanishads, and it is with Brahm that the philosophy of Hinduism is chiefly concerned.. Brahm is pure being. He is the highest self. But He cannot be defined. Every attempt to do so always breaks down. And few phrases appear more frequently on the pages of Tulsidas than the phrase he has borrowed from the Upanishads. In response to the efforts made to explain this *primal entity*, these scriptures answered, *Neti, Neti*. It is not this; It is not that. And so when Tulsidas speaks of Brahm, he does not tell us what He is. He tells us what He is not. He is beyond speech and understanding. He is without qualities and attributes. He is without passion and without desire. He is not touched by virtue or defect; by sin or merit. He is without form and without name. He is beyond measure and beyond change. Phrases such as these constantly occur in every part of the poem. The poet seems to exercise all his ingenuity to find a new one. But the one he employs most is the term, *Nirgun Brahm*—that is, Brahm without qualities.

There is yet another phrase which is employed very often. We are told that Brahm is Sachchidanand. That means He is existence (*sat*), thought (*chit*) and joy (*anand*).

But these terms are only of negative import. The existence, thought and joy, which belong to a passionless, partless, quality-less Brahm, must be very cold indeed. And Monier Williams is justified in saying that such *existence* as is attributed to Him can only be the negation of *non-existence*, just as the *thought* is the negation of *non-thought*, and the *joy* is the negation of *non-joy*.

This is the doctrine of monism. Based on the Creation hymn of the *Rig-Veda* (10, 90) which says that Purusha himself is this whole (universe,) whatever has been and whatever shall be,[1] it is expressed with greater distinctness in the well-known phrase from the *Chhandogya Upanishad*, 6, 2 : *there is but one being without a second* (advaita). The quality-less Brahm is all that is. Nevertheless there is a world around us. But this world which we see around us, and we who see it, or who think we see it, are all the products of illusion. The illusion is called Maya. Tulsidas has a great deal to say about Maya. It is Maya, he tells us, who creates, preserves and destroys the world.

So long as Brahm remains Nirgun Brahm—that is, Brahm without qualities—nothing happens or can happen, because nothing exists except this solitary, impersonal Spirit. But the balance is sometimes disturbed. When the Impersonal God is associated with Maya (and, strange to say, Maya is said to be eternal), He becomes a personal God and is spoken of as Sagun Brahm, *i.e.* Brahm endowed with qualities. These qualities are three in number: goodness (*sattva*), activity or passion (*rajas*) and darkness or ignorance (*tamas*).[2] But when Nirgun Brahm becomes Sagun Brahm as a result of His association with Maya, the

[1] Muir, *O.S.T.* vol. i. p. 9.

[2] The character of each soul depends on which of these three qualities predominates (*Laws of Manu*, 12, 24). "Dominated by activity (*rajas*), the One Universal Spirit is Brahma the Creator; by goodness (*sattva*), it is Vishnu the Preserver; by indifference (*tamas*), it is Rudra the Destroyer." Monier Williams, *Brahmanism and Hinduism*, p. 36.

Universe which has resulted is only apparent. If He is a Personal God, He is only a Personal God in a world of illusion. Brahm alone is real, even when we allow, as the Vedantists do, a practical existence to external things, to gods and men. In face of such a situation the wise man is he who by the way of knowledge (*gyan marg*) is able to recognise that his soul is one with the Supreme Spirit.

By the time of Shankaracharya, born in A.D. 788, these monistic speculations had hardened into a system which secured increasing favour in many quarters. But side by side with the way of knowledge there had always run another path, the way of faith or devotion, *bhakti marg*, of which we have an early and impressive illustration in the *Bhagavadgita*. And those who wished to travel by that more satisfying path had come to realise that the doctrine of bhakti could not be permanently maintained if the theory of monism or advaita were allowed to prevail. In Southern India, in particular, there were among the followers of Vasudeva (Vishnu) not only poets who wrote hymns in adoration of the special object of their worship, but philosophers who declined to accept the interpretation which Shankara and his school had put upon the Upanishads. They refused to believe in a God destitute of all qualities and for ever shrouded in Maya.

Among these protestants the most outstanding name is that of Ramanuja who was born in A.D. 1017. In opposition to Shankara, he condemned the doctrine of Maya and asserted his belief in a personal God. At the same time, he acknowledged that God contains within Himself everything that exists. But he held this belief with a difference, and in consequence his system is called *Vishishtadvaita*. He taught that within the Unity of God there are three distinct eternal principles, the individual soul (*chit*), matter in all its forms (*achit*), and the Supreme soul (*Ishvar*);

that *chit* and *achit* are attributes of the Supreme and constitute His body. In his own words, as given in his commentary upon the *Vedanta Sutras,* Ramanuja taught that:

> "The highest Brahm is essentially free from all imperfection whatsoever, comprises within itself all auspicious qualities and finds its pastime in originating, preserving, re-absorbing, pervading and ruling the universe; that the entire complex of intelligent and non-intelligent beings (souls and matter), in all their different estates, is real, and constitutes the form, *i.e.* the body of the highest Brahm." [1]

These doctrines, as well as others, all of them modifications of the *advaita* school, spread to Northern India, and exercised a wide influence among the worshippers of Vishnu. Bhandarkar is careful to insist over and over again that the great object of these Vaishnava teachers was to confute the theory of Maya, and to establish the doctrine of Bhakti.[2] The only name which concerns us here is that of Ramananda, who died in A.D. 1411. A disciple of the school of Ramanuja, he broke away and founded a sect of his own, called the Ramavats or worshippers of Rama. By identifying Rama and not Krishna with the Supreme God, he rendered an inestimable service to the people of Northern India, a service which was made the more permanent by the fact that he and his followers used the vernaculars in propagating their views, and

[1] *Vedanta Sutras* with Ramanuja's commentary, translated by Thibaut, *S.B.E.* vol. xlviii. p. 88. See also Berriedale Keith's article on Ramanuja, *E.R.E.*; Monier Williams's *Brahmanism and Hinduism,* pp. 119–124; and Banerjea's *Dialogues on the Hindu Philosophy,* Dialogue IX.

[2] Bhandarkar, *Vaisnavism, Saivism,* pp. 51, 52, 54, 57, 58, 62, 67. *E.g.* A strong feeling of Bhakti or love, and a fear of the dangerous consequences of the doctrine of Maya or illusion, were the guiding principles of the new development, p. 62.

admitted not only Brahmins but outcastes to their fellowship.

Tulsidas (born 1532) belongs to this great succession. He also believed in a personal God, very different from the Sagun Brahm of an earlier day, and he was devoted to this personal God in a very real fashion. But the fact remains that Tulsidas's thought continues to be coloured by the very conceptions from which his school had been expected to deliver him. He believes, as Ramanuja believed, that the God he worships is all-knowing and all-merciful; that He is antagonistic to all evil. Nay, more, he believes that He is a real Saviour of mankind. He also passionately believes in the personal immortality which Rama grants to all His devotees. And time after time he says that he has no wish to hear or to sing the praises of Nirgun Brahm. Indeed his poem, as Growse says, is a passionate protest against the virtual atheism of philosophical Hindu theology. Nevertheless, he frequently uses the language of that philosophy. Maya is seldom absent from his thoughts. He seems to be haunted by it. It has enveloped the world. It is always perplexing and deceiving men. He has personified it in Sita. He looks on it as eternal. His one consolation is that Rama is greater than Maya. He is Maya's lord. He sends it forth. Controlled by Him, it can make even Brahma, Vishnu and Shiva to dance like puppets. But He who sends it forth can also recall it, and not only recall it, but save His worshippers from its power. Devotion to Rama is able to set its victims free. When Tulsidas writes in that manner, it is impossible to avoid the belief that he has surrendered much that his predecessors had gained. It cannot be said of him, as was said of them, that his great object is to confute the theory of Maya. He can only tell us how to evade its power. On the other hand, we have to recognise that Tulsidas did not claim to be a philosopher. When he attempts to philosophise, he is often uninteresting and sometimes absurd. But he believes that the Supreme Spirit has become incarnate in Rama, that the Nirgun has become Sagun, and that Rama at least is real, if all else is a dream.[1] He believes also that those who worship Rama will not be absorbed in the godhead, but will pass to Rama's own heaven. For the rest, he is content to know that "the actions of Sagun Rama are not to be comprehended by thought or human strength of speech." Lanka, 85 (70) 95. And then he adds what looks like a taunt at somebody's expense: "That is the reason why the wisest ascetics discard theological speculations and simply adore."[2]

And it is because he did that with so much devotion, and wrote of it with such power and beauty, that his poem has exercised so great and healthy an influence among the Hindi-speaking population of Northern India.[3]

[1] In Aranya, 64 (33) 49 Shiva says to Uma: "The worship of Hari is real; the world is a dream."

[2] Growse's translation.

[3] Farquhar remarks: "It has been frequently assumed that Ramananda taught the Vishishtadvaita system of Ramanuja. This is one of the many points with regard to the leader on which no direct evidence is available; but the indirect evidence which does exist, scarcely points to that conclusion. One of the characteristics of the whole movement that springs from him is a constant use of *advaita* phrases, a clinging to *advaita* concepts, while holding hard by the personality of Rama. The teaching is usually a sort of compromise between theism and strict monism." *Outlines of the Religious Literature of India*, p. 326.

IX.

RAMA, THE INCARNATION OF VISHNU AND OF BRAHM, THE SUPREME GOD.

In our examination of the various religious ideas of the poem, we have been all along leading up to what is its very heart and centre—the birth of Rama and the work he achieves in the world. The poet's claim is that he is not only an incarnation of Vishnu, the second member of the Triad, but of Brahm, the uncreated, the invisible, all-pervading Brahm, the Supreme Spirit of the universe, who has taken on himself a visible form. When Tulsidas makes this double claim, he is merely following the example set him by other writers. It has been argued that the original kernel of Valmiki's *Ramayana* did not contain any reference to Rama as an incarnation, even of Vishnu; and it is true that in certain sections of the poem Rama is spoken of as if he were merely a human hero. On the other hand, in the Epic as men have read it for many centuries, there are passages where Rama is spoken of not merely as an incarnation of Vishnu, but is identified with the Supreme Spirit. Thus in the sixth book of that poem we read that the Creator told Rama who he really was.

> "Thou art . . . the true, imperishable Brahm. . . . Thou art the source of being and the cause of destruction. . . . I am thy heart; the goddess Sarasvati is thy tongue. The gods have been made by Brahma the hairs on thy limbs. The night is called the closing, and the day the opening, of thine eyes. The Vedas are thy thoughts. . . . Thou

art called the highest soul. . . . Sita is Lakshmi, and thou art Vishnu."[1]

The *Bhagavadgita* makes the same claim for Krishna. He also was an incarnation of Vishnu. And he is reported as saying of himself:

> "I am the producer and the destroyer of the whole universe. There is nothing else higher than myself; all this is woven upon me like pearls upon a thread. I am the taste in water. I am the light of the sun and moon. . . . Know me to be the eternal seed of all beings."[2]

Tulsidas, then, is merely following the example of others before him when he identifies his hero not only with Vishnu, but with the Supreme Spirit. How he relates them to one another we must now endeavour to examine. And in doing so it will be desirable that we should take the various periods of Rama's life in turn, on the lines which the poet himself has laid down: his birth and childhood; his life in Avadh; his exile in the forest; his alliance with the monkeys; his attack on Lanka with the defeat of Ravan and the rescue of Sita; and the return to Avadh. In following this method we shall be able the more easily to watch the movements of the author's mind, and to discover a different outlook and atmosphere in more than one section of the poem.

Prior to that, however, we have to examine the first section of the first book, which may be reckoned as the prelude to the whole poem. Here we have a very important series of passages. Because Tulsidas is undoubtedly trying to meet in advance those who are disposed to doubt the claims he puts forward on behalf of his hero; or to satisfy those who find that they need to have their difficulties explained.

[1] Muir, *O.S.T.* vol. iv. p. 181.
[2] *Bhagavadgita*, chap. vii., Telang's translation (*S.B.E.*).

Prelude.

It will be remembered that in the earlier part of the Bal Kand, or book of childhood, there is a long passage relating to Shiva. There we read that Shiva and Uma one day saw Rama searching everywhere in the forest for his lost wife. It is not without a purpose that the poet makes the goddess cross-examine her husband with regard to the mystery of Rama.

> "Is Rama the son of the king of Avadh, or is he some uncreated quality-less (*nirgun*) invisible being? If he is a king's son, and in distress for the loss of his wife, how can he be Brahm? Tell me, my lord, and cause me to understand with regard to him who is passionless, all-pervading and omnipresent. Do not be angry at my ignorance. But act in a way that will remove it. In the forest I saw the majesty of Rama. I was so amazed that I did not tell you. My stupid mind could not grasp it then, and I got the reward [1] I deserved. To-day, again, there is some doubt in my mind. Have mercy on me, I beg of you, with joined hands. You have indeed told me already, and in a variety of ways. But do not be angry. At that time I was in a sort of infatuation from which I am now free. And first of all, after due thought, tell me the reason why the quality-less Brahm assumed a body with qualities (*sa-gun*)." Bal. 117 (115) 131.

We have here a frank recognition on the part of the poet that the common man at least feels the mystery connected with such an incarnation, and that he is entitled to some explanation. And it is interesting to observe that when

[1] The reward was separation from her husband. This question was put thousands of years after, when in a later birth Uma was reunited to Shiva under the name of Parvati.

he sets himself to remove his wife's doubts and answers her questions Shiva manifests a certain amount of diffidence.

> "Seeing you are so eager, I shall tell you in accordance with what is taught in the books of revelation and as far as my intelligence permits. Your questions are natural and proper, pleasing both to the saints and to me." Bal. 123 (121) 137.

But there was one question which Shiva was sorry to hear. He had no doubt his wife had spoken under the power of delusion. It was when she asked: "Is there some other Rama of whom the books of revelation sing, and on whom holy men meditate?" The god thereupon proceeded to denounce all those who entertained such thoughts, as—

> "Heretics and enemies of Rama's feet, who do not know falsehood from truth; ignorant, undeserving, blind and reprobate; people on the mirror of whose minds nothing remains, lustful, deceitful and very perverse, who have not even in a dream seen an assembly of the saints. They teach doctrines contrary to the Veda. They understand neither gain nor loss. They cannot discern between *agun* and *sagun*. They babble words of their own invention and at great length; under the influence of Hari's illusion (*maya*) they go astray in the world. In speaking of them you cannot use language that is improper. They are full of wind, possessed by devils and drunken. They never say anything of value. They have drunk of the liquor of strong delusion (*moh*). No one should listen to anything they say." Bal. 124 (122) 138.

The thought at once occurs, to what extent did Tulsidas find that his feelings for Rama were not shared? Whatever the answer may be to that question, Shiva proceeded to give his own views on the matter, and in the statement he makes we probably have the poet's beliefs better expressed than anywhere else in the poem.

> "There is no difference between *sagun* and *agun*, so the saints, Puranas and wise men say. The quality-less (*agun*), the invisible, the formless, the uncreated, for the love He had for those devoted to Him, became *sagun* (endowed with qualities). How can that which is without qualities (*agun*) become endowed with qualities (*sagun*)? Even as there is no difference between water and ice (though their form is changed). How can He, whose name is the sun that dispels the darkness of ignorance, be associated with sensual delusion? Rama who is Sachchidanand and the lord of day; in Him there is not an atom of the night's delusion. The very embodiment of light, the adorable, in him there is no dawn of understanding. Joy and sorrow, knowledge and ignorance, conceit and pride, which belong to life, are not to be found in Him. The world knows that Rama is the all-pervading Brahm, the supreme bliss, the god of gods, the primeval. He is Purush, the ocean of glorious light, the lord of the universe revealed, the jewel of the house of Raghu, my Lord. And having said this Shiva bowed his head." Bal. 124 (122) 138.

These long quotations from the Prelude of the poem show that while Vishnu continues to be remembered, were it only by his name of Hari, he is very much a vanishing quantity. It is Rama who is thought of as wholly and entirely God. And the rest of the poem does not fail to substantiate that idea, though from time to time, especially in the portions dealing with his childhood, his relation to the lesser god is recalled.

RAMA'S BIRTH AND CHILDHOOD.

In the chapter dealing with Vishnu, we have seen how the voice from heaven declared :

> " Fear not ye saints, sages and Indra, for your sakes I shall assume a human form and descend as a man with every element of my divinity incarnate." Bal. 192 (198) 218.

And with unusual abruptness, after mentioning that the gods took birth as monkeys and in vast troops awaited the coming of Hari, we are introduced to Dashrath, king of Avadh.

Nothing is said of his being an incarnation of Manu, or of that sage's wife and the promise made to her. Three queens are spoken of, however—obedient wives, devoted to their husband and earnest worshippers of Hari. Unfortunately they were childless. But when the king spoke to his family priest [1] of his regret that he had no son, he was told not to be anxious.

> " You will have four sons, who will be famous throughout the world and will remove the fears of the faithful." Bal. 194 (200) 220.

In accordance with the holy man's instructions a sacrifice was performed, with the object of procuring a son. When the oblation had been offered, Agni, the god of fire, appeared and said to the king : " Go and divide this offering as you think proper." Bal. 194 (200) 220. The king did as he was commanded ; and calling the queens he gave to Kaushalya half the oblation, to Kaikeyi a quarter of it. What was over he divided between these two, but they gave it to the third queen, Sumitra. As a result, the three queens became pregnant.

[1] His name was Vasishth. He was for sixty generations family priest to the royal house of Avadh.

"From the day Hari was conceived in the womb, all the worlds were filled with happiness and prosperity." Bal. 195 (201) 221.

Though the promise was to the effect that in the house of Dashṛath will become incarnate four brothers, we find three of them already forgotten, for it is said that it was under an auspicious star, and in an auspicious month, and on an auspicious day, that Rama, the root of joy, was born. The gods were present at his birth, seated in their cars, the celestial minstrels sang his praise, the drums of heaven began to beat, and flowers fell from the sky. And it is Rama's mother alone, and not the mothers of the other children, who, like Mary the mother of Jesus, gives voice to her gratitude in a hymn of praise. As she looks at the child in her arms and is amazed at his wonderful form, his beautiful eyes, his body dark like a cloud, his weapons and his four arms, his ornaments and garland, she recognises him to be the enemy of the demons and calls him the husband of Lakshmi. She addresses him as immortal, and says he is beyond the understanding of men. In particular, she tells her child that in every hair of his body there is a multitude of worlds, fashioned by Maya. Bal. 198 (204) 224.

A few pages farther on we have another account of the child's beauty, and there again he is identified for the moment with Vishnu, because mention is made of the imprint of a holy man's feet on the body of that god. But this statement is preceded and followed by these two declarations:

"The all-pervading Brahm, void of emotion, without attributes, without sensations of pleasure, the uncreated . . . lay in Kaushalya's arms." Bal. 206 (210) 230.

"Rama, the father and mother of the world, the giver of joy to the people of Koshal, though his enemies try without end, they will never escape from the bonds of existence. Maya, who has brought under her power all souls, both what moves and what does not move, trembles before the Lord who makes her dance to the playing of his eyebrows." Bal. 205 (211) 231.

Still more wonderful is another story recorded of Rama's infancy :

" Once when his mother had washed and dressed him, she put him in his cradle. She then prepared an offering to present to Bhagwan, her own family god. When she had worshipped the god and made the offering, she went to the place where she had prepared the food. But on returning to where she had made the offering, she saw there Rama eating the offering. Overcome with fear, she went to (where she had left) her child, and there found him asleep. Again she came and saw her son eating. She trembled in her heart and courage departed. Here she saw a child ; there she saw a child. 'My mind is in a maze' (she said) ; 'what has happened ?' When Rama saw his mother's perplexity, he laughed and showed to her his entire marvellous form, with hundreds of millions of worlds in every single hair, with innumerable suns and moons, Shivas and Brahmas, with many mountains, rivers, oceans, lands and forests, with Time, Karma, attributes, demerits, natural dispositions (*svabhav*). She saw even what had never been heard of. As she looked at this Maya, very incomprehensible in every way, she stood with joined hands and very afraid. She saw that which causes life to dance ; she saw the *devotion* that sets it free. Her body trembling, and with not a word from her mouth, she closed her eyes and bowed her head at his feet. Seeing his mother in a state of amazement, Rama again took the form of a child. She sang his praises, but her terror did not leave her."

> " 'The father of the world! I thought he was my son,' she said. In many ways Hari exhorted her. 'Listen, mother, do not speak of this to any one.' And over and over again Kaushalya besought her son with joined hands, 'And do you never again, oh Lord, pervade me with your Maya.' " Bal. 206 (212) 232.

And yet he was a very human child. He and his brothers played at every kind of children's game. But the poet cannot fail to wonder that it should be so.

> "The lord whose thoughts, actions and words are beyond comprehension played in Dashrath's courtyard. When the king was eating he would call for him. But he would not come and leave his play. He came running, however, when Kaushalya went to bring him. Him, whom the scriptures call Neti, and whose mystery Shiva cannot solve, his mother ran and laid hold of, in his peevishness. He came, his body covered with dust. The king smiled and seated him in his lap." Bal. 208 (214) 234.

The passage just quoted is the final incident recorded of Rama's early childhood. And we next hear of his school-days, but only in the very briefest way.

> "Rama went to his teacher's house to read. In a very short time he had acquired all knowledge. It was very much a joke for Hari to study, seeing the four Vedas are nothing but his breath." Bal. 209 (215) 235.

In other matters we read that Rama was obedient to his parents, a source of joy to the citizens of Avadh, and went hunting with one of his brothers. The interesting statement is added that every beast that died by his hand, on leaving its body, went to heaven. But despite the brevity of the poet's account of this period of Rama's life, he gives vent to his feelings thus:

> "The all-pervading, the indivisible, the passionless, the

uncreated Nirgun, with neither name nor form, did many wonders for the sake of those devoted to him." Bal. 211 (217) 237.

In strange contrast to the brief and somewhat chastened paragraph dealing with Rama's school-days, the poet or rather Shiva thereafter begins a long story of how Vishvamitra the royal sage came to the palace and asked the king to allow Rama and Lakshman to go with him to his hermitage and slay certain demons who were disturbing his prayers and sacrifices. The sage had said to himself:

"'Without the help of Hari, these wicked demons cannot be killed.' Then the saint reflected in his mind, 'The Lord has descended to remove the earth's burden.'" Bal. 211 (217) 237.

And as he approached the palace he cried: "I shall gaze my fill at the Lord, the abode of all virtues, knowledge and absence of desire."

It was the help of both Rama and Lakshman that he asked for. And it is in connection with this request that the poet, for the first time since the brothers were born, remembers that Rama was not the only son of Dashrath, who was an avatar of God. Because, as the two boys went forth to fight against the demons, we read:

"The two lion-hearted heroes set out, glad to remove the alarm of the sage. Oceans of compassion, firm of purpose, the primary and secondary causes of the whole universe." Bal. 214 (220) 240.

It was on this expedition that they came to the abandoned hermitage of the sage whose wife had committed adultery with the god Indra. Her husband's curse had changed her into a stone. But whenever the feet of Rama touched the stone the curse was broken, and the woman restored to life. Her first act was a hymn of praise, in which she called him Prabhu, Hari and Raghupati, the protector of the world, the fount of knowledge, the giver of joy to all, and the enemy of Ravan. In particular, she said it was from his feet that the Ganges arose, when the waters of that river poured down from heaven on Shiva's head, and asked that his feet might rest for ever on hers. Tulsidas points the moral by an interjection of his own :

> " Thus you see the Lord Hari is merciful and a friend of the poor, without regard to their deserts. Worship him and abandon all hypocrisy and strife." Bal. 217 (223) 244.

The defeat of the demons did not take long. Rama slew their two leaders. So mighty was the blow with which he smote them that the head of one of them fell to the ground at a place on the other side of the ocean, seven hundred miles distant. Lakshman is credited with the overthrow of the rank and file. It was when they were on this expedition that the two lads heard from the sage about the bow of Shiva, and how, on an appointed day, the person who was able to bend it would gain the hand of Sita, the daughter of Janak, king of Videha.

As Sita was not only Rama's future wife, but his supreme energy (*param shakti*) and his Maya (illusion), this is the place to tell of her wonderful birth. When Ravan was oppressing gods and Brahmins, he remembered that he had never made any of the forest dwellers pay him tribute. Accordingly he sent four of his followers to a certain hermitage. In response to the demand for tribute, the hermit filled a jar with his own blood, and said : " Go and tell Ravan when this jar is opened, destruction will fall upon you and your family." Bal. 188 (194). To avoid such a catastrophe, Ravan told those who brought the jar to take it to the capital of Janak and bury it in a field. Some time after, when Janak was ploughing the field as part of a religious ceremony, Sita emerged.[1] She was adopted by the king, and though it was intended at first to call her by another name, she was eventually spoken of as Sita, which means a furrow. She is frequently referred to as the earth-born, or daughter of the earth, because of her strange origin.

The two brothers, when they reached the capital of Videha, made a great impression. The king, taking the sage apart, said :

> "Tell me, oh holy one, who are these two boys ? Are they the glory of a saint's home or are they the support of a royal house ? Or is it that Brahm, who, the scriptures say, is *Neti*, has taken a twofold disguise and come hither ? " Bal. 221 (227) 248.

The common people were equally enthralled, and declared :

> "As for Vishnu with his four arms, Brahma with his four heads, Shiva with his strange attire and five faces, and all the other gods, there is not one of them whose beauty can be compared to theirs." Bal. 225 (231) 252.

Great numbers of people had gathered to witness the contest, and many preparations were made for seating the spectators. Rama showed a boyish interest in all he saw. But Tulsidas's comment on this action of his is :

> "He, by whose command Maya created the worlds in a moment in the twinkling of an eye, showed amazement at the sight of the arena, for the sake of those devoted to him." Bal. 230 (236) 257.

When the great day arrived, kings and princes, one after the other, tried to raise the bow ; but they could not even move it as it lay on the ground. Indeed, not less than 10,000 kings, when they applied their united strength,

[1] This incident is not given in the Allahabad edition. Growse and the Bombay edition record it but recognise that it is an interpolation.

found themselves helpless. But when Rama's turn came, he not only lifted it from the ground ; he raised it above his head and drew it with such force that it snapped in two. The crash was so tremendous that the sound of it re-echoed round the world. The great serpent and the tortoise, on whom the earth rests, trembled ; the horses of the sun went out of their course, while gods, saints and demons had to put their hands to their ears.

It was at this stage that Rama of the Axe appeared. This is one of the incarnations of the god Vishnu, and in the Lanka Book, 126 (106) 135, when the celestials were expressing their gratitude to Rama for all he had achieved, they included Parashuram or Rama of the Axe among his avatars. When Rama of the Axe appears on this occasion, however, the poet makes no reference to the fact that he also is an incarnation of Vishnu. And he follows Valmiki in his omission. Certainly it would be difficult to explain the presence of two incarnations on the earth at the same time.[1] Apart from that, the whole story is very remarkable, because both brothers indulged in a type of badinage somewhat incongruous with the character of the hero. Rama of the Axe was very angry when he found that Shiva's bow had been broken. But Rama suggested that it had perhaps been broken by one of Parashuram's own servants, while Lakshman added fuel to the fire by asking why he made such a fuss about the breaking of a bow. What was the difference between this one and any other ? The situation became even more acute when the prince refused to fight the angry visitor on the ground that he was a Brahmin. But such a suggestion was scornfully repelled. He was no ordinary Brahmin. He had slaughtered many thousands of the warrior caste. He was no common ascetic. He was the enemy of the whole

[1] According to Hindu chronology, a period of a million years divides their descents.

Kshatriya race. Time after time he had robbed the earth of its rulers and given it to Brahmins. Eventually Rama was invited to try and bend the bow of Vishnu which Parashuram had brought with him. As soon as the boy had taken the bow into his hand it became taut of its own accord. This wonderful miracle filled Rama of the Axe with amazement. His pride was at once humbled, and he began a hymn of praise in which he sought pardon for his foolish arrogance. He called the brothers temples of forgiveness. He said that Rama, whom he had formerly spoken of as an enemy of Shiva, was the swan that dwelt in the lake of Shiva's soul; the friend of the gods, of cows and of Brahmins. He called him the ocean of all the virtues. But he did not address him in the lofty terms which others so frequently employ. He never says that he was an incarnation of either Vishnu or the Supreme God. As has been said, the whole narrative is very mysterious. Nevertheless one point is made plain, that Rama, prince of Avadh, was very much the superior of Rama of the Axe, who was born in a Brahmin's house. And one feels that we have here some attempt at atonement for the grievous slur which inevitably attaches to the warrior caste from the legends recorded in the *Mahabharata*.

The result of bending Shiva's bow was that Sita placed the garland round Rama's neck, and arrangements were made for their marriage. When speaking of Sita, the poet refers to her on several occasions as the mother of the world; and says of Videha that it was the city where the goddess Lakshmi lived in the false guise of a woman. Bal. 291 (297) 322. Dashrath is referred to as "*the king whose son is sagun Brahm.*" 304 (310) 336. But the father of the bride says of his son-in-law:

"Rama, how can I sing thy praise? Thou art the swan of the Manas lake of the souls of saints and Mahadev, for whose sake yogis practise yoga, abandoning anger, delusion (*moh*), selfishness and pride. Thou art the all-pervading Brahm, the invisible, the imperishable, Sachchidanand, devoid of qualities (*nirgun*) and endowed with qualities (*sagun*), whom neither thought nor speech can understand, whom philosophers are unable to explain, regarding whose glory the scriptures can only say *neti*, and who remains the same in the past, the present and the future." Bal. 339 (345) 373.

Rama's Life in Avadh.

The second book of the poem describes Rama's life in Avadh up to the time when, in obedience to his father's reluctant command, he went into exile in the forest.[1] In atmosphere and outlook it is very different from the earlier book, and has a much wider appeal. Its greater attractiveness lies in the fact that it is so much more human. The supernatural in its cruder forms is not in evidence. From time to time, no doubt, the narrative is broken by Tulsidas's characteristic declarations, similar to those we have already quoted, that Rama is the Supreme God, or that he is Vishnu incarnate. But apart from such assertions we feel that we are face to face with a real man, whose words and doings are essentially human. But it is his very humanity which shows him most divine. There are no marvellous revelations of his godhead, such as he showed to his mother in his infancy, no amazing slaughter of demons performed by a boy in his sixteenth year; no bending and breaking of a bow which a great multitude of kings combined could not raise from the ground. But in contrast to that, we have a very beautiful and attractive picture of an obedient son, a loving husband

[1] Its name is the Ayodhya Kand. It also deals with the first months of Rama's life in the forest.

and a large-hearted brother. Rama displays a wonderful patience, an amazing magnanimity. Sita, in her wifely devotion, is not a whit behind. And the story of two such noble and unselfish lives, recorded first by Valmiki in his Sanskrit *Ramayana*, and in later centuries by Tulsidas, has been a great influence for good on the moral and spiritual life of Northern India. The critic may think that Rama should have satisfied the desires of his father's subjects rather than yield to the intrigues of a wicked woman. But all criticism is silenced in presence of Rama's simple confidence that there was only one path he could tread; the determination not to render void his father's promise, however foolish, coupled with the modesty of his conviction that the brother who would supplant him was as capable of ruling Avadh as himself.

In studying this part of the poem, it is necessary to remember the main points of the story as recorded in the introductory chapter. Here it is our purpose to present some of the passages which help best to illustrate the character of Rama. Two will be sufficient to show his conception of filial obedience. When told by his step-mother that he was to go into exile that very day, and be displaced by his brother, he replied:

> "Listen, mother, that son is fortunate who obeys the command of his father and mother. A son who cherishes his parents is not easily found in this world. It will be good for me in every way to live with the hermits in the forest. There is my father's command that I should do so; and it has your approval. And Bharat, whom I love as I love my own life, will obtain the kingdom. The Creator in every way is favouring me to-day." Ayodh. (40) 41.

When reflecting on what he had done, the old king was in a strait betwixt two. He knew the disgrace that would attach to him should his son refuse to obey his orders. And yet he prayed to Shiva :

> "You direct the hearts of all. Give to Rama such understanding that he will ignore my commands and stay at home, forgetting his natural disposition and love." Ayodh. (44) 45.

But there was not a moment's hesitation on the part of Rama. He told Dashrath when they met, not to be distressed.

> "The man, who loves his father and mother as he loves his own soul, holds in the palm of his hand the four objects of life. By obeying your commands, I achieve the purpose of my existence." Ayodh. (45) 46.

Rama, in his unselfishness, wished to go into exile alone, but he was met by a pertinacity greater than his own. Sita and Lakshman accompanied him. In urging Sita to remain in Avadh, he was thinking of his wife's comfort ; in desiring that Lakshman should stay behind, he was thinking of the situation in Avadh, his father old and heart-broken ; the other two brothers absent from the capital. Rama's treatment of the citizens deserves to be noted : his kindness to those he met on the road, his treatment of the ferryman who rowed them across the Ganges, and of the low castes and their chieftain in the forest. A prince of royal blood in India to-day would not make an outcaste sit down beside him. But the finest trait in his character is his treatment of Bharat. When Bharat followed the exiles to the forest, Lakshman was afraid that he had come for sinister ends. Sita also was anxious.

> "If there were no deceit and evil purpose in his heart, why does he come with carriages and horses and elephants? And why should we blame him? The world goes mad when it secures dominion." Ayodh. (218) 228.

But Rama refused to believe it.

> "Lakshman, listen. In all that the creator has made, I have never heard of or seen as good a man as Bharat. He would not be intoxicated with kingly power were he to attain the dignity of Brahma, Vishnu and Shiva." (222) 232.

It is less easy to admire the way in which Rama assured his brother, when they met, and Kaikeyi herself [1] somewhat earlier that she was not to blame.

> "Rama first greeted Kaikeyi and softened her heart by his sweet disposition and piety. Falling at her feet, he comforted her again, saying, 'The guilt rests on the heads of Time, Karma and the Creator.' Raghubar met all the mothers and comforted them, saying, 'The world is under the control of God (*ish*); blame nobody.'" (234) 244.

> "Brother, do not grieve in your heart. Know that the ways of life are under the control of God (*ish*). Whoever accuses you of evil he will perish both in this world and in the next. The people who blame your mother are fools, who have never studied in the school of the learned or of the saints." (252) 263.

We have, then, this very human and often very attractive Rama presented to us. But it must not be forgotten that the other Rama, the Rama who is a manifestation of Brahm, is never absent from the poet's thoughts. Indeed he brings the two sometimes very close together, and in such a fashion that it is difficult to reconcile them. And more than once he realises that he has attributed to his hero mortal weaknesses and limitations for which he must offer some explanation.

The principal passages in this section which emphasise the conviction that Rama is God, are as follows :

[1] Kaikeyi and the other queens also went to see Rama in the forest.

When the prince was bidding farewell to his father before going into exile, Dashrath said :

"Listen, my son, saints say regarding you, 'Rama is the lord of creation, both what moves and what does not move :' they say that God (*ish*), after due consideration, gives the fruit according to good or bad Karma. According to what one does, so does one find the fruit. Such is the teaching of Scripture and the verdict of mankind. But for one to sin, and another to find the fruit! The ways of God are very wonderful! Who is there on earth who can comprehend them ?" (74) 77.

Again, when Rama came with Sita and Lakshman to the Ganges we are told how they bathed in the sacred waters, and were refreshed.

"They bathed in the stream, and the weariness of the journey disappeared. They drank the holy water, and their spirits were made glad. But how can you say of him, by the remembrance of whom the world's burden is wiped out, that he was tired ? It is a mere play of words. Rama, the banner of the Solar race, is the holy Sachchidanand, the bridge over the sea of transmigrations, though he acts after the fashion of a man." (85) 88.

When Rama and Sita were lying asleep on the bare ground Lakshman explained to the forest chieftain who Rama really was. Guha was perplexed by the seeming cruelties of life, and he talked at length of the luxury with which they had been surrounded in Avadh, and the amazing contrast afforded by the condition in which they now were. This caused him to cry out, "To whom is the Creator not hostile ? People say with truth that Karma is supreme." (88) 91.

To this lament, Lakshman replied :

"Who is the cause of another's pain or gladness ? All men, my brother, experience the fruit of their own doings. Union, separation, pleasure, good and evil, friendship, enmity and indifference, are all snares of error's weaving. Birth and death, in which the world entangles us, prosperity and adversity, Karma and Time, land, houses and wealth, city and kindred, heaven and hell, whatever the interests in which men are involved, what they see, what they hear, what enters into their minds, delusion (*moh*) is their root. The *supreme reality* (*paramarth*) is not there. In a dream a beggar becomes a king, the god of heaven becomes poor; they awake, and there has not been either gain or loss to any one. In like fashion you should look upon the world around you. Reflecting thus, be not angry, and make no false accusation against any one. All are sleepers in the night of delusion (*moh*) and see many kinds of dreams. In this world of night, they who keep awake are those who engage in abstract meditation on *supreme reality*, in a state of detachment from the world. Reckon that soul to be awake where there is absence of desire for every sensuous enjoyment. From this results discernment and escape from the errors of delusion; then love for the feet of Raghubir. Ah, my friend, the height of *supreme reality* is this—in mind, deed and word to love Rama's feet. Rama is Brahm, *supreme reality* embodied, all-pervading, invisible, without beginning, beyond compare, devoid of all change, indivisible. The Veda investigates, but it ever says, *Neti*. For the sake of those devoted to him, the earth, Brahmins, cows and gods, the merciful assumed a body, and performs actions. The hearing of his deeds destroys the snares of the world." (89) 92.

Rama's kindness to the primitive people of the forest calls forth the poet's wonder:

"The Lord, whom the Veda cannot express in words,

nor the minds of saints understand, in his compassion listens to the words of the Kirats, as a father to the voice of his child." (131) 137.

When the gods were alarmed lest Bharat would persuade Rama to return to Avadh and render impossible his encounter with Ravan, Indra said to the priest of the celestials, " Do something to prevent this meeting of Rama and Bharat." But the priest smiled to think that the " god with the thousand eyes was without eyes," and replied :

" You distress yourself to no purpose ; leave tricks alone. On this occasion deception would be ridiculous. Illusion (*maya*) practised on a servant of the lord of illusion recoils on those who attempt it. I once formerly attempted something of the kind, knowing that it was in accordance with Rama's desire. To do anything crafty now would be disastrous. It is Rama's nature not to be angry at any offence against himself, but those who offend his devotees are consumed in the fire of his anger. Tradition, the Veda and history prove it. Durvas knows this to be characteristic of him. Who is there like Bharat in his devotion to Rama ? The world repeats Rama's name ; Rama repeats Bharat's. Do not think to do harm, oh lord of the immortals, to a devotee of Rama ; if you do, disgrace in this world and suffering in the next will be your portion, with sorrow that grows from day to day. . . . Although Rama is always alike, without passion, and without desire, and is not touched by sin or merit, by virtue or defect ; and though he has made Karma lord of all that is, and as we act, so must we taste the fruit, nevertheless, he plays at odds and evens, according as hearts are devoted or hostile. Without qualities (*agun*), without form, beyond measure and unchangeable, Rama, conquered by the love of his devotees, has become endowed with qualities (*sagun*). The Veda, Puranas, saints and gods, testify to the fact that Rama has always given heed to the wishes of his servants. So knowing that such is the case, abandon guile." (209) 218.

When Bharat reached his brother's presence, accompanied by many of the citizens and the widows of the late king, he was reminded by one of the great sages who Rama was, and of the obedience to which he was entitled :

"The upholder of religion, the sun of the Solar race, king Rama, the self-controlled Bhagwan, the sea of truth, the protector, the bridge of revelation, Rama has taken birth for the happiness of the world ; obedient to the word of his religious teachers, his father and mother, the destroyer of the armies of the wicked, the well-wisher of the gods, . . . Brahma, Vishnu, Shiva, the sun, the moon, the guardian of the spheres, Maya, life, karma and all the ages ; the lord of serpents, the lord of the earth and whatever lords there be, the spells and magic of the Vedas and Tantras—consider it well in your minds and understand—they are all obedient to Rama." Ayodh. (243) 254.

The most striking passage, however, is from the lips of Valmiki :

"Rama ! you are the guardian of the bridge of revelation—you are the lord of the world. Sita is Maya, who, in accordance with your will, creates, preserves and destroys the world, and Lakshman is the lord of serpents with a thousand heads who upholds the world with all that moves and all that does not move ; for the sake of the gods, and assuming a regal human form, you have come to destroy the hosts of the wicked. Rama ! your form is beyond speech and understanding : it pervades all things : it cannot be described ; it is boundless ; the scriptures say, Neti, Neti. Life is a play, and you are its beholder ; you make Brahma, Vishnu and Shiva to dance, even they do not know your secret. Who then can know you ? . . . For the sake of holy men and gods, you have taken a human body, and speak and act like an ordinary king." (121) 126.

There at once follows this declaration, one of those utterances which constitute a peculiarly valuable contribution to the spiritual development of India, because it links religion and morals together in a fashion not so common as one could wish, showing how clearly the poet realised that a clean heart was needed to be the dwelling-place of God. It is true that portions of this utterance strike a somewhat ambiguous note. But for that very reason it is desirable to give it in full, that we may appreciate the better both its light and shade. The very fact that Tulsidas puts this statement in the mouth of Valmiki, whose earlier *Ramayana* had inspired him to write his own, makes it the more valuable. Rama had asked the sage to tell him what place he should choose as their dwelling during their exile in the forest, and Valmiki replies :

"You ask me, 'Where shall I dwell ?' With awe I answer, 'Show me the place where you are not present.' Hearing the words of the holy man so full of love, Rama was abashed and smiled in his heart. Then Valmiki, laughing, said in loving accents, 'Listen, Rama, I will tell you the home where you with Sita and Lakshman dwell. They, whose ears are like the ocean and the story of your doings are like the rivers that flow into it ; they are for ever filling it, but it is never full ; their hearts are always your home. They, whose eyes are like the chatak bird, full of desire for the rain clouds, holding in scorn, ocean, river and lake, when they obtain the raindrops of your presence, they are content. In their hearts make your home, oh, giver of happiness, with Lakshman and Sita. He whose tongue is like the swan, which gathers the pearls in the lake of your virtues, make his heart your home. They whose nostrils always reverently are breathing in the beautiful and blessed offerings of the Lord, who feed on what is offered to you, who wear the garments and ornaments offered to you, who when they see religious teachers, gods and Brahmins, bow their heads before them, and treat them with special love and honour, whose hands ever worship Rama's feet, whose hearts have no other hope than hope in Rama, whose feet go to Rama as their place of pilgrimage, dwell in their hearts, oh, Rama. They who ever repeat your name as their mantra, and with their family adore you, who offer oblations and sacrifices of various kinds; who feast Brahmins and give them many gifts; who in their thoughts pay more regard to their religious teachers than to you, and serve them with all love and honour; who ask of all one fruit that they may be lovers of Rama's feet, dwell in their hearts as your temple, oh, Sita, and you two sons of Raghu. In whom there is no lust, anger, passion, pride, delusion (*moh*), covetousness, excitement, envy, violence, deceit, arrogance, Maya, in their hearts dwell, oh, Raghuraya. They who are beloved of all and are the well-wishers of all; to whom pain and pleasure, praise and abuse, are all one; who are careful to say what is both loving and true; who waking and sleeping make you their shelter: (believing that) apart from you there is no salvation, in their hearts, oh, Rama, make your dwelling. They who look on another man's wife as their mother, and another man's wealth as more poisonous than poison; who are glad at another's prosperity and sad at another's misfortune; to whom you are dearer than life, may their hearts be your auspicious abode. Those to whom you are everything, master, companion, father, mother and religious teacher, dwell in their hearts as your temple with Sita, you brothers two. Those who, overlooking men's bad qualities, choose out the good; who for the sake of Brahmins and cows endure suffering; for whom perfect behaviour is their path in the world; their hearts are your natural home. They who know your virtues and their own faults; whose trust is in you, in every way, and who love all who are devoted to you, dwell in their hearts with Sita. They who, abandoning everything, caste, sect, wealth, their familiar beliefs, honour among men, friends and relatives, houses and all, continue with constant craving for you; in their hearts dwell. They to whom heaven and hell, and emancipation from rebirth are all the same, if they can see the bearer of the bow and arrows, and who in deed, word and thought are your disciples, in their hearts raise your tent. They to whom nothing is ever necessary, except sincere love for you, dwell in their hearts always, for there is indeed your home.' " Ayodh. (122) 128.

This statement from the lips of Valmiki gives expression in unmistakable fashion to the belief that faith in or devotion to Rama will bring about great changes in a man's heart and life. And it is supported by others in all parts of the poem, sometimes at great length, but often in brief phrases. The gods, for example, were told by their priest, " The man devoted to Rama is eager for the good of others. He suffers pain when others suffer pain, and is full of sympathy." (211) 220. While somewhat later a sage says to Bharat: " Rama is mercy itself; without Rama there is no happiness even in a dream." (245) 256. It is, however, by no means easy to recognise any ethical significance in the repeating of Rama's name.

" The all-merciful, the single remembrance of whose

name takes a man across the boundless ocean of existence, makes a humble request to a ferryman ; he who crossed the universe in less than three steps. At the sight of his toe nails, the river Ganges rejoiced." (97) 100.

"Even an ordinary person finds the highest objects in life easy to get if he repeats Rama's name when he yawns." (299) 312.

"The man who says 'Ram, Ram,' when he yawns will find that his many sins will not confront him. . . . The world knows that Valmiki became equal to Brahma because he repeated Rama's name backwards. A dog-eater, a Shavar, a Khas, a fool, a foreigner (*yavan*), an outcaste, a Kol, a Kirat, by repeating Rama's name, become altogether pure and famous in the world."[1] (186) 194.

But there is a preface to the last quotation which deserves to be set down, to let us see how wisdom and what we reckon foolishness can go together. The great forest chieftain who befriended Rama, also befriended Bharat, when he came in search of his brother. The prince was so delighted to see one who had seen Rama so recently and helped him, that he clasped the outcaste to his breast. This demonstration of affection called forth the admiration of the gods. Raining down flowers and shouting their approval, they said :

"According to the world's ideas and the teaching of the Veda, this man is an outcaste in every way. If his shadow touches any one it is necessary to bathe. Nevertheless Rama's young brother has embraced him and thrilled all over with joy at meeting him."[2]

In conclusion, reference requires to be made to the

[1] Yavan is originally a *Greek* (*Ionian*), hence a foreigner !

[2] When Rama returned from exile, he also embraced the outcaste chieftain. Lanka, 146 (117) 133.

position which Lakshman acquires in this section. As we have seen, he is linked with Rama and Sita in Valmiki's speech. No mention is made of his relationship to Vishnu, but he is spoken of as "the lord of serpents with a thousand heads, the earth holder."[1] This is a reference to the old idea that the world rests on the head of a serpent called Anant. In pictures this serpent is represented as Vishnu's couch, on which he rests in the intervals between one creation and another, while from the god's navel a lotus springs, out of which Brahma is born. Lakshman is referred to by this name, Anant, in other parts of the poem, especially in the Lanka book. As it will be unnecessary to make further mention of this conception of Lakshman as the great serpent, the most remarkable statements in that book may be given here. In the fight with Rama we are told that the demon struck Lakshman with a bolt given him by the god Brahma.

> "The very powerful arrow, the gift of Brahma, struck Anant on the breast. The hero fell in a faint. The ten-headed one tried to raise him, but the unparalleled weight did not move. The foolish Ravan tried to raise the lord of the three worlds, on one of whose heads rests the whole created universe, as if it were a grain of sand." Lanka, 98 (79) 107.

Somewhat earlier in the battle, Lakshman, once more spoken of as Anant, had an encounter with Ravan's son. On that occasion also, as the result of a blow, he became unconscious. But when the enemy tried to lift him from the ground, they found they could not.

> "An hundred million soldiers, the equal of Ravan's son, attempted to raise him. But they could not raise

[1] Lakshman is addressed in Bal Kand, 23 (21) 31, as an *avatar,* who descended, for the sake of the world, to remove the fears of the world, in the form of a serpent with a thousand heads.

Anant, the world's upholder. 'Listen, Gauri (says Shiva to his wife), 'who can conquer in battle him, the fire of whose anger burns up the fourteen spheres of creation, whom gods and men, things that do not move, and things that do move, worship. This mystery only that man knows on whom Rama has mercy." Lanka, 67 (53) 75.

Some of Rama's complimentary references to Bharat have been already recorded; one passage in particular deserves special attention, where the prince says:

"All sin, delusion and the burden of every misfortune are wiped out: glory in this world and happiness in the next are obtained by remembering your name. Be Shiva my witness, I speak the truth, brother; the earth exists by your support." Ayodh. (253) 264.

The gods were also conscious of Bharat's power and were told by their priest that devotion to his feet was the root of all happiness Ayodh. (255) 266; and by the wife of Brahma that though the Maya of Brahma, Vishnu and Shiva was very great, it could not comprehend Bharat's purpose. Ayodh. (283) 295. There is another passage also where it is possible that the poet is comparing Bharat to *Purush*, the primeval man, or, it may be, the Soul of the Universe. But it is equally possible that Tulsidas is merely expressing the opinion that Bharat is a *man* (purush) without a peer. Ayodh. (277) 289.

The fourth brother, Shatrughn, who was Lakshman's twin, and who would possess an equal portion of the godhead, is practically ignored throughout the poem.

Rama in the Forest.

The first months of Rama's exile in the woods are, as we have seen, described in the Ayodhya book. This section will deal with the contents of the Aranya Kand or Forest book up to the point where we read of the abduction of Sita.[1] The contents of these two books form a striking contrast. We return to the atmosphere of the Bal Kand. The Rama we are now to read about is surrounded by miracle, the human hero is almost entirely forgotten, and his words and actions are predominantly the words and actions of a god. This is strikingly manifest in the opening pages. There we are told how a son of the god Indra—his name was Jayant—resolved to test the power of Rama. Assuming the form of a crow, the foolish creature, like an ant wishing to find out the depth of the ocean, approached Sita, bit her foot and flew away. When he saw his wife's foot bleeding, Rama discharged an arrow after the miscreant. Changing into his proper shape, the son of Indra flew to his father for protection. But Indra refused to shelter him. With the arrow still closely pursuing, Jayant went to one place after another. He went to Brahma's heaven and to the city of Shiva. He journeyed to every corner of the three worlds. No one asked him to sit down. They could not give hospitality to one who was Rama's enemy. In such a case "a man's mother becomes death to him and amrit changes to poison; the Ganges is as baleful as the river of hell, and the world burns hotter than fire." Broken by terror and remorse, with the arrow still close at his heels, he resolved to seek Rama himself and ask to be forgiven. Returning to the forest, he cast himself at the divine feet; and Rama had mercy. The only punishment he inflicted was to deprive Sita's assailant of an eye.

The poet next goes on to tell us of how Rama, realising that their settlement was too near Avadh, decided, after a few months' stay at Chitrkut, to travel farther south. The first hermitage they came to was the dwelling of Atri.

[1] The numbers will refer to that book.

After being greeted in a lengthy hymn of praise, Rama asked his host in what part of the forest he would advise them to settle. This called forth another outpouring on the part of the sage.

> "Oh, Rama, it is your favour that Brahma, Shiva and the other gods seek after, as do also those who speak of the supreme reality. Now I know the cunning of Lakshmi; she forsook every other god and worships you only. How is it possible that I should tell you where to go? Oh, Lord, you are Antaryami." 5 (2) 4.

This term, *antaryami*, is an epithet of God. It means checking or regulating the internal feelings, and thus refers to the Supreme Spirit as regulating and guiding mankind. More commonly it means acquainted with the heart. Very naturally we find it used of Rama over and over again. The desire to use such language in reference to Rama is specially strong when he professes himself ignorant of something, and asks for information, as if he were an ordinary mortal. Thus, very soon after the incident about to be recorded, we read that when in the company of certain sages he saw a heap of bones lying on the ground, and asked what they were, they answered:

> "'You know—Why do you ask? You see all things, you know all that is in the heart (*sab antaryami*). These are the bones of saints whom demons have devoured.' On hearing this, tears filled the eyes of Raghunath. He raised his arms and vowed that he would rid the earth of demons."[1] 12 (5) 13.

The three exiles resumed their journey. Wherever they went, the rivers, forests and mountains knew their master

[1] Shortly before Rama had killed a cannibal Rakshas (demon), as big as a mountain and a hundred times swifter than the wind. As a result of seeing Rama, the demon assumed at death a beautiful form, and the hero sent him to his own heaven! Aranya, 9 (3) 10.

and made a path easy to his feet. Even the clouds gathered to give the travellers a welcome shade from the sun's rays. In course of time they reached another hermitage, where they found another holy man impatiently awaiting their coming. This individual had resolved to go to heaven, and the funeral pyre had been prepared for him. But he would not go until he had seen Rama face to face. When Rama did appear, he said :

> "I was setting out for the dwelling-place of Brahma when I heard that Rama had come to the forest. I have been watching the path day and night ; now I have seen the Lord, my heart is at peace. I am altogether lacking in achievement (*sadhan*), but recognising that I am a humble person you have had mercy. I therefore make no request, oh god (*dev*). I had made my vow, oh stealer of the souls of men, to wait until I met you, the friend of the humble, and then abandon my body. The meditation, sacrifices, prayers, penance and fasting I have performed, I did for the Lord, and I have obtained the gift of devotion. . . . May the Lord, whose body is dark as a raincloud, who has become endowed with qualities as the blessed Rama, live for ever in my heart with Sita and Lakshman." 12 (5) 13.

What followed is told very briefly and in obscure words, but it gives expression to what is taught elsewhere, that the worshippers of Rama do not seek absorption in God, but conscious communion with Him :

> "When he had said this, the fire of Yog consumed his body. By the favour of Rama, he went to Vaikunth (the heaven of Vishnu). The saint was not absorbed in Hari, for this reason, that from the first he has received the gift of devotion." 12 (5) 13.

As the story proceeds, we are again and again made to

realise the spirit of devotion roused in Rama's worshippers. A disciple of the great Agastya hears of his approach :

"In thought, word and deed he was a servant of Rama's feet ; not even in a dream had he thought of any other god. When his ears heard of Rama's approach, he rushed out, full of desire. 'Oh Vidhi,' he cried, "will Raghuraya, who is a brother to the lowly, have mercy on such a worthless thing as I ? The holy Rama and his younger brother will meet me as if I were their own servant. In my heart there is no steadfast trust, no devotion, no self-control ; in my mind no knowledge, no association with good men, no meditation, no prayer, no watchings, no constant love for the lotus feet ; only the word of him who is the treasure-house of mercy. *He is my loved one who goes to no other*. To-day my eyes will be rewarded by seeing him who liberates from existence.' " 14 (6) 14.

Eventually he came to a standstill. He could neither advance nor retreat. He was in so great a maze, that when Rama did arrive, nothing could rouse him till Rama put off his human form and showed himself as the four-armed god. Then the hermit awoke. He fell at Rama's feet, overwhelmed with love and gladness. The hero raised him from the ground and folded him to his breast :

"I adore Rama, Nirgun and Sagun, like and unlike, beyond thought, speech and comprehension, pure and faultless, everywhere and illimitable ; the breaker of the world's burdens ; a grove of the trees of heaven [1] for those devoted to him ; the destroyer of passion, greed, pride and lust ; the bridge over the ocean of life ; the banner of the Solar race. May he be always our protector. . . . Though he is without passion, all-pervading, eternal, and dwells for ever in the hearts of

[1] In Indra's heaven there were trees which yielded all one's desires.

all, nevertheless may he dwell in my heart as the wood-wandering enemy of demons, along with Sita and Lakshman. Those who know, know you, oh master, to be Sagun, Agun, Ur antaryami (with qualities, devoid of qualities, the knower of the heart)." 15 (7) 15.

Rama next passed to the hermitage of Agastya. From this holy man the hero asked for a strange boon. "Give me a charm by which I may destroy the persecutors of the hermits." When he heard this strange request, the sage smiled and said :

"You ask of me ? My lord, what do I know ? Oh, destroyer of sin, because of my worship of you, I know something of your greatness. Beholding the play of your eyebrows, men ever remain enchanted with your lotus feet. With your own hand you cast down various Brahmas, saints and Shivas. Your power is very great, as all the world knows. But there is something else I wish to say. Listen, Bhagwan. Your Maya is a wide-spreading fig tree ; the many multitudes of worlds are its fruit ; while all things that have life are like insects that dwell within (the fruit). They know nothing else. This fruit is consumed by harsh and formidable Time ; Time, who, in his dread of you, is always afraid. You, who are the lord of all the worlds, ask a question of me, as if you were only a man. I ask this boon, oh mine of mercy ; dwell in my heart with Sita and Lakshman. Give me steadfast devotion, compassion, fellowship with pious men and a love for your lotus feet that cannot be broken. Though you are Brahm, indivisible, eternal, beyond the reach of perception, whom holy men worship, nevertheless I know you and declare your manifestation as Brahm and Love embodied."

Of the long years that follow we learn nothing except the statement that, as a result of Rama's presence, the holy men who lived in the forest had no further cause to be afraid. In this ensuing peacefulness birds and beasts, rivers, trees and mountain shared. Even of the conversations in which the exiles would indulge we obtain only one glimpse, though we are told that some days were spent in talking about asceticism, knowledge, virtue and conduct. This single glimpse is, however, of great value and must be recorded in full.

> "Once upon a time, as Rama was seated at his ease, Lakshman said very meekly : 'Oh king of gods, men and saints, of all that moves and that does not move, I wish to ask you a question. You are, as it were, my own life. Give me an explanation, oh god ; I have abandoned all to serve the dust of your feet. Describe to me knowledge, self-control and Maya. Describe to me that *devotion* to which you show mercy. Tell me, my lord, and explain it all, the difference that subsists between God (*ishwar*) and the soul, by means of which arises love for your feet, and grief and error vanish.'" 20 (10) 18.

To this appeal Rama replied :

> "Listen, brother, and apply your intelligence and heart (to what I say). *I and mine, thou and thine*, are the product of Maya. Maya has brought the multiplicity of souls into its power. The senses and the objects of sense, as far as the mind can reach, are all Maya. Understand that, brother. Listen while I tell you of its divisions. They are two, namely, knowledge and ignorance, the one exceedingly evil, grief embodied, by whose control the soul falls into the pit of existence ; the other, which created the world, dominated by the three qualities. It did so by the direction of the Lord, not by its own power. Knowledge, in which there is not any self-confidence, sees the form of Brahm in every-

thing. He is called the greatest ascetic who surrenders the fruit of asceticism, and the three qualities as if they were a blade of grass." 21 (11) 16.

"Soul is that which because of Maya does not know itself to be God, the giver of bondage and of liberation, God over all, the sender forth of Maya, the boundary. From the practice of religious rites, asceticism springs; from the practice of meditation, knowledge. Knowledge is the giver of liberation, so the Veda says. But that by which I quickly exercise mercy, brother, is *devotion* to me, it yields happiness to my devotees. It is self-sustaining, it needs no other support. Both knowledge and ignorance are subordinate to it. Devotion! brother, there is nothing to be compared to it as a source of happiness. It can be obtained if holy men (*sant*) are favourable. I shall describe how *devotion* can be realised. It is a path easy to travel, by which men find me. First a great love for the feet of Brahmins and, in one's own actions, taking delight in the teaching of revelation. Having done this the result is a mental aloofness from the things of sense; then there springs up a love for my feet. The nine acts of devotion exercised by means of the ear, etc., become strong, and there is born in the mind a great love (*rati*) for my exploits and a great love (*prem*) for the lotus feet of holy men. In mind, deed and word, worship becomes a confirmed purpose. Father, mother, relative, master, god, all treated like myself, receive steadfast service. When singing my virtues, the hairs of the body stand on end, the voice trembles, water flows from the eyes. I always come under the control of those in whom there is no lust, pride, deceit or other vices. Those who in word, deed and thought guilelessly sing the praise of my incarnation (*gati*), in their lotus hearts I take my rest for ever." 22 (12) 20.

This discourse afforded great satisfaction to Lakshman, who bowed his head at his brother's feet. He said : "My lord, listening to your words has removed my doubts, knowledge has come. New love has grown in my heart."

The Abduction of Sita.

Agastya advised Rama to settle near the river Godavari. And it was from there in the thirteenth year of his exile that Sita was carried off by Ravan.[1] How that happened has been already described in the first chapter. Here it is our business to relate how Rama himself acted, and what were the opinions of the demons with regard to him.

When Khar and Dushan, the brothers of Ravan, came to avenge their sister, they first sent heralds to the prince, demanding the surrender of Sita. Rama replied: "Though I am a man, I am the destroyer of the demon race ; though I am a child, I am the protector of holy men and the exterminator of the wicked." 28 (14) 22. In the battle that followed, Lakshman and Sita retired to a cave, and Rama engaged a host of fourteen thousand demons, single-handed. The difficulty of slaying them was increased by the fact that no sooner were they killed than, by virtue of their magical powers, they came to life again. This alarming situation filled the gods with dread, but their fears were allayed when Rama, the lord of illusion, exercised his own still greater powers and brought the battle to an end by destroying every one of his opponents. As the souls of the demons parted from their bodies, they cried out, "Ram, Ram," and thus attained *nirvana*.

"When Ravan heard of his brothers' death, he said, 'Gods, men, demons, serpents, there is not one of them equal to my servants. Khar and Dushan were equal to

[1] The abduction of Sita is described in the second half of the Forest book. The numbers refer to that book.

me in strength. Who can have killed them, if it was not God (*bhagwan*) ? If the lord of the world (*jagdish*), the giver of joy to the gods, and the remover of the earth's burden, has become incarnate (*avatar*), then I shall go and fight with him. By means of the arrow of the Lord, I shall cross the ocean of existence. For this demon shape of mine, prayer is of no avail. . . . If he is only a man, some king's son, I shall defeat them and carry off the woman.' "

To assist him in his enterprise, he called upon his friend Marich. The advice he received was discouraging :

" He is the god of all that moves and all that does not move. Don't fight with him, my son. If he kill you, you die ; if you live, it is he who gives you life." 38 (20) 32.

When he saw argument was of no avail, Marich consented to assume the form of a deer, and beguile the princess. But he knew that his deceit would have a fatal issue.

" Thus pondering, he went with the Ten-headed. Undivided love was in his heart for Rama's feet. He was very glad, but he did not show it. 'To-day I shall behold the one I love best. . . . I shall place in my heart the feet of the abode of mercy, with Sita and Lakshman. His anger confers *nirvana*. His devotees bring him under their control. Hari, the ocean of happiness, will fit an arrow to his bow with his own hands and slay me.' " 39 (21) 33.

In the meantime, knowing what was about to happen, Rama, in the absence of Lakshman who had gone in search of herbs and fruit, said to Sita :

" 'Listen, oh beloved, faithful and amiable spouse. I am about to play a part after the fashion of a man. Make your dwelling in fire until I destroy the demons.'

When Rama had said all he had to say, Sita placed the Lord's feet on her breast and entered into fire. She left behind her shadow only, but it was the same in appearance, amiable and gentle. Lakshman did not know the secret or what God (*bhagwan*) had planned." 37 (19) 31.

The poet represents what follows as unreal. So far as one can judge, Sita's desire to secure the skin of the lovely deer was real. But Rama knew that the deer was not a deer, that it was the demon in disguise. And so when Sita begs her husband to secure it, the poet tells us :

"Raghupati knew the reason of it all. He got up, glad in heart to accomplish the purpose of the gods. . . . The deer, seeing the Lord coming after him, ran away. Rama pursued him. He, whom the Veda calls Neti, and whom Shiva cannot fathom, ran after a mimic deer." 40 (22) 34.

As the deer fell dying before the shaft of Rama, he called out in a loud voice, "Lakshman!"

"At the hour of death, as he abandoned his body, he remembered Rama and Sita. The benevolent lord understood the love that was in his heart, and gave to him a condition which saints find it difficult to attain. The gods rained down a great many flowers, and sang songs in praise of his virtues, saying, 'Raghunath, the friend of the humble, has given a place in his own heaven to a demon.'" 42 (23) 35.

When Sita heard the demon calling out the name of Lakshman, she thought her husband was appealing for help. She begged her brother-in-law to go to his assistance. But he replied, "By the play of his eyebrows, the world is destroyed. Even in a dream he cannot fall into trouble." 42 (23) 35. When Lakshman at length did go, it was because his resolution was shaken by the contrivance of Hari.

The absence of the two brothers gave Ravan the opportunity he sought. Sita was carried off to Ceylon. When the prince returned and found the hermitage empty, "he became as distressed as an ordinary man." He went searching everywhere. He appealed to the birds and beasts, to the trees and flowers, to tell him where Sita was hiding. He cried aloud and begged her to ease him of his pain.

> "Rama, whose desires are all satisfied, who is the dwelling-place of joy, the unborn, the everlasting, conducted himself like a man." 52 (25) 38.

All through the poem, up till now, the picture presented to us of Rama's love for Sita is both beautiful and sincere. It is therefore matter for wonder that at this stage Rama should be made to speak in such bitter disparagement of women. Both to his brother and to Narad, who is brought quite unnecessarily upon the scene, he uses language difficult to reconcile with his normal attitude. In a later chapter more detailed reference will be made to some of these utterances. Here it is enough to record one of them:

> "Lust, anger, greed, pride and other passions form the mighty torrent of delusion (*moh*). But of them all, the most horrible and the cause of greatest pain, is illusion (*maya*) in a woman's form." 71 (38) 56.

Rama's opinions on this and other matters, however, excited the mingled wonder and admiration of the god Shiva, for he said to his wife, "The lord of creation, devoid of qualities, Rama, who knows all hearts, showed the distress of a lover as well as steadfastness and absence of desire." 64 (33) 48.

The search for Sita continued, but she was nowhere to

be found. It is strange that the god, so often spoken of as *antaryami*, did not know where she was. But he obtained two valuable clues. The vulture, who tried to rescue Sita from the clutches of Ravan, was able before he died to tell who was her captor.

> " It is the ten-headed one who did this. He is the wicked one who carried off Sita. He went carrying her towards the south." 53 (26) 39.

And somewhat later, a female hermit with whom they had a long interview advised Rama to seek the help of Sugriv. The incident is peculiar. The prince made no mention of what he had heard from the vulture, and it is only at the close of their conversation that he asks her: " Lady, have you any news of Sita ? If you know, please tell me." The woman was surprised that he did not know. Rather she was convinced that he did know: " Sugriv will tell you everything, oh god Raghubir. You know already, and yet you ask ! " 59 (30) 44.

Rama's encounter with the vulture and the female hermit, who was an outcaste, " the lowest of the low and a woman to boot," deserves very special attention. Not because of the information they gave, but because of their feeling for Rama and the gracious treatment which they received at his hands, it is manifest that Tulsidas wishes us to realise that these two incidents are important. It is not by accident that he puts them together. He is determined to make his readers understand his purpose. Nor does he leave us in doubt what conclusion we are to draw. It is that there is no barrier of race or caste or condition which can shut out any one, however vile, from Rama's presence and from Rama's grace. Thus we read that Rama offered the dying vulture the gift of life:

> " Rama said, ' Continue to live, father.' He answered with a smile, ' He has appeared before my eyes, the

muttering of whose name at the hour of death confers salvation on the most contemptible; so the books of revelation declare. Why should I continue to live?' Tears filled the eyes of Raghurai, and he replied, 'Father, your own deeds (*karma*) have achieved for you this rank. There is nothing in the world difficult to secure by those who are eager for the good of others. When you surrender your body, go to my heaven. What can *I* give? You have got your desire.'" 54 (26) 39.

An immediate transformation of the vulture's shape took place. He changed into the very form and fashion of Vishnu. His body was dark blue in colour and had four great arms. He wore a yellow garment, and was adorned with jewels. And his hymn of praise was not behind those of the greatest sages in its understanding of the mystery of Rama's person. "He is Nirgun and Sagun Brahm, the all-pervading, the eternal." But what is specially worthy of remark is the emphasis on that part of the hymn which reminds us of the toil which saints and ascetics endured in their efforts to know God. Knowledge, meditation, penance and abstraction, the subduing of the mind and of the senses, Rama now has provided a better way than they afford. He has revealed himself to give delight to the whole universe. And so he says:

"May Rama who is the husband of Lakshmi, and is ever under the control of his servants; he who is the lord of the three worlds, dwell in my heart; whose pure praise brings transmigration to an end." 54 (26) 39.

With the result that:

"The vulture, having asked for the boon of unbroken devotion, went to Hari's heaven. Rama with his own hands performed the funeral rites according to the rules laid down. The very merciful and tender-hearted

Raghunath, who is merciful without a cause, gave to an unclean, flesh-eating bird, a rank which ascetics crave." 55 (27) 41.

As for the female hermit, she belonged apparently to one of the jungle tribes. And here again the poet labours to make us realise how base was her origin. Yet when the prince enters her hut, he sits down on a seat which she places for him, and allows her to bathe his feet. More than that, he takes from her hand and eats the food she brings. And this is what she says :

"'How can I praise thee ? I am a low caste person and I am very stupid. I am the lowest of the low caste ; I am very low, a woman ! and besides all that, I am very ignorant.' But Raghunath replied : 'Listen, lady, I recognise one relationship only, that of devotion. Caste, family, religion, reputation, wealth, power, connections, good qualities, cleverness ; if a man has these and has not devotion, he is like a cloud without water in it.'"

And here again, perhaps with even greater emphasis, the poet is resolved to make his purpose plain. He chooses the most unclean of unclean birds, a creature that lives on carrion, and perhaps even more, he chooses a woman reckoned as outside the pale of all decent society, to proclaim his doctrine at its best and highest : that the greatest of all endowments is the love men cherish for God. The woman also attained beatitude.

"Gazing on Rama's face and placing his lotus feet in her heart, she surrendered her body on the fires of Yoga, and became absorbed in Rama's feet. She went whence there is no return. Oh, men, forsake your various works, which are unrighteousness, and all your sects, which are a source of sorrow ; exercise faith (*bishwas*) and fall in love with Rama's feet ; this is Tulsidas's plea. He gave salvation (*mukti*) to such a woman, an outcaste and of sinful birth. Foolish indeed you are, if you desire peace of mind and forsake such a Lord." 59, 60 (30, 31) 44, 45.

Rama's Alliance with the Monkeys.

Rama's alliance with the monkeys is described in the fourth book of the poem. It is one of the shortest, and is called Kishkindha, from the name of Sugriv's capital. When the two brothers approached the home of the monkey king, their arrival occasioned much alarm. Sugriv was afraid they had come at the instigation of his brother Bali, with whom he was at strife. He therefore asked his friend Hanuman, who was a son of the wind god, to go and interview them. Hanuman, assuming the appearance of a young Brahmin, went forward, and said, "Are you two of the three gods, or are you Nara and Narayan? Or are you the lord of all the spheres who has taken human form and come down, for the sake of the world, to be its saviour and to break its burdens?"

Rama replied that no one could wipe out the writing of the Creator. They were the sons of Dashrath, king of Koshal, who, in obedience to their father's command, had come to the forest. Their names were Rama and Lakshman. His wife Sita was with them. But a demon had carried her off, and they were seeking her in every direction. He ended by saying, "We have told you who we are. Tell us, Brahmin, your story." Hanuman, however, could not be deceived. He fell at Rama's feet and said:

"I am an ignorant person, that is why I asked. But you, why do you ask, as if you were a man? Under the influence of your illusion (*maya*) I wandered in error. That is why I did not recognise the feet of the Lord. I am stupid and ignorant in the grasp of error to begin with, and then the merciful Lord Bhagwan led me astray. Life is fascinated by your Maya; then it is released by your affection. For this reason I cry to Raghubir. I know no other way of breaking my bonds. As a child has trust in his father and mother, so we abide without anxiety, nourished by the Lord."

Rama raised his worshipper and took him in his arms, saying :

"Listen, monkey, don't consider yourself less (than others). I love you twice as much as I love Lakshman. Every one says that I treat all alike. He who has no other resort (but me) is a servant beloved. And he who has *no other resort* is the man who never doubts in his mind that he is the servant of Bhagwan, the lord of all created things, manifest in many forms." (2) 4.

In the alliance which was made between the monkey king and Rama, the former promised to send out millions of spies to search the world for Sita's hiding-place, while Rama promised to kill Bali : "Though he take refuge with Brahma and Shiva he will not survive." 9 (6) 8. Sugriv, however, had not Hanuman's faith, and Rama had to perform several miraculous deeds before the monkey king could believe that the prince would be more than a match for his brother.

"Knowledge arose in his mind and he said : 'By the Lord's mercy my mind is established. I will surrender pleasure, wealth and family to serve you. All these interfere with devotion to Rama, so say the saints who worship thy feet. Enemy, friend, pleasure, pain, are the products of Maya and not the chief end of life. Bali is my greatest friend.'" Kish. 9 (6) 8.

Bali, the prospective victim of Rama's prowess, had a truer conception of him from the first than his brother. Because when his wife warned him against encountering Rama in battle, he answered :

"Listen, my timid dear, Raghunath treats all alike.

Even though he slay me, he will still be my lord."
11 (7) 9.

While the brothers fought, Rama watched the duel from behind a tree. But when he saw his ally being worsted, he stepped out and smote Bali to the ground. It is a conflicting statement on the part of the poet that follows :

"He sat up and saw the Lord in front of him. . . . Again and again he gazed and placed his soul at his feet ; he reckoned that his birth had been worth while ; he knew his Lord. His heart was full of love, but his words were severe. He spoke, his gaze in Rama's direction : 'For the sake of religion you have become incarnate. Why then have you killed me in hunter fashion ? Sugriv is your friend. I am your enemy. For what reason did you take my life ?' " 12 (8) 10.

Rama's defence is scarcely conclusive :

"Fool, you knew that Sugriv relied on the strength of my arm, and in your pride you sought to slay him !"

But in any case he offered, as he had offered the vulture, to give him back his life. The monkey declined the proffered gift.

"Listen, fountain of mercy. In birth after birth the saints try their hardest, and in the end Rama never comes near them. But he, by the power of whose name Shankar at Benares gives to all the same imperishable state, has appeared before my eyes. Shall I ever have such an opportunity again ? The Lord has told me to retain my body ; who would be so foolish as to cut down the tree of the gods and water instead a babul tree ? Now, oh Lord, look upon me in mercy and give to me the boon I crave, that in whatever womb I may be born in the grip of Karma, I may be a lover of Rama's feet."
13 (9) 11.

He chose the easier and better part. Rama sent him to his own heaven. As for the disconsolate widow:

> "Seeing her distress, Hari instructed her and removed her Maya. 'Earth, water, fire, air and wind, of these five elements are our base bodies composed. The corpse, which you see before you, is asleep. The soul is eternal; why do you weep?' Knowledge sprang up. She embraced his feet. She asked and received the gift of perfect devotion. The Lord makes us all dance like dolls. There is no well-wisher like Rama in the world—son, father, mother, kinsman. Every one else—gods, men and saints—profess affection for selfish reasons. . . . The man who forsakes such a Lord must fall into the net of affliction." 15 (10) 12.

With the end of the rainy season, Sugriv was slow to implement his promise. When finally roused, he excused his delay by saying:

> "Lord, there is no guilt on my part. Your Maya is very powerful. If any one escape from it, it is because you are merciful. Gods, men and saints are without control with regard to the senses. I am a low beast, a most lascivious monkey."

To which Rama replied:

> "You are as dear to me as my brother Bharat. Now apply yourself, and try in what way you can get news of Sita." 25 (20) 23.

When eventually the monkeys did gather, there were so many of them that, as Shiva remarked, only a fool would attempt to count them. Nevertheless there was not one of them after whose welfare Rama did not inquire. But "this is no great matter for the Lord to do. Raghurai is manifest in all things and pervades all." 26 (21) 24. Associated with the monkeys there was the king of the bears, and on his lips also are placed words in praise of Rama, quite equal to anything spoken by others. It was in response to a remark made by one of the monkeys suggesting that Rama was only a man :

> " My son ! don't think that Rama is a man. Reckon him to be Nirgun Brahm, the unconquerable and the unborn. We his servants are all very fortunate, having as a lover the everlasting Sagun Brahm. Of his own desire, the Lord has come down for the sake of gods, Brahmins, cows and the Earth. As Sagun he dwells among his worshippers, surrendering beatitude and all its joy." 30 (26) 29.

The Finding of Sita.

The finding of Sita is described in the fifth book of the poem.[1] When Hanuman after his first interview with Sita allowed himself to be seized and carried into Ravan's presence, he told the demon :

> " It is by Rama's power that Maya creates the multitude of worlds ; it is by Rama's power that Brahma, Vishnu and Shiva create, protect and destroy them. It is by his power that the thousand-faced serpent bears on his head the world-egg's shell, with its mountains and forests. He assumes various bodies for the protection of the gods, and to give a lesson to scoundrels like you. . . . By his power, the very smallest atom of it, the whole creation exists. . . . Death, who devours gods, demons and all created things, fears him with a great fear. Don't become his enemy. Listen to me, and give up Sita. The jewel of the house of Raghu is a protector of the suppliant. He is an ocean of compassion. Go to him for shelter ; the Lord will protect

[1] This book is called Sundar or *the Beautiful.*

you and forget your sins. . . . If Rama is hostile to you, there is no saviour from his wrath. Shiva, Vishnu and Brahma cannot protect you when Rama is your foe." 20 (20) 20.

The wife of Ravan, especially after Hanuman burned down the capital, gave her husband similar advice, while a pious brother who was a fervent worshipper of Vishnu pleaded with him to surrender Sita before it was too late.

"Lust, anger, pride, avarice, all are paths that lead to hell. Abandon all of them, and worship the feet of Raghubir. Rama is not a man. Rama is not a king. He is the god of the universe He is Time, its very self personified. He is Brahm, the imperishable, the uncreated Bhagwan; the all-pervading, the unconquerable; without beginning and without end, the friend of cows, Brahmins, gods and the earth. The sea of mercy has assumed a man's body to give gladness to men, to destroy the companies of the wicked; to protect the Vedas and religion; to be the saviour of the gods." 37 (37) 37.

This book closes with an account of the gathering of the monkey hosts, which Rama and Sugriv brought to the southern shores of India. The problem was how to get them across the intervening ocean to Ceylon. Ravan's brother, who had taken refuge with Rama, proposed that they should address their prayers to the ocean:

"And Rama said, 'Friend, you have made a good suggestion. If the god (*daiv*) will help us, it will be well.' But Lakshman did not approve this proposal. When he heard Rama's words he was very grieved. 'Sir,' he said, 'what confidence have you in the god? Show your anger and dry up the ocean; it is the one idea of a coward and a lazy man to cry, god! god!'". 53 (50) 50.

Rama, however, was determined to try what prayer would do.

"He went down to the shore, reverently saluted the ocean, and having spread sacred grass, sat down. Three days passed, and the stupid ocean paid no heed to his entreaty. Then Rama in wrath said, 'There will be no kindness unless he is made afraid.'" 61 (57) 60.

And so he called on Lakshman to bring his bow and arrows. The arrows soon produced a response. The ocean appeared in the guise of a Brahmin, and casting himself at Rama's feet, asked to be forgiven.

"The firmament, the wind, fire, water, earth, have all sprung up for the sake of creation at the instruction of your Maya, so the Scriptures sing. They are what they are, in accordance with the Lord's command, and their happiness depends on their so remaining. The Lord has done well in teaching me a lesson. Nevertheless the keeping within my proper limits was appointed by you. A drum, a villager, a low caste, a beast and a woman are entitled to a beating. For the glory of the Lord, I shall be dried up. The army will cross over, but it will not be to the increase of my fame. The Lord's commands cannot be evaded. So the books of revelation declare. Do then quickly what you think right." 62 (58) 61.

Rama was pleased with this very modest appeal. Nothing more was said about drying up the ocean, and it was resolved instead to build a bridge.

The Death of Ravan and the Rescue of Sita.[1]

The proposal to build a bridge called forth a variety of moralisings on the part of the king of the bears. "Sir,

[1] The Lanka book deals with these. It is one of the long books of the poem.

your name is the bridge by which men cross life's ocean. What obstacle is there in crossing this little sea ?" If the builders remembered Rama's fame, their toil would be as nothing. With Rama's lotus feet placed on their hearts, it would be a pastime and no more. When the bridge was completed, Rama, as has already been mentioned, erected a phallus (*linga*) of Shiva, and worshipped it. But in addition he made the promise :

> "The people who will make a pilgrimage to Rameshwar when they leave their bodies, will go to my heaven. Those who will bring Ganges water and offer it will obtain the salvation of absorption (*sayujya mukti*).[1] Those who serve me without an object, and forsaking guile, Shiva will give to them devotion for myself. Those who make a pilgrimage to the bridge that I have made will cross the ocean of existence without any difficulty." (3) 5.

The bridging of the ocean and Rama's arrival in Ceylon led to fresh attempts on the part of Ravan's wife to persuade him to surrender Sita. The queen said :

> "Do not fight against him in whose hands are Kal, Karma and Gun. . . . He is the creator, preserver and destroyer of the world. Rama is gracious to those who reverence him. Give up your selfishness and pride and worship him for sake of whom holy men endure afflictions, and kings surrender their kingdoms and become ascetics. The king of Koshal has come to manifest his mercy to you. If you will be persuaded by me, you will become famous in the three worlds." (7) 9.

She made somewhat later another appeal, which is remarkable for the fact that Tulsidas borrows freely the

[1] See Monier Williams's *Sanskrit Dictionary*, p. 1109. One does not expect Rama to promise *absorption*.

terminology of the Sankhya philosophy which, so far, he has scarcely ever used.

"Put away your pride and do not think he is a man. The jewel of the house of Raghu, his form is the universe. The Vedas say that in every limb of his body a world is framed. His feet are hell; his head is the dwelling-place of Brahma, and in the rest of his limbs there are other worlds. The play of his eyebrows is terrifying Time; his eyes are the sun, his hair is the gathering of clouds, his nostrils are the two Ashwins; night and day are the twinkling of his eyes; the ten regions are his ears, as the Veda says; the gods of the storm are his breath; and the words of the Veda are his very voice. His lips are the lower world; his teeth are the fearsome god of death; his smile is Maya, his arms are the rulers of the different regions, his mouth is fire, his tongue is Varun; creation, preservation and destruction are his acts; the hairs across the middle of his body are the leaves of the forest; his bones are the mountains, his veins are the rivers, his belly the sea, his anus is hell. All that the world contains is the fashioning of the Lord. Shiva is his consciousness (*ahankar*). Brahma is his intellect (*buddhi*), the moon is his mind and the great principle (*mahat*) is his soul. Consisting of everything that is, he dwells in men, a multitude of forms, Bhagwan." 18 (15) 20.

The many incidents related in this book with reference to the battle between the forces of Rama and Ravan call for no detailed comment. Shiva reminds his wife in familiar phrases that the play of Rama's eyebrows creates and destroys the universe, while it is frequently stated that Brahma and Shiva both worship Rama. One more tribute from a demon, however, deserves to be recorded. It will be remembered that in addition to Ravan's pious brother there was another who in response to his asceticism was told to ask a boon. The boon he desired was that he might sleep for six months at a time. He was sound asleep when Rama invaded Ceylon, and it was with great difficulty that Ravan succeeded in wakening him. His purpose was to demand his help. But the awakened brother was very angry when he heard what Ravan had done.

> "Fool, you have carried off the mother of the universe, and expect to succeed. You have not done well, and now you have come and wakened me. Give up your pride. Worship Rama, and you will be happy. You must not set yourself against that Lord, whom Shiva, the Creator and the gods all worship. . . . Now take me to your bosom, brother, and let me depart. For I go to fill my eyes with the sight of him who delivers from the three kinds of suffering.[1] Calling to mind Rama's form and qualities, he was for a moment filled with joy. Then he asked for ten million jars of liquor and many buffaloes." 74 (59) 84.

When these had been consumed he went forth to fight —and to fight against Rama. On the way he met the brother who had already gone over to Rama's side, and told him that he had conferred a great honour on the demon race by having been a real worshipper of Rama in thought, word and deed. For himself he was in the grasp of Time. When eventually he died by Rama's hand, "his glory entered the Lord's mouth."

> "As for the demon rank and file, when they fell, Rama sent them to his own heaven. Man-eating demons thus obtained a rank which ascetics desire. Rama is tender-hearted and full of mercy to demons who invoke his name, even when they are moved to do so by hatred.

[1] They are bodily affliction, affliction sent by God, affliction arising from existence or contact with the world.

Who is so merciful as he? The man who does not give up his error and worship such a lord is foolish and accursed." 56 (43) 64.

The poet's refusal to believe that Rama could be hampered in any way by human limitations, places him time after time in serious difficulty. We have seen it in the assertion that the real Sita entered the fire, leaving only a shadow to be carried off by Ravan.[1] And we saw how, when the very human and very attractive Rama mourned sincerely for his lost wife and searched for her everywhere, those he met are represented as refusing to believe that he could be ignorant as to her whereabouts. Indeed, rather than believe that Rama could be ignorant of anything, Tulsidas declares that he was merely playing a part. And in this book also he finds it necessary to remind us that that is so. "By the play of his eyebrows everything comes to be, and again everything is destroyed. He makes a thunderbolt out of a blade of grass, and a blade of grass out of a thunderbolt." 44 (33) 52. He is omniscient and dwells in all hearts. 11 (17) 23. And yet, when Lakshman was wounded, Rama's distress was very great: "The unconquerable god of the universe, the all-pervading Brahm, the abode of mercy, asks: 'Where is Lakshman?'" 67 (53) 75. He sends Hanuman to the Himalayas to bring healing herbs, and when the monkey seems long in returning, he sits by his brother's side lamenting "after the fashion of a man."

"If I had known that going to the forest would mean

[1] Long before the days of Tulsidas it had been difficult to "reconcile the entirely human words and actions of Rama and Sita in Books ii.–vi. of the *Ramayana* (of Valmiki) with the belief that Rama is the eternal God." And, in consequence, the *Adhyatma Ramayana* was written, telling the whole story afresh with a view to meet these difficulties. In that book we find Sita entering the fire, leaving only an illusory Sita to face the demon. See Farquhar's *Outlines of Religious Literature of India*, p. 250. Adhyatma means *the Supreme Spirit*.

the loss of my brother, I would not have obeyed my father's command. Sons, wealth, wives, houses and relatives, these come and go time after time in this world ; but a true brother is not so easily found. . . . If a stupid god (*daiv*) keep me alive, what kind of face can I take back to Avadh, after losing a brother beloved for the sake of a woman ? Better to endure dishonour in the eyes of the world. The loss of a woman is no great loss . . . Rama the indivisible, the merciful, thus displayed the appearance of a man." 72 (58) 81.

With regard to Rama's own part in the fight, the same idea is maintained that it is only make-believe.

"When Rama plays at being a man, it is like Garud playing with the snakes. . . . How can he acquire glory from taking part in such a battle ? It is because the fame of it when spread abroad purifies the world, and men who sing of it will cross the ocean of existence." 77 (62) 87.

We are told at one stage that when fighting with Ravan's son the youth shot arrows at him which changed into snakes.

"Rama was in the power of the serpents' coils. The self-controlled, the eternal, the unchangeable one ; like a dancer he plays many parts, but he is never subject to another. . . . It was to give glory to the battle-field that he allowed himself to be bound in the serpents' coils. But when the gods saw it, they were afraid. The Lord, the repeating of whose name cuts the coils of existence, how could he be bound, the all-pervading, who dwells in all things ! The deeds of Sagun are beyond the comprehension of our understanding, strength and speech. When they ponder on that fact, the greatest ascetics give up all discussions and simply worship Ram." 84 (69) 94.

The bird of Vishnu, Garud, who was an age-long enemy of the snake race, was summoned by the gods and rishis.

> "He went to Rama at once, seized and ate up all the snakes fashioned by Maya, and the illusion (*maya*) departed." 85 (70) 95.

We get one glimpse of Sita during the battle. One of her guards who had become a friend, told her how it was proving impossible to kill Ravan. As soon as a head or an arm was cut off, it grew on again " just as sin does even at a place of pilgrimage." 113 (94) 122. To this Sita replied:

> "What will happen? Why don't you tell me? When his heads are cut off by Raghupati's arrows, he does not die! The Creator is making everything contrary. It is my bad luck that keeps him alive and separates me from Hari's lotus feet. The god (*daiv*), who made the false, deceitful, golden deer, is still angry with me. The Creator, who causes me to suffer pain so difficult to endure, made me speak cutting words to Lakshman . . . it is the Creator who keeps me alive and no other." 114 (95) 123.

There is real poetry in the answer with which the demon sought to comfort her. "If an arrow strike his heart, the enemy of the gods will die. But the Lord will not strike there, because in his heart Sita dwells."

And this is followed by a chant, placed, as it were, on Rama's own lips: "Sita lives in my heart; I live in Sita's; and in my stomach there are many worlds. If an arrow were to strike there the worlds would all be destroyed."

When Ravan's death was at last secured by the method explained in the preliminary chapter, his widow, after reproaching her husband for thinking that the self-existent Hari, whom Shiva, Brahma and all the gods worship, was a man, said;

"From your birth rejoicing in doing injury to others; your body is one mass of sin; and Rama has sent you to his own heaven. I worship Brahm free from stain. Is there any one like Raghunath, the ocean of mercy? He has given you the highest state which saints with difficulty secure." 120 (100) 129.

Rama's treatment of Sita in saying that she must once more enter into fire is mentioned very briefly. When she was brought from her prison-house, "First of all, Rama placed her in the fire. He wished that the internal witness might be revealed. It was for this reason that the *abode of mercy* spoke with some severity." When Lakshman was told to assist, he showed reluctance. But his brother's look silenced all opposition. He ran, brought wood and lighted it. Sita was not the least afraid. She was glad of the opportunity to testify to her loyalty to Rama in deed, word and thought. In giving this account of the testing by fire, Tulsidas in one sense has made a great advance on the earlier narrative of Valmiki. Because there Rama is represented as showing himself as unworthily suspicious of his wife. He won't take her back till she has been tested by fire. The gods are amazed and protest against such treatment. Here there is that element also but in a very slight degree. There was the stain which the world would attach to her. But the main purpose was to bring back the real Sita. Since she had entered the fire in the forest at her husband's command, the real Sita had been elsewhere. It was only a shadow of herself which Ravan carried off, and only a shadow which Rama rescued. But when she emerged from this second fire, it was the divine goddess her very self once more.

"The fire became (cool) like sandalwood, as Sita entered it remembering the Lord. . . . Her shadow and the stain which the world would attach to her were consumed in the fierce fire. Gods, sages and saints all stood around. They had never seen such action on the part of the Lord. The fire, assuming the form of a Brahmin, took by the hand and brought to Rama the real Lakshmi whom the books of revelation sing, and who as Indira emerged from the Sea of Milk.[1] She shines forth on Rama's left side, her glory very beautiful and excellent." 125 (105) 134.

In Sita's case as in Rama's, Tulsidas is unwilling to face the consequences of a real incarnation. When Rama acts like a man, he does so in sport. When he is weary, when he swoons, when he finds it difficult to defeat Ravan, when he asks questions as if he did not know, some explanation must be found. It is said that it was Rama's pleasure that it should seem so. And to that extent his incarnation is not real. The same has to be said with regard to Sita. The poet cannot bear the thought that the goddess should be carried away and live in the demon's house. He therefore invents the plot we have described. It is here that he falls below Valmiki. With the Sanskrit poet, it is the real Sita who is carried off, and it is the real Sita who is compelled to face the fire. No wonder the gods entered a protest. Rama's treatment was very cruel. He told the princess that he would have nothing more to do with her. She could go where she liked. He had come to rescue her that the insult to his name might be removed. But no self-respecting man could take back a wife who had lived so long in another's house.[2] If Rama's reputation suffers at Valmiki's hands in connection with this incident, Sita's is correspondingly increased, and it is remarkable that Sita is the most human and the best portrayed character in the earlier work.

[1] This refers to the legend that Lakshmi was one of the products secured by churning the Sea of Milk.

[2] See my *Ramayana of Valmiki*, p. 272.

Tulsidas then escapes from these embarrassing situations which caused discredit to his hero, and which seemed to cause discredit to Sita, and everybody was pleased. The gods in particular appeared in person.

> "Then came the gods, selfish as they always are, and spoke as if they were in search of the highest good. 'Friend of the humble, merciful Raghurai, a god yourself, you have had pity on the gods. . . . You are omniscient, Brahm the imperishable, ever the same, untouched by the world, without parts, without qualities, without sin, without defect, unconquerable, full of compassion. Assuming a body, as the fish, the tortoise, the boar, the man-lion, the dwarf, as Parashuram, whenever the gods were in trouble, you have been born in bodies of various kinds and destroyed what troubled them. As for Ravan, the very root of sin, the oppressor of the gods, addicted to lust, anger, pride and desire, you have sent him to your own heaven. This is an act which causes us to wonder. We gods are possessed of very great authority. But out of desire for our own selfish purposes we have neglected devotion to you, and have fallen into the ever-flowing flood of existence. Lord, we come to you now for refuge.'" 128 (104) 133.

The Creator also is made to confess his former foolishness.

> "A curse on the life we gods have lived. Without devotion to you we have wandered, and come to grief in the world. Have mercy upon me now, oh merciful one, dispel my mind's bewilderment, by which it will be different from what it was, finding pleasure in what was pain, and living happily." 128 (107) 137.

Rama's father, Dashrath, next appeared. His two sons received him with great respect and obtained his blessing. They said that it was by the power of their father's religious merit that they had been able to conquer the unconquerable demon. The very important statement is then added :

> "Raghupati, beholding the greatness of his father's love, gave to him firm conviction. He did not obtain release from existence (*moksh*) ; Dashrath applied his mind to devotion's secret. Those who worship God endowed with qualities (*sagun*) do not obtain release from existence. Rama gives them devotion to himself." 129 (108) 138.

Indra, the king of heaven, then presented himself, and in view of what Tulsidas has to say of that god's character, it is interesting to find him seated on the penitent's stool.

> "I was very proud. I thought there was no one equal to me. But now that I have seen the Lord's lotus feet, my grief-causing pride has ceased. Let others worship the invisible Nirgun Brahm of whom the Vedas sing. But my choice is Koshal's king, the divine Rama endowed with qualities and real . . . receive me as thine own servant and give me devotion." 130 (109) 139.

Indra was thereupon invited to restore to life the bears and monkeys who had been killed in the battle. This request fills the poet with wonder.

> "This is a very great mystery which only learned saints can understand. The Lord, if he wish, can destroy the three worlds and bring them to life again. He merely wished to give glory to Indra. He rained down *amrit* on the monkeys and bears, and they lived. Delighted, they all got up and went to the Lord. The amrit fell on both armies. It raised the bears and monkeys, not the demons. The likeness of Rama was imprinted on the souls of the demons, and, abandoning their bodies, they went to the place of Brahm. The

monkeys and bears were partial incarnations of the gods. They all came to life again by the will of Raghupati. Who is so kind to the distressed as Rama, who gave salvation to the demons? And that abode of filth, the lascivious wretch, Ravan, obtained a rank which only saints secure." 131 (110) 140.

Shiva was the last of the gods to speak. His eyes were full of tears. He spoke with difficulty, because of the greatness of his emotion. He said that Rama was both Agun and Sagun, that he was the remover of doubt, and the joy of the gods. He besought him to dwell in his heart for ever, and convey him to the other side of life's ocean, so difficult to cross.

Rama was now impatient to return to Avadh. They were to travel in the aeroplane which had formerly belonged to Kuver, the god of wealth, but had afterwards been stolen by Ravan. The demon's brother, who had gone over to Rama's side, filled the car with garments and jewels. But Rama told him to rise up into the air and then cast these down. The demon did so. This at once produced a great scramble among the monkeys.

"Whatever they fancied they seized. They crammed jewels into their mouths, then threw them on the ground. Rama, Sita and Lakshman laughed. The abode of mercy is very playful. He whom saints cannot find by contemplation, whom the Vedas say is *neti*, *neti*, he, the ocean of compassion, sports and plays with the monkeys. Oh, Uma (says Shiva), profound meditation, the repetition of prayers, the giving of gifts, the practice of asceticism, the various kinds of abstinence, sacrifice and vows, do not secure Rama's compassion as love alone can do." 138 (114) 148.

RAMA'S RETURN TO AVADH.

Rama's return to Avadh [1] was eagerly awaited. And when he appeared the joy of Bharat and the citizens was very great. It was increased, if that were possible, by a specially gracious act.

"Seeing the great love of the people, the merciful Rama created a diversion. He revealed himself in countless forms and in appropriate fashion met them all. As he looked at the people with eyes of kindness, he made every man and woman happy. In a moment, Bhagwan met each of them. This is a mystery which no one can understand." 13 (6) 14.

The ceremonies connected with the coronation were attended by Brahma and Shiva, who, along with other gods and sages, mounted their cars and came to gaze at Rama. Before returning to heaven, they severally sang his praise. On this occasion we are not told what they said. The poet contents himself with recording the hymn uttered by the Vedas, who appeared in the guise of bards.

"The omniscient Lord, the ocean of mercy, received them with great respect. Nobody knew their secret as they began to sing his virtues: 'Hail to Sagun, Nirgun embodied, Rama without compare, the jewel of kings. By the strength of your arm you destroyed the ten-headed and other terrible and powerful demons; descending as a man, you broke the world's burden and consumed its terrifying pain. Hail, merciful Lord, protector of your worshippers, we worship you along with your *shakti*.[2] Gods, demons, serpents, men and

[1] The story of Rama's return is told in the first half of the Uttar Kand.

[2] Sita is Shakti, the power or energy of the god personified. See the chapter on Vishnu, where Sita is called *param shakti*, or the god's supreme energy.

every living thing (*ag-jag*) are all in the grip of your fearful *maya*. Night and day they wander exhausted in the path of existence, sated with *kal*, *karm* and *gun* (Time, the fruit of their past deeds and the three qualities). Those on whom you look with compassion are freed from the three kinds of suffering. Oh Rama, able to destroy fear and sorrow, protect us, we pray. Those who, intoxicated with pride of knowledge (*gyan*), treat with dishonour your world-conquering devotion, may obtain a rank greater than that which the gods find it difficult to secure, nevertheless we have seen them fail.[1] On the other hand, those who repeat your name cross the ocean of existence without difficulty. It is Rama we worship. Shiva and Brahma adore his feet. . . . We worship the eternal Tree, whose root is the unmanifest (*avyakta*), whose bark is fourfold, as the religious books declare, whose boughs are six in number, and whose branches are twenty-five, with many leaves and many flowers. Its fruit is of two sorts, bitter and sweet. One creeper clings to it. A tree full of fruit and flowers, the everlasting tree of the world.[2] Those who meditate on Brahm, the unborn, the one without a second (*advaita*), accessible only by inference, beyond understanding, let them talk of what they know, oh Lord ; but we shall always sing the glory of your qualities (*sagun yash*).

[1] The idea is that they lose their heavenly rank and have to resume the weary round of transmigration and rebirth, from which Rama alone can guarantee release.

[2] *Avyakta* is the primordial element from which all the phenomena of the material world have developed. It is another name for Prakriti, the first of the twenty-five principles here referred to. Tulsidas is back to the terminology of the Sankhya school. The bark is the four Vedas. The two fruits are pleasure and pain. The creeper is Maya. The six branches, says Growse, are either the six stages of existence—conception, birth, childhood, manhood, old age and death — or the six natural impulses—hunger, thirst, sleep, etc. Kabir has a similar passage in his Bijak.

Oh, seat of mercy, Lord, oh, mine of all that is good, oh god, this boon we ask, that in thought, word and deed we may be unchangeably devoted to your feet.' When the Vedas had uttered this eloquent prayer, in the sight of all they became invisible and went to Brahma's heaven." 28 (13) 27.

This is a passage of the very greatest importance. It is the poet's most impressive utterance as to the truth he holds on the comparative value of devotion and knowledge. He admits that the way of knowledge (*gyan marg*) has its uses. He knows that the wise men of his country have often spoken of it as the method by which the soul is able to achieve union with God, and cross the ocean of existence. He admits that sometimes it has been successful. But it is at best a long and laborious process, attended by precarious results. The man who seeks absorption in Brahm may find that all his efforts have been in vain. They have not carried him over the sea of life. He will have to come back again and resume the weary round of birth and death. He has not escaped the nightmare of transmigration. And so he says the world by wisdom knows not God. There is a better and a surer way—the way of faith or devotion (*bhakti marg*). It achieves definite results, and it is foolish to treat it with contempt. The man who puts his trust in Rama will be able to cross life's ocean and there will be no coming back. But when he proclaimed this earnest belief the poet had another reason for doing so. And that reason was to be found in the cravings of his own heart. The worship of Nirgun Brahm could not satisfy his needs. He wanted a God whom he could see and love. The God of the philosophers, the monism of the schools, might be enough for others, but he desired something more. He wanted a God who could dwell in his heart, overcome life's delusions and strengthen his soul.

And it is not without a reason that Tulsidas makes the Vedas themselves the vehicle of these convictions. The Vedas, as we have seen, are constantly referred to as the authoritative books of revelation. Neither Tulsidas nor his hearers may have known much about them. But they were recognised to be the inspired word. They are not *tradition* (*smriti*), the name applied to lesser books, like the Epics and Puranas. They are *shruti*, what has been heard, or, as Christians would say, the *Word of God*. It is therefore a skilful and, to his hearers, a very effective plea, when the poet makes the Vedas themselves claim Rama for their own. No wonder he calls their hymn an eloquent prayer, or the best of prayers. What stronger argument could he use in favour of the worship of a personal God who understands all the needs of men, and who is able and willing to help them when they call ?

The poet's task is now nearly over. And he tells us what great blessings will accrue if we read or listen to the story of Rama's deeds. But his narrative would be incomplete if he did not describe the happiness and virtue which filled the world when, as he says, God Himself ruled over it. The days of the Golden Age returned when Rama was king. The trees bore every kind of fruit. The air was always pleasant. The cows yielded as much milk as heart could desire. Abundant harvests were always sure. The rivers were full of water. The clouds gave rain when they were asked. And if the lion and the lamb did not lie down together, as Jewish prophets pictured, the elephant and the lion did so. As for the inhabitants of the world, they walked in the paths of the Vedas, devoted to the rules laid down, each person acting in accordance with the regulations of his own caste and stage in life. They found continual joy in doing so, and suffered from no kind of fear, sorrow or sickness. The three ills that afflict mankind—those that come from the body, those that come from God and those that come from existence itself—never afflicted any one in Rama's kingdom. No one died young, no one was ever sick, every one was beautiful, every one was healthy. There was no poverty, there was no sorrow. No one was ignorant, no one was unfortunate. All were free from pride. Men and women alike were clever and doers of good deeds. No one ever dreamed of doing wrong. They all appreciated one another's merits. They were grateful for what others did for them. Indeed they already enjoyed the highest state.

> "When Rama reigned, throughout all creation there was no pain caused to any one as the result of Time or as the fruit of past deeds, or flowing from natural disposition and qualities. The earth with its girdle of the seven seas, had only one king, Raghupati of Koshal. But that was no great lordship for him, in every hair of whose body there is a multitude of worlds. Those who know the glory of the Lord will think this account of mine very deficient. . . . The king of the serpents and the wife of Brahma even, could not describe the happiness and prosperity of Rama's kingdom. Every one was very good, desirous of the welfare of others, and served Brahmins. Each man was faithful and loving to his single wife. Each woman sought her husband's good in thought, word and deed." 42 (21) 43.

Another aspect of the teaching of Tulsidas now presents itself. And as it appears at the very close of Shiva's account of Rama's earthly life, it may be reckoned as of more than ordinary importance. It will be recognised that in some respects it is difficult to reconcile it with opinions expressed in other parts of the poem, especially with reference to a man's responsibility for what he has done. Attention has already been called to this contradiction, and a portion of the text has been quoted. The attitude also is at times peculiar. Rama seems to stand aside and speak of God as some one other than himself. It is, therefore, necessary to give it in full. Rama was addressing a meeting in Avadh. It consisted of religious teachers, Brahmins and citizens, whom he himself had summoned. When all were seated :

" The dispeller of the fears of the devout spoke and said : 'Listen to my words, men of the city. There is no self-seeking in what I say. There is no injustice. There is no attempt to assert my own authority. Listen, and do what you think right. The servant I love best is the servant who obeys me. If I say anything that is improper, brothers, do not be afraid to interrupt. The sacred books say it is great good fortune to be born in the form of a man. That is a condition which the gods find it difficult to reach. It is in that condition that one can realise oneself. It is the gateway of salvation. And yet when men do not secure salvation and go to the other world and there suffer torment, beating their heads they falsely lay the blame on Time, Karma and God (*ishwar*).[1] A human body is not obtained in order that we may enjoy the fruits of sense. These fruits yield heaven for a very little while. But the result in the end is pain. The receiver of a human body who gives his mind to the things of sense is like the man who takes poison in exchange for amrit. No one ever speaks well of such a person. He gathers peppercorns and loses the best of all precious stones. His life, which cannot be destroyed, continues to wander in the womb of the 8,400,000 births, revolving for ever at the will of Maya, surrounded by Time, Karma, his natural disposition

[1] Ishwar is the name Shankaracharya gives to Brahm when he is associated with Maya. It is his lower Brahm or personal God. Ramanuja also employed it for God.

(*svabhav*) and the three qualities (*gun*). But some time or other God (*ish*) takes mercy on him and, without any reason except affection, gives him a man's body. And this human body is the boat by which he may cross the ocean of existence. With my grace as the favouring wind, true religious teachers as the helm and steadfastness as his vessel he finds easily the means of transport which otherwise would be difficult to obtain. The man, then, who finds the means of transport in this fashion and fails to cross life's ocean is an ungrateful fool. He is a destroyer of his own life. Those then who wish happiness in the other world and in this should listen to my words and fix them in their minds. It is an easy and pleasant path, brothers, the *path of devotion* to me. The Puranas and the Vedas sing its praise. The *path of knowledge* is very difficult to traverse. The obstacles are numerous. The means of accomplishment are severe. It has no support for the soul. And when a man has endured many afflictions, what does he obtain? The man who is without devotion is not loved by me. The *path of devotion* is free. It is a mine of every happiness. But no one can find it unless he associates with good men. And good men are not to be found unless you have acquired merit. Association with good men brings transmigration to an end.'" 64 (43) 66.

At this point there is a curious anticlimax. One wonders why it was introduced: "There is one act of merit in the world and not a second. Worship the feet of Brahmins in thought, word and deed. Munis and gods are favourable to the man who serves Brahmins in sincerity. There is one other mysterious thing I say to you all with joined hands. Unless a man worship Shiva, he will not secure devotion to me."

Having made this announcement with regard to Brahmins and reasserted his own affection for Shiva, Rama resumes:

"Tell me what are the hardships that are connected with the *way of devotion*. Profound meditation, sacrifices, the repetition of prayers, asceticism, fasting, none of them are necessary. What is required is a sincere disposition, a mind devoid of guile, always content with whatever happens. . . . But why should I continue to lengthen my remarks further? Here is the manner of life which brings me under control. The man who is influenced by neither hatred nor strife, neither hope nor fear, his condition is always full of tranquillity. He begins nothing. He has no home. He is without pride, without sin, without anger. He is clever and wise. He always loves the society of good men. He reckons the things of sense, heaven and emancipation from rebirth (*apvarga*) as of equal value to a blade of grass. He is an advocate of Bhakti. He lives remote from perfidy and every kind of wickedness. In love with my name, which is a home of all the virtues, free from selfishness, arrogance and infatuation, the happiness of such a man as I have described is the sum of supreme felicity." 67 (46) 68.

X.

THE CROW'S PHILOSOPHY.

THE second half of the Uttar Kand may be reckoned as a summary of the poet's own religious attitude. It is placed in a very strange setting. When Shiva began to tell the story of the deeds of Ram, he said that he was merely repeating what had been related by an inspired crow. And when his narrative was finished, he repeated that assertion. This not unnaturally afforded Uma the opportunity of expressing her surprise that a crow should be possessed of such unparalleled devotion. Her experience had been that among the many millions who practise religion, it was difficult to find one possessed of perfect knowledge and absorbed in Brahm. But it was still more difficult to find a true and steadfast devotee of Rama. Uttar, 76 (54) 77.

In view of the poet's frequent assertion that the path of devotion is a pleasant and an easy road, that seems a very pessimistic utterance. But it may be due to the fact that Tulsidas is about to address himself to the task of dealing with the doctrines of Maya and Bhakti more fully and more exclusively than he has previously attempted. He has often set them side by side. Now his special purpose is to show how devotion to Rama robs Maya of its power, and makes his worshippers free. And he does not achieve his purpose by minimising the strength of that mysterious influence which plays such havoc among gods and men. Indeed at times he seems to take pleasure in emphasising it. On the other hand, one feels that he detracts from its power by ceasing to personify it in Sita, and associating it with sin and evil. In particular he does more than suggest that it is a species of blindness for which we are ourselves responsible, when we yield to its power. This section of the poem, because of its association with the crow, may seem fantastic to Western minds. But it is the poet's own method for bringing Maya and Bhakti together, and when he thus seeks to contrast them he is dealing with his central theme. He is presenting his message from another angle. He has found that a belief in Maya is woven into the very texture of Indian thought. It is present in his own. But he is persuaded, nevertheless, that faith in Rama will give men the victory and satisfy their needs.

When Shiva was asked to explain what he knew about the crow, he took his wife back to the time in her previous existence when she had performed Sati at the sacrifice of Daksh. Distressed at the loss of his wife, Shiva had journeyed to the northern mountains where he lived the life of an ascetic. Among these mountains he saw a crow who did not die even at the end of a Kalpa.[1] This crow was engaged day and night in worshipping Rama, and telling the story of his deeds to large gatherings of birds who flocked from every quarter. Shiva himself assumed the form of a swan and spent some time in their society that he might share in the privilege. How Garud, the king of birds, came to follow Shiva's example is, however, another story. In the account given in a previous chapter

[1] According to Hindu calculations, there are four ages, whose combined length is equal to 4,320,000 years. The first is the Golden Age, the fourth is the Iron Age. When the Iron Age comes to an end, a Golden Age begins. A Kalpa is a period of time equal to 1000 of such four ages, and is therefore 4,320,000,000 years in length. At the end of a Kalpa the existing world is destroyed. But in due course another comes into being.

of the battle with Ravan, it will be remembered that Rama allowed himself to be bound in the serpents' coils. On that occasion, Garud, who is the vehicle of Vishnu, had to come to his relief. He did so by swallowing the snakes, but the fact that he had to do so filled him with amazement.

> "I have heard that the all-pervading, passionless Brahm, the lord of speech, the supreme God, beyond the influence of Maya and delusion (*moh*), has descended to the earth, but I see nothing of his glory. By the repeating of his name, men escape from the bonds of existence. Can this Rama be he, when a base-born demon binds him in serpent coils?" Uttar, 80 (58) 81.

In his perplexity Garud went to Narad, who said:

> "Rama's Maya is very powerful. . . . That which time after time has made me dance, has spread itself over you. The great delusion (*moh*) has sprung up in your mind. It won't be erased quickly by any words of mine. Go to Brahma. Do what he advises you to do." 81 (59) 82.[1]

Garud, in accordance with this advice, went to the Creator, who bowed his head at the mention of Rama's name. As he meditated on his glory, love filled his heart, and he said:

> "Poets and learned pandits come under Maya's power. The power of Hari's Maya cannot be measured. It has often made me dance. Although everything that moves and does not move was created by me, it is no matter for wonder that it should be so. Then the Creator spoke in a sweet voice: 'Shiva knows Rama's

[1] "Having said this, the rishi of the gods departed, proclaiming the virtues of Rama: time after time he, who is supremely wise, declared the power of Hari's Maya." Uttar, 82 (60) 83.

power. Go to Shankar. Do not enquire from any one else. There your doubts will be dispelled.' " 82 (60) 83.

When he went to Shiva, that god, as he himself reports, said :

" I told him, Bhavani . . . until you have spent some time in the society of good men, this delusion and error (*moh-bhram*) will not be destroyed. There listen to the sweet story of Hari, which the seers sing in diverse ways. The theme in its beginning, middle and end is the Lord Rama Bhagwan. . . . Except in the society of good men, you do not hear the story of Hari, and without the story of Hari delusion (*moh*) cannot be dispelled. Unless delusion disappears, there is no steadfast love for Rama's feet. Without love there is no meeting with Rama, even though you engage in profound meditation, repeat prayers, possess knowledge and subdue the senses." 83 (61) 84.

Shiva accordingly sent him to interview the crow, very old and very wise, who spent all his time in singing the praises of Rama.

In commenting on this part of the story in which he was so personally involved, Shiva observes :

" The Lord's Maya is powerful. Who is so full of knowledge that delusion does not touch him ? The vehicle of the lord of the three worlds, the jewel of the wise and the devout, Maya deluded him. No wonder sinners are perplexed. It deludes Shiva and the Creator : what then are others ? helpless and weak ! Know that this is so. Seers worship Bhagwan, who is the Lord of Maya." 85 (62) 85.

As soon as he arrived at the crow's dwelling-place,[1]

[1] " The virtues and vices in their various forms, fashioned by Maya, along with delusion, love and the other errors of judgment which envelop the whole world, never go near that mountain." Uttar, 79 (57) 80.

Garud experienced an immediate change. The power of Maya disappeared, and he felt happy. Bathing in the lake and drinking some of the water added to his joy. His arrival was happily timed. The crow was about to begin a recital at that moment. And the poet gives a brief summary of Rama's deeds. When it was completed, Garud told the reason why he had come. The crow refused to believe that the king of birds could have been the victim of Maya :

> "You had no doubts, delusion, Maya. In sending you under the pretence of being deluded, Raghupati did me a kindness." Uttar, 96 (69) 98.

Nevertheless, he proceeded to declare :

> "And yet it is no wonder, because there is no one, including Narad, Shiva, Brahma, Sanatkumar and others, the great sages, who speak about the soul, whom delusion has not blinded, whom Love (*kam*) has not made to dance, whom desire has not made mad, whose heart anger has not set on fire. Among wise men, ascetics, brave men, poets, pandits, people endowed with good qualities, who is there in this world whom greed has not deceived, whom the intoxication of success has not made crooked, whom the possession of authority has not made deaf, whom the arrows of beauty have not pierced, whom achievement has not benumbed, whom pride and vanity have not overshadowed, whom the fever of youth has not made crazy, whose glory selfishness has not ruined, in whom envy has not found some blemish, whom the winds of sorrow have not shaken, whom the serpent tooth of care has not bitten ; who is there in the world whom Maya has not pervaded ? There is no one so strong but desire lays hold of him, even as the weevil worm does with wood. The desire for a son, for wealth, for a woman ; whose understanding have not these

three soiled ? These are all Maya's appointed followers. Her power is unmeasured. Who can describe it ? When Shiva and Brahma see it they are afraid. What need to take account of others ? The mighty army of Maya pervades the world. Her generals are lust and other kindred evils ; her warriors are pride, hypocrisy and heresy. She is the servant of Raghubir, and though we recognise her to be false, yet there is no escape without the mercy of Rama. I say this, sir, and defend it with a wager. The Maya who causes all the world to dance, and whose doings none can comprehend, it is by the play of the Lord's eyebrows that she dances like an actress with all her company. Rama is *existence, thought, joy* (*sachchidanand*), entire, the unborn, knowledge personified, the abode of the qualities. He is the pervader. He is that which is pervaded, the indivisible, the eternal Bhagwan, of universal, unerring power, free from the qualities, free from deceit, beyond the reach of speech or of the senses, all-seeing, unconquerable, faultless, formless, free from delusion, everlasting, void of passion, the accumulation of joy, the Lord who transcends Prakriti, and who dwells in all hearts, Brahm devoid of effort, free from desire, the indestructible. He is not the cause of delusion. Darkness can never oppose the sun. For the sake of those devoted to him, the blessed Lord Rama has assumed the body of a king, and like a common man, has done highly purifying deeds. Like an actor assuming various disguises and playing different parts, he also acts a pantomime, but in himself it is not so. Such, then, is the pastime of the Lord, a cause of bewilderment to demons, a cause of joy to men. Those whose minds are unclean, lascivious, who are in the grip of the senses, attribute such delusion to the Lord, just as a man whose eyes are sick says that the moon is yellow, or, when confused about direction, declares that the sun rises in the West, or as one who has gone on board a ship, the victim of delusion, sees the world moving and thinks that he himself is stationary. Children at play go spinning round. It is not houses and other things that revolve, though they say so falsely among themselves. Such is delusion, so far as it relates to Hari; not even in a dream can he be associated with ignorance. Stupid and unlucky persons, in the power of Maya and with a curtain over their minds in their foolish obstinacy, raise doubts and attribute their own ignorance to Rama. How can fools addicted to lust, anger, pride, greed, involved in household cares, themselves personifications of misery, fallen into the well of darkness, how can they understand Raghupati?" 96 (69) 98.

To this long quotation there immediately succeeds what every one must recognise as a very penetrating observation. It is a thought to which the poet returns. If we are content to believe in a God who can be described in the language of negation and is remote from human affairs, it is easy to believe in Him. But think of Him as one who is near at hand, and questions at once arise.

> "It is easy to understand the conception of God devoid of all attributes (*nirgun*), but no one can comprehend God endowed with qualities (*sagun*). When saints hear of His many actions, ordinary and extraordinary, their minds are bewildered." 103 (73) 106.

The crow next proceeds to describe his personal experience with Rama, and he gives expression to an opinion already referred to by Shiva that Rama had appeared as Rama times without number. "Rama is infinite, his virtues are infinite. His births, his actions, his names, cannot be numbered." 73 (52) 74. When Shiva spoke in this way he may have been thinking of Rama as the god who, in many and distinct incarnations, has appeared in the world. But with the crow it is otherwise. He speaks of Rama being born in Avadh over and over again, and says, "Whenever Rama assumes a human form and for the sake of those devoted to him plays many sports, on these occasions I go to Avadh . . . and stay for about five years. The child Rama is my own special god." 106 (74) 109. The crow found it easy to be often very near to Rama.

One day the divine child tried to catch the crow. The bird flew away, but it was tempted back with a piece of cake. When the bird flew away a second time, Rama began to cry. "I came near and the Lord laughed. I flew away and he cried. I went near to lay hold upon his feet. He ran off, but turned round time after time to look." This very human and natural conduct on the part of the child bewildered the crow.

> "Does the Lord, who is the sum of thought and joy, act in this fashion? Such thoughts came into my mind. *Maya* enveloped me by the contrivance of Rama. But the *Maya* caused me no pain. Existence was not as it is to other souls. There was a reason for this to which I wish you to listen with attention. The bridegroom of Sita is knowledge, one and indivisible. Souls, that which moves and that which does not move, are in the power of *Maya*. If all were of the same degree of knowledge, what would be the difference between God (*ishwar*) and the soul? The soul in his pride is in the grip of *Maya*. *Maya*, which is the mine of all the qualities, is in the grip of God. The soul is in the grip of another (*parvash*). Bhagwan is free (*svavash*). The soul is manifold. The husband of Lakshmi is one. Though the distinctions made by *Maya* are unreal, they will not disappear without the help of Hari, even if you make a million attempts. The man

who desires salvation (*nirvana*) apart from prayer to Hari, wise man though he be, is like a beast without tail and horns. . . . The troubles that afflict the soul cannot be wiped out. Ignorance does not envelop the worshipper of Hari. Knowledge that is caused by Hari pervades him. There is no destruction for a servant of his." 110 (77) 113.

With these and other comments the crow went on to relate how he flew into the air, but Rama was close behind. He had seen that the bird was perplexed, and smiled, stretching out his arms. He flew so high and so far that he reached Brahma's heaven and other worlds beyond. But every time he looked, Rama was there, with outstretched arms, no farther away than the breadth of two fingers. He closed his eyes from fear. When he ventured to open them, he was back in Avadh.

"Rama looked at me and smiled. He laughed and at once I jumped into his mouth. In his belly I saw a great multitude of universes and in them a variety of very wonderful worlds, the fashioning of each more strange than the other, with a hundred million Brahmas and Shivas, with innumerable stars, suns and moons, with innumerable guardians of the spheres, gods of death, and Time personified, with innumerable mountains and widespread plains, seas, rivers and forests without limit, the expanse of creation in many forms. Gods, sages, saints, serpents, men, kinnars, the four kinds of life,[1] what moves and what does not move; what no one ever saw or heard, what never entered the mind; such were the marvels that I saw there. How can I describe them? In each universe I lived an hundred

[1] The four kinds of life are: (1) those born from vapour (worms); (2) those born from an egg; (3) those born from the womb; (4) those born by sprouting (plants).

years; and in this manner, moving about from one to the other, I saw them all." 117 (80) 120.

In each of these multitudinous worlds he found a separate Creator, a separate Vishnu and a separate Shiva. In each of them he saw a city of Avadh with men and women, with Dashraths and Kaushalyas and others. In each of them there was a Rama who had become incarnate (*avatara*), whose childlike sports he was privileged to see.

"I visited in my wanderings countless worlds, but it was Rama and no other whom I saw." 118 (81) 122.

It seemed as if he had spent an hundred Kalpas travelling from universe to universe, and what he saw cannot be described. Yet everywhere he saw Rama, the merciful Bhagwan, the Lord of Maya. It seemed as if he had spent an hundred Kalpas in this amazing task, nevertheless it all happened in the space of two hours, because it was at the end of that short time that he jumped out of Rama's mouth when he laughed, and found him engaged as he had been before, at some children's game. The divine child, however, saw the perplexity of his devotee; he restrained the power of his Maya, and, placing his hand on the crow's head, told him to ask a boon. He could have anything he liked: miraculous powers, untold wealth, salvation from rebirth. But naturally the crow asked for devotion to Rama.

"A pure unbroken devotion (*bhakti*) to thee, of which the Vedas and Puranas sing, and which the greatest of ascetics and sages seek after, and only a few, by the favour of the Lord, find." 124 (84) 128.

In granting this request, Rama told the crow that every other blessing would be added. He had shown his wisdom by making such a petition, because devotion was the mine that contained every sort of happiness.

"Sages cannot secure it, though they make a million attempts, repeating prayers, practising asceticism, and giving their bodies to be burned. Every good quality will dwell in your heart—devotion, knowledge, wisdom, self-control. You will know every secret, and in the accomplishment of it, by my grace, there will be no pain. The errors produced by Maya will not pervade you. You know me to be Brahm, without beginning, the unborn, without qualities, with qualities."

Rama thereupon began to instruct the crow. What he said was in accordance with the teaching of the Vedas and other religious books, though he also speaks of it as his own doctrine.

"Apply your mind to it and listen ; leave all others and worship me. My Maya is the cause of the world, living creatures of every kind, both what moves and what does not move. They are all dear to me ; they are all created by me. But of them all, *man* is the one I like best ; of men, Brahmins ; of Brahmins, those who uphold the books of revelation ; of these, those who walk in accordance with their teaching ; of these, I love learned sages, who are ascetics ; and of those who are learned, those who know Brahm are especially dear. But more than all these, my own servant is dear to me. He comes to me and has no other hope. I tell it to you again. It is the truth. No one is so dear to me as my own servants. If the Creator were lacking in devotion, of all creatures he would be unloved by me ; whereas the very lowest soul if he have devotion is very much beloved indeed." 127 (85) 130.

When Rama had spoken in this fashion for some time longer,[1] he resumed his play. Then with tears in his eyes

[1] "My mercy is over all. But of them all, if any one abandon intoxication and Maya, and worship me in thought, word and deed, be

and twisted mouth, he looked at his mother as if he were hungry. His mother rose and took him to her breast. "She placed him in her lap and gave him suck."

In bringing this amazing narrative to an end,[1] the crow declared that from the time he obtained Rama's boon, Maya had never troubled him, and he warned the king of birds that his troubles would never cease until he worshipped Hari. He would not destroy the fear of life.

> "Without faith (*bishwas*) there is no devotion (*bhakti*), without devotion Rama does not exercise mercy, without the mercy of Rama, not even in a dream can one think of peace. Reflect on these things, and abandon all false doctrines and doubts." 130 (88) 138.

To this exhortation the king of birds replied that he was completely satisfied. He repented his former delusion when he had supposed that the eternal Brahm was a man. He added the opinion, to which the crow had already given expression, that:

> "No one can cross the ocean of existence without a teacher, though he were the equal of the Creator and Shiva." 133 (90) 142.

The king of birds had another question to ask. He had heard from the god Shiva that at the dissolution of the universe the crow continued to live when all other creatures perished. Shiva did not tell lies, nevertheless such a statement caused great perplexity. Serpents, gods and men, indeed the whole creation, perished. Time had swallowed up innumerable worlds. How was it that when others died, he did not die?

he man or eunuch, male or female, animate or inanimate . . . he shall be most loved by me." 128 (86) 131.

[1] "I have sung to you the whole mysterious story, how Hari's Maya caused me to dance." Uttar, 129 (87) 132.

"Tell me, was it through the power of knowledge or by the strength of abstract meditation, and why was it that when I came to your hermitage my delusion and error disappeared ?"

The crow's reply is very interesting. It confirms what has already been suggested, that in this section we have the summing up of the poet's outlook on religion and life ; and here in particular, and in a very real sense, we have the record of the conclusions he arrived at, moulded and coloured by the beliefs and the philosophies of his own time and country.

" 'As I listen to your loving and gracious questions,' said the crow, 'I remember my many former births. I will tell you all my history. . . . The repetition of prayers, asceticism, sacrifices, quietude, self-restraint, acts of religious merit, gifts, detachment from the world, discrimination, abstract meditation, knowledge, the fruit of all these is love for Rama's feet : without it none can find comfort. It was in this body I found devotion to Rama. That is the reason why I have a special liking for it. I do not surrender this body, though I can do so when I wish, because without a body worship is not possible, as the Vedas declare. At first delusion (*moh*) submerged me often. With Rama opposed to me, I had no pleasure even when asleep. My births were many. My acts (*karm*) and works of merit were many. I engaged in profound meditation ; I repeated prayers. I practised asceticism. I made sacrifices. I gave gifts. In what womb have I not been born in my constant roaming through the world ? I have seen everything in the accomplishing of my *karma*, but I was never so happy as I am now. I can remember many of my former lives. By the grace of Shiva, delusion (*moh*) has not enveloped my mind.' " 136 (92) 149.

One of these previous lives the crow described in detail. It was in a former Kalpa, which means in an earlier creation, and in one of the fourth ages, the age when religion is always at a low ebb :

"In a former Kalpa, there was an age of Iron. It was the root and essence of wickedness. Men and women were in love with unrighteousness and opposed to the Vedas. In that Iron Age I went to Koshal and was born in the body of a low caste Shudra.[1] I was a worshipper of Shiva in thought, word and deed, and in my pride a blasphemer of other gods. I was intoxicated with the haughtiness that comes from wealth, very boastful, of a fierce disposition and great arrogance. Although I lived in Rama's own capital, I knew nothing of his glory." 138 (93) 151.

After dwelling at great length on the evils that afflict the world when the revolution of Time brings the fourth age once more, the crow said :

"The Iron Age is the very dwelling-place of iniquity of all kinds. But it has also many excellencies. In the Iron Age salvation can be got without difficulty. In the ages of Gold, Silver and Brass,[2] worship, sacrifice and profound meditation are the means of attaining it ; but in the Iron Age people secure salvation by the repetition of Hari's name. In the Golden Age all men engage in profound meditation and are endowed with knowledge ;

[1] The Shudras are the fourth of the four castes. It is their duty to serve the other three.

[2] The four ages are called Krit, Treta, Dwapar and Kali. The *Vishnu Purana* compares the merits of the four ages in quite the same fashion, and tells us in practically the same words that while in the former ages, worship, sacrifice and meditation were needed, in the Iron Age all that one had to do was to repeat Krishna's name. See my *Vishnu Purana*, p. 225.

by meditating on Hari they cross the sea of existence.[1] In the Silver Age men offer a variety of sacrifices; by means of these acts, they cross the sea of existence. In the age of Brass they worship Rama's feet; by no other expedient do they cross the sea of existence. In the age of Iron they have only to sing the praise of Hari. By singing it men fathom the depths of existence. In the Iron Age profound meditation, sacrifices, knowledge, are not necessary. To sing Rama's praise is the one prop. Those who abandon every other hope and worship Rama, singing his praise with love, cross the sea of existence; of that there is no doubt. The glory of his name is manifest in the Iron Age. It is its one purifying glory." 149 (99) 163.

After living for many years in Avadh, but still ignorant of Rama's fame, this low caste Shudra was driven by famine to seek refuge in another country. He settled in Ujjain. In that city he acquired wealth, and, as before, continued to worship Shiva. He also became the friend of a learned Brahmin who, though a devotee of Shiva, never spoke disrespectfully of Hari. Thanks to the kindness of this holy man, who treated him like a son, he learned the sacred formula employed in the worship of Shiva, and when he went to the temple of the god, repeated the phrase he had acquired. But his heart was full of pride and arrogance, so much so that when he saw any one worshipping Hari, he would become very angry and pour insults on Vishnu. The kind-hearted Brahmin rebuked him for his foolishness and said:

"My son, the reward for serving Shiva is a sincere love for Rama's feet. Shiva and the Creator worship Rama . . . not to speak of sinful men. How can you

[1] In the Golden Age, religion (*dharm*) is in the hearts of all by the contrivance of Hari's Maya. Uttar, 151 (100) 165.

expect happiness if you insult him whose feet Shiva and Brahma adore ?" 154 (102) 169.

The Shudra's heart, however, did not change. And one day he was so rude as to remain seated when the man who had been so kind to him entered the temple of Shiva. The Brahmin said nothing and showed no signs of anger. But such an insult roused the indignation of the god. A voice was heard—it was the voice of Shiva—declaring that the unhappy wretch who had dared to sit in the presence of his religious teacher would have to crawl as a snake for the rest of his life. The Brahmin was horrified at such an awful penalty, and begged the god to be merciful. In the appeal which he addressed to Shiva he employed a great many of the epithets which belong to the Supreme Spirit, and said he was Nirgun Brahm. "Those who do not worship the feet of Uma's lord can find neither in this world nor in the next, happiness or peace." Moved by this appeal, Shiva said that though he could not recall the curse it would be changed into a blessing.

> "My curse cannot be rendered false. He will have a thousand lives. But the terrible pain which attends birth and death will not attach to him in the least. In no birth will his knowledge fail. Listen, Shudra. You were born in Rama's city. . . . Devotion to Rama will spring up in your heart." 162 (105) 174.

And so it came to pass. In whatever body he was born he was an earnest devotee of Rama. Beginning as a snake among the Vindhya hills, he at long last was born a Brahmin—"a rank which it is difficult for a god to acquire." When in that rank he gave all his mind to the worship of Rama, visiting holy men in their hermitages and asking them to tell him all they knew about Rama. His one thought was, "When I see Rama's lotus feet I shall consider that my life has reaped its reward." But when he spoke to those various sages about Rama, they always said to him, "God (*ishwar*) is in everything that exists." This response, however, gave him no satisfaction or, as it is expressed in the text, "The religion of Nirgun was not agreeable to me. Love for Sagun Brahm had a greater hold on my heart." 166 (106) 181.

In the course of his travels he came to the heritage of the rishi Lomas, and said to him as he had said to others, "Tell me how to praise Sagun Brahm." The rishi's attitude and response deserve very careful attention.

He was a philosopher devoted to *Brahm gyan*, and he began to instruct his questioner on the knowledge of Brahm. Many of the terms he employed have been quoted already. He is the unborn, devoid of qualities (*agun*), without form, without a name, without desire, without change, and so on. He is also called *advait*, one without a second, which is peculiarly the word applied to Brahm by the monistic school; and to make it all the plainer, in expounding Brahm, the rishi says, "Between Him and you there is no difference, like water and the wave." 170 (107) 185. But the religion of the Absolute (*nirgun mat*) made no appeal to this earnest seeker after truth. "It did not satisfy my heart." And he said once more, "Tell me how to worship the God endowed with attributes; devotion to Rama is the water, my heart is the fish. How can they be separate? Take mercy on me and show me how I may see Rama with my own eyes. When I have seen my fill of the king of Avadh, then I shall listen to your discourse on the Absolute (*nirgun*)."

The result was that both grew angry. The rishi denounced the religion of Sagun, declaring that God was Nirgun. Rama's devotee asserted the opposite, giving an answer to everything that was put forward. Among his very pertinent questions he asked how various things were possible if the monistic theory were true. "How can there be anger without duality; or how can there be ignorance without duality? How can a soul in the grip of Maya, cut off from others, and stupid, be the same as God?" 172 (108) 186.

At last the rishi could contain himself no longer, and he cursed the pertinacious Brahmin to be changed into a crow. The rishi, however, was not to blame. It was Rama who had led him to speak as he had done, confusing his mind as a means of testing the other's devotion. Indeed, he proved to be an earnest worshipper himself of Rama, and inviting the crow to come near, he gave him the Rama mantra, taught him how to meditate on Rama in the form of a child, and told him the whole story of the Ramcharitmanas. It was by the grace of Shiva he had acquired it, and he promised that the crow, whatever form he wore, would never cease to be an unflinching devotee of Rama.

It was first the curse of Shiva, and next the rishi's curse which had secured for the crow so many privileges. His hermitage for a distance of seven miles round had been made free from the power of Maya. He could change his shape at any time, but he preferred the form in which he then was. He could die when he liked, but he chose to live on. Twenty-seven kalpas had passed since he began to dwell among the mountains, singing Rama's praise. He never lived anywhere else, except when Rama took the form of a man and was born at Avadh. On these great occasions he hastened to that city and gladdened his soul by witnessing the child at his play, and renewing his image in his heart.

> "The great rishi cursed me for the obstinacy with which I clung to my belief in *bhakti*. But I obtained the boon which saints find it difficult to secure." 177 (111) 192.

XI.

THE MORAL TEACHING OF THE POEM.

THE sacred books of India contain moral teaching of a high order. And many passages could be quoted, especially from the *Mahabharata* and the *Laws of Manu*, to show with what earnestness men have pondered over the conduct of life. In few countries have wiser words been spoken on the need of practising self-control, on the dangers of pride and anger and greed, on the attractiveness of kindness, purity and truth. And when we turn to the pages of Tulsidas, we realise how deeply he has drunk at those ancient springs. He also has the gift, which his predecessors had, of uttering his thoughts in pregnant phrases which linger in the memory :

"To a good man happiness envelops the earth. Just as rivers flow into the sea, although it has no craving for them, so do peace and prosperity come without asking for them to the virtuous." Bal. 295 (301) 326.

"If you are good, the world is good. If you are bad, the world is bad." Ayodh. (208) 217.

"There is nothing in the world difficult to secure for those who from their hearts desire the good of others." Aranya, 54 (26) 39.

"The touchstone tries gold and there is a test for precious stones. But it is opportunity which discovers a man's real nature." Ayodh. (271) 283.

"An animal can dance, and a parrot is clever at talking,

but their quality and acting depend on the person who taught them." Ayodh. (287) 299.

"The parrot and the maina when they live with good people learn to say, 'Ram, Ram.' When they live with bad people they learn to give abuse. In the company of the wind dust flies up to heaven. When it associates with water, it becomes mud and sinks." Bal. (7) 12.

"Good men and bad men both cause pain, but there is a difference between them. The one robs you of life by separation from his presence. The other when he meets you causes grief. The lotus and the leech both grow in water. But their natures are different." Bal. (5) 10.

"The virtuous acquire virtue; the vicious acquire vice. Nectar confers immortality; poison causes death." Bal. (6) 11.

"The man who is selfish and unclean can never reach the joy of Brahm." Ayodh. (217) 226.

"In this world there are three kinds of men similar to the trumpet-flower, the mango and the bread-fruit tree. One yields flowers, one has both flowers and fruit, one has only fruit. One man talks and does nothing; one both talks and acts; the third acts and says nothing." Lanka, 105 (86) 114.

"Can you get rid of filth by washing it with filth? Can you get butter by churning water?" Uttar, 70 (49) 71.

"When a vile person humbles himself it is that he may do harm. The loving speeches of the wicked inspire fear." Aranya, 37 (19) 31.

"A man without devotion is like a cloud without water in it." Aranya, 57 (29) 43.

"Knowledge without love for Rama is like a boat without a boatman." Ayodh. (265) 276.

Phrases such as we have quoted are to be found throughout the poem, sometimes standing alone, sometimes as parts of a long discourse on the attractiveness of goodness or the ugliness of evil. In the course of our study many such passages have already been quoted. They show how the poet strove to reach the heart of morality, and to discover the motives which underlay men's actions. It is true that like other preachers he is sometimes more eloquent when he is denouncing wickedness than when he is commending virtue. But the inwardness of his exposition seldom fails to be apparent. For example, he speaks of good men endowed with calm and equal minds who make no distinction between friend and foe : like the flower which, when held in the hollow of the two hands, imparts its sweetness to both. Such men he calls the world's well-wishers. They have sincere natures and loving dispositions. And he contrasts them with evil men who reckon another's prosperity a misfortune and are glad when they hear that a house has been made desolate. They have a thousand eyes to see another's faults and a thousand ears to hear of them. They would be glad to die if by doing so they could cause injury to another. Bal. (3) 8.

In the Forest book, Rama himself is asked how good men may be recognised. It is manifest from the answer which he gives that the *good men* referred to are ascetics who have left the world and are free from its sorrows, because they care neither for their bodies nor their homes. But the fact that Rama is the speaker makes his reply of more than ordinary value as an estimate of what constitutes virtue.

"When they hear themselves praised they are ashamed. When they hear others praised, they rejoice. Calm and cold in disposition, they never abandon the practice of morality. Gentle in their natures, they have love for all. They practise prayers, penance, fasting, self-control, continence and vows. They love the feet of their religious teachers, of Govind[1] and Brahmins. They exercise faith (*shraddha*), forgiveness, friendship and compassion. These things afford them joy and a sincere love for my feet. They are free from *Maya* and worldly desire. They possess discrimination, humility and knowledge. Their opinions are in accordance with the Vedas and the Puranas. They are never guilty of boastfulness, arrogance and pride, nor do they set their feet even by accident in the path of evil. They are always singing or hearing of my exploits. And without any selfish motive they seek the good of others." Aranya, 73 (40) 58.

In the very striking description of the wickedness which affects the world when the Iron Age comes round, the poet's exposure of wrong-doing shows by contrast what he had hoped for, but never saw. The passage occurs in the crow's account of the time when he lived in Avadh, as a member of the Shudra caste.

"It was a very evil age. Men and women were wholly occupied with sin. Its filth had swallowed up all piety. The sacred books were obsolete. Heretics fashioned religions of their own and started many sects. Every one was in the power of delusion. Greed had devoured good deeds. . . . No attention was paid to the rules of caste and the four stages of life. All men and women were intensely hostile to the Vedas. The Brahmins sold these sacred books, and kings devoured their subjects. No one gave heed to the commands of the Vedas. Every one went his own way, as it pleased his fancy. A pandit was the one who talked most. The deceiver and the boaster were said to be saints. The wise man was he

[1] This reference to Govind, another name for Krishna, a later incarnation of Vishnu, is surprising.

who stole his neighbour's goods. The man who showed off was the man who was most religious. The man who could raise a laugh by his falsehoods however feeble was reckoned a fine fellow in the age of iron. The man who observed none of the rules of life, and abandoned the path of Revelation was supposed to be endowed with knowledge and to have subdued all worldly passions. If a man's nails were long and he had wide-spreading, matted hair, he was assumed to be an eminent ascetic. He who wore filthy clothes and other finery, who ate both lawful and unlawful food, was a yogi ; he was a saint, he was worthy of worship. Evil-doers were treated with respect and honour. Those who were false in thought, word and deed, were the preachers in that evil time. Men were all in subjection to their wives, who made them dance as the juggler does with a monkey. Shudras gave instruction in knowledge to the twice-born. They wore the Brahminical cord and received their base rewards. All were in the power of sensuality, greed and anger ; hostile to the gods, Brahmins and saints. Wives forsook handsome and virtuous husbands to follow after other and worthless men. Women whose husbands were still alive, ceased to wear ornaments. Widows adorned themselves with newly purchased jewels. Teachers and pupils were deaf and blind. The one did not listen, the other did not read. A teacher who takes money from his pupil and does not remove his difficulties, falls into a deep hell. Fathers and mothers summoned their children and taught them that the object of their lives was to fill their bellies. People who are destitute of the knowledge of Brahm can say nothing else. In the power of greed as they are, they would kill a Brahmin or a religious teacher for the sake of a farthing. Shudras argued with the twice-born and said, 'Are we any lower than you ? The man who knows Brahm is the best of Brahmins.' It is thus they browbeat and threaten. Libertines, in pursuit of other men's wives, wise only in deceit, in the grasp of delusion, violence and selfishness, these are the men who are learned talkers on the doctrine of monism. I have seen the manner of life that prevails in the age of iron. Ruined themselves and seeking to ruin others who keep to the path of Revelation, those who reject the Vedas and speak evil of them will have to live in each separate hell for the period of a Kalpa. Low caste people like oil-men, potters, dog-feeders, Kirats, Kols and manufacturers of strong drink, who, on the death of their wives, or when they lose their household goods, shave their heads and become *sannyasis* (religious mendicants), and cause Brahmins to worship their feet, destroy themselves with their own hands, both in this and in the other world. A Brahmin is unlettered, covetous, lustful and pays no attention to the rules of conduct, is wicked and marries a Shudra. A Shudra on the other hand repeats prayers, practises penance, fasts and receives gifts, sits on a lofty seat and reads the Puranas. Every one fashions his own way of life. The immoralities that prevail are beyond counting and cannot be described." Uttar, 139 (94) 152.

The poet goes on to declare that such disregard for the laws of religion and morality bore its natural fruit. The sins of which men were guilty resulted in suffering, sorrow, sickness, fear and death. Life was very short. No one lived longer than fifteen years. And yet, in their pride, men hoped to live to the end of a Kalpa. Ascetics grew rich. Beggars built for themselves fine houses. Kings, engulfed in sin and paying no heed to their religious duties, punished their subjects, regardless of justice. The powers of darkness were worshipped by prayer, penance, sacrifice, vows and gifts, the rites that had been employed in connection with a purer faith. Deceit, violence, arrogance, heresy, lust, anger, covetousness, and every kind of evil desire enveloped the world. All thought of paying respect to caste, the four modes of life, religion and moral conduct disappeared. And as a natural consequence the gods (*dev*) rained no rain on the earth. Seed was sown, but it never sprouted.

The moral teaching of the poem at its best is not expressed, however, in words or maxims, but in the portrayal of men and women. Rama and Sita, Bharat and Lakshman, by their unflinching obedience to what they believed to be their duty, by their love of truth, purity and righteousness, by their thoughtfulness for others, have set before India a very high ideal.

It is true that in his delineation of the hero, with his wife and brothers, Tulsidas was to some extent a copyist. He is drawing over again the picture drawn by his predecessor, Valmiki. And it must be confessed that in certain respects, his copy is less effective than the original. Tulsidas, as we have seen, was often unwilling to acknowledge the reality of Rama's incarnation. He could not endure the thought that the object of his worship should be exposed to any limitations, should suffer weariness, should manifest ignorance, should even seem to run the risk of defeat in battle. The result is that, except in the Ayodhya book, we feel that we are often face to face with a phantom and not a man. The same is true of Sita. We would love and honour her more whole-heartedly if we were allowed to believe that she is a real woman. But he refuses to forget that she is the mother of the world, and he will not entertain the idea that such as she could be carried off by Ravan. He therefore uses the conceit that it was not the real Sita, but only an image of her who lay a prisoner in Lanka. Valmiki knew none of these evasions.

Both Rama and Sita are so human in his eyes, their humiliation is so complete, that the Rama of the earlier poem has to be told by the Creator that he is God and not a man.

And yet in spite of himself and his philosophisings Tulsidas has succeeded for the most part in making his characters live. And this is specially striking in the Ayodhya Kand, the finest book in the poem, and the one that is most read. When speaking of Rama's life in Avadh, the poet only very seldom stops to tell us that he is merely acting a part. He is suffering a real sorrow ; he is undergoing real acts of self-renunciation. He has no thought for himself. He is thinking of his father's honour. He is concerned about his wife's comfort. He is rejoicing in one brother's generosity. He is planning for another's advancement. He shows compassion, sympathy, forgiveness, kindness, when they are required. In the description of Rama, which Tulsidas gives us there, and not in the battling with demons, or in the amazing manifestations of his divine form, or in the exercise of his Maya, do we see a real incarnation at its highest and best. And the same is true of Bharat and Lakshman and Sita. It is in their treatment of others, their unselfishness, the purity of their affections, their attitude to the citizens and to the outcaste tribes of the forest, that they are most attractive. It is when they reveal the human side of their natures that they are most divine.

There is this also to be said, and it cannot be said with too much emphasis, that it is not only in this visible embodying of the virtues that the poet excels. There is something even more valuable than that: the way, namely, in which he links religion and morality together. He has made religious enthusiasm the inspiration of right living. Faith without works is dead. Religion, if it is real, must work a change of heart. A change of heart can only come through faith in God. Devotion to Rama must produce good men. This is set forth with peculiar beauty in the passage which has been given in full at page 116. When the exiles asked a rishi to tell them where they were to live, he answered :

> " Dwell in those hearts, where there is no lust, anger, passion, pride, delusion, covetousness, excitement, envy, violence, deceit, arrogance, *Maya*. . . . They who look on another man's wife as their mother and on another man's wealth as more poisonous than poison, who are glad at another's prosperity and sad at another's misfortune, may their hearts be your auspicious abode."

In his enthusiasm for the power of Rama's name, it is true that the poet sometimes forgets this high ideal, and speaks as if the mere repetition of the name could cleanse the soul. But the prevailing conviction is that the inspiration to all goodness is devotion to Rama's feet. That does not mean that he is blind to the value of religious instruction. He recognises the need of education and training, or, as he expresses it, the society of good men. He magnifies the office of the religious guide or guru. Living with such persons, he says, is like going on a pilgrimage to a holy place. Wonderful results ensue. The crow becomes a parrot and the goose becomes a swan. But it is made clear that such beneficial intercourse is only possible through the mercy of Rama. Bal. (2) 7.

And what he proclaims on the first pages of his poem, he proclaims as the work draws to a close. Rama himself is made to say :

> " What is required is a good disposition, a mind devoid of guile, always content with whatever happens. In love with my name which is a home of all the virtues, free from selfishness, arrogance and delusion, the happi-

ness of such a man as I have described, is the sum of all felicity." Uttar, 68 (47) 69.

It is not suggested that Tulsidas surpasses the more ancient scriptures in the inwardness of his moral teaching. We could quote passages from the *Great Epic* and the *Laws of Manu* which dwell on the need for repentance with more intensity and directness than Tulsidas does. But when all has been said, it has to be realised that the moral teaching of those ancient scriptures has been like that of other scriptures. It is given by way of precept and exhortation, expressed in pithy proverbs and sententious aphorisms, conveyed by means of parable and allegory. Such teaching is very valuable wherever it may be found. It is a confirmation of the eternal verity of the moral law. It is another proof that God has not left Himself without a witness in the heart and conscience of mankind. Good men everywhere have been marvellously at one in the views they hold as to the principles which should govern human conduct. But the precept does not always express itself in practice. The exhortation is too often disobeyed. They are only too apt to remain cold and barren unless there is some fructifying heat.

It was only when the Hindu found in Rama one who embodied his own best thoughts and ideals that religion and moral conduct could be linked together in a satisfactory fashion. How convinced the poet was of the close connection that must subsist between religion and morality is well illustrated by what he says in the beginning of his poem. The story of Rama which he has to tell deserves our study, he says, because it gives rest to the intellect ; it delivers the mind from doubt, delusion and error ; it carries the soul across the sea of existence ; it removes sorrow ; it is the true teacher of knowledge, asceticism and profound meditation ; it heals the diseases of life ; it wipes out sin, pain and sorrow ; it destroys lust, anger and uncleanness ; it burns up deceit, hypocrisy and unbelief ; it is the seed from which grow all religious rites, fastings and vows.[1]

It is true that the same close connection between religion and morality is asserted in the *Vishnu Purana,* a book devoted to the worship of Krishna. "He who lives pure in thought, free from malice, contented, leading a holy life, feeling tenderness for all creatures, speaking wisely and kindly, humble and sincere, has Vasudeva ever in his heart." [2]

It is difficult, however, to concede to Krishna such a home. The god's own life on earth was such that his worshippers had felt they must find some excuse for it. It is different with Rama. He towers above his devotees in every virtue. He offers no unworthy ideal, and so to the Hindu who believes in him and loves him, there comes a spiritual impulse and a moral strength. Faith in Rama contributed what was required to change precept into practice, a theory into life. Religion and morality are the two sides of the same shield. This is reckoned a commonplace in the Christian religion. "If ye love me," said Jesus, "ye will keep my Commandments." And Paul declared, "If any man be in Christ he is a new creature." It is one of the glories of Tulsidas that with certain aspects of his mind he strove to bring a similar truth home to the heart of India.

If we are to form a balanced estimate of the poet's teaching, however, we must take into consideration those other elements where it cannot be said that religion and morality go hand in hand. The most influential of these is Karma. A detailed examination has already been made of the strong hold which that doctrine had upon

[1] These are selections merely from a long passage in Bal Kand, 40 (38) 50.

[2] *Vishnu Purana,* iii. 7 (Wilson's translation).

the people of Avadh. They were constantly abusing Karma, and Rama repeatedly followed their example. It is a theory which seems to offer an attractive explanation for the inequalities of life, but in practice it proves an only too easy refuge for those who would apologise for their own or other people's sin. The poet's belated awakening to his blunder in the last book of the poem is very interesting, but it does not atone for the harm he has done by his earlier teaching. It is well that he should have made Rama his mouthpiece :

> "And yet when men do not secure salvation and go to the other world and there suffer torment, beating their heads they falsely lay the blame on Time, Karma and God." Uttar, 64 (43) 65.

The enthusiasm again which Tulsidas shows for sacred places is very wonderful. The Ganges, especially at Tribeni, Prayag and Benares, is particularly holy. It is true that the river is sometimes addressed in the definite language of prayer and that it gives an answer which its worshippers can hear and understand.[1] But in the majority of cases a place or stream is in itself reckoned holy. It is not thought of as being alive as a god is alive, nevertheless the very sight of it confers beatitude.

> "I reverence the holy city of Avadh and the river Saraju which destroys the sins of the Iron Age." Bal. 21 (23) 31.
>
> "By the power of his name I make happy those whom I see dying at Kashi." Bal. 127 (125) 142.
>
> "How is it possible not to render service to Kashi, knowing that it is the birthplace of salvation, the mine of knowledge, the destroyer of sin." Kish. invocation.

[1] Sita prayed to the Ganges both before and after her exile. On both occasions she got an answer. Ayodh., (99) 103. Uttar, 190 (117) 208. Bharat also had a similar experience. Ayodh. (195) 204.

> "The river Mandakini is a branch of the Ganges. It destroys sin as readily as a witch destroys a child." Ayodh. (126) 132.
>
> "Thus Rama came to the Tribeni, the remembrance of which gives every kind of good fortune. With joy he bathed in its water and worshipped Shiva. With appropriate rites he worshipped the god of the place." Ayodh. (102) 106.
>
> "Who can describe the power of Prayag, the lion that destroys the elephant mass of sin." Ayodh. (162) 106.

When Rama was returning from exile in his aeroplane, he told Sita that the Jumna removed the impurities of the Iron Age, and continued as follows :

> "Again behold Prayag, the lord of tiraths, the sight of which puts away the sins committed in an hundred million births. See again the most holy Tribeni that dispels sorrow, the ladder to Hari's heaven, and look ! look ! the very holy city of Avadh, the destroyer of the three kinds of pain and the disease of existence." Lanka, 144 (116) 154.

There is only one passage which suggests that the worshipper himself should be in a correct mental attitude. It is when Atri describes to Bharat the discovery of a forgotten *tirath* :

> "This has been a holy place from all eternity, but Time concealed it and no one knew of its existence. Then my servants saw that it was an auspicious spot and made a well for the sake of the excellent water. Under the control of Vidhi, the whole universe has benefited, and a religious purpose very difficult to secure has become very easy. From henceforth people will call it Bharat's well, a very purifying tirath, because of the union of the waters. Those who with love and

religious observances bathe in it will become pure in thought, word and deed." Ayodh. (297) 310.

The magic influence belonging to sacred places is surpassed by the power attached to Rama's name. In the Bal Kand particularly, the poet dwells on the sweet and gracious name easy to remember which satisfies every wish, affords profit in this world, and procures salvation in the next. (23) 35. He tells us indeed :

> "The glory of the name is boundless. It is greater even than Nirgun. Yes, in my opinion the name is greater than Rama himself. . . . By repeating his name with love, those devoted to him become dwellers in the abode of happiness and bliss. Rama himself saved only one person, the ascetic's wife. His name has reformed the evil deeds of millions of wicked men." Bal. 29 (27) 39.

Much of this is merely the language of exaggerated devotion, and it would not be impossible to find somewhat similar expressions in Christian literature with reference to the name of Jesus. But the poet is not content with expressions such as we have quoted. He finds it necessary to declare that the demons slain by Rama obtained salvation because they happened to utter his name at the hour of death :

> "Rama sent them to his own heaven. Demons who devour human flesh obtained a rank for which ascetics crave. Rama is tender-hearted and full of mercy to demons who invoke his name, even when they are moved to do so by feelings of hate. Who is so merciful as he ? The man who does not give up his error and worship such a lord is foolish and accursed." Lanka, 56 (43) 64.

The poet's mind, as we have seen, had many points of

view. The ancient wells at which he drank afforded water of various qualities, and he did not always discriminate as we should have liked. It is not unnatural that the sacred literature of any country should contain a great deal of diverse teaching, that passages which carry the soul up to God should stand beside teaching that repels. This is true, for example, with regard to the Old Testament. The moral teaching of the Prophets is very different from what we find in some of the historical books. The Psalter contains not only hymns which dwell on the beauty of holiness; it has others which call down calamity and punishment on the heads of the writers' enemies. The God who was supposed to sanction some of the deeds recorded in Exodus and Samuel was not the God of whom Jesus tells us in His Gospel. The Ten Commandments were rewritten in the Sermon on the Mount. The explanation of such glaring contrasts in the sacred books of any nation is that they are a compilation. The writings they contain represent a long development. And though we may wonder how any compiler could put them in the same book and attribute them to the same divine source or to the same human author, we remember that they have been sanctified by the reverence of centuries, and that a multitude of different minds have shared in their composition.

Tulsidas, however, was his own compiler. And it might have been expected that he would have used more discrimination in the choice of his materials. But it must not be forgotten that with all his spiritual insight and healthy moral fervour, he remained an orthodox Hindu. The feelings he had for what he called the Vedas were similar to those entertained by the average Christian for the Bible. Those Scriptures were *Shruti*, or "what had been heard." They were more than a tradition to him. They were the Word of God. That he did discriminate in the choice of his materials, is, however, quite evident.[1] Attention has been called to his attitude with reference to the lesser gods. He continued to believe in their existence, but he had little or no respect for some of them. And as we have seen, he did not hesitate to express his opinions. When Tulsidas did that he rendered a service to religion and morality. The pity is that he had not the strength to do more. He speaks without restraint of the character and conduct of the lesser gods. And yet when he tells us what Vishnu and Shiva did on certain occasions it would appear as if he had no feelings of disapproval, at least as regards Vishnu. With reference to Shiva, it is manifest that he was seized with some qualms of conscience, and he offers the old apology, in words which have passed into a proverb, coupled to a warning :

> "The powerful can do no wrong. They are like the sun, like fire and the Ganges. But the fool who in his pride wishes to copy them, saying that a man is like a god, will fall into hell for the period of a Kalpa." Bal. 80 (78) 92.

When we read the account of Shiva's wedding, or the methods which the other gods adopted to persuade that deity to marry ; when we read the description of what Vishnu did to cure the pride of Narad and rob him of his phantom bride, we ask, How was it possible that the man who wrote so beautifully in praise of purity and truth and the love of God, could, in other parts of his poem, put together conceptions so unworthy ? It is no excuse to say that these narratives belong to the mythological stage in

[1] Tulsidas often confirms his statements by saying, "So the Vedas sing," or, "so says *Shruti.*" *Shruti* includes the hymns of the Vedas, the Brahmanas and Upanishads. Tradition (*smriti*) includes the *Laws of Manu,* the two great Epics and the Puranas. Smriti is ***what is remembered,*** in contrast to *what is heard* (Shruti).

the history of religion. That is merely to repeat a platitude. The wonder is that a man who had travelled so far and risen so high, did not realise that such stories were undesirable. And this also has to be noted, that the poet is not merely repeating old stories in which he has no real interest. Shiva is one of the great gods. He is an object of the poet's own worship; and as for Vishnu, when he describes that god's treatment of Narad, he repeatedly identifies him with Rama. The name of Rama is used time after time interchangeably with that of Vishnu. Not only so, but when Rama was in the forest and there met with Narad, the rishi, reverting to his old disappointment, asked the incarnate god why he had treated him as he did.[1]

For semi-divine beings also, the poet had apparently a standard that differed from what he demanded of ordinary humanity. In Sanskrit literature Narad is represented as an inquisitive, unattractive old man, a gossip and a fomenter of quarrels, constantly moving between earth and heaven. And yet he seems to have a strange attraction for Tulsidas. He plays a prominent part. Vishnu receives him with the greatest respect when he appears in heaven, rising from his seat and inquiring after his welfare. It was he who helped to arrange for Parvati's second marriage. And despite his earnest devotion to Rama, it was the strength of his curse that brought about Vishnu's incarnation. The seven rishis are also made to indulge in language which the poet would not sanction in common life. It will be remembered that they were sent by Shiva to make trial of Parvati's love. They approached and asked her why she was engaged in such arduous

[1] It was this practice of attributing to the gods conduct which their purer-hearted worshippers felt it necessary to disown, that made the Latin author say:

"*Tantum religio potuit suadere malorum.*"

penance. She replied that she was trusting to the truth of Narad's promise and hoped to secure Shiva for a husband.

> "When they heard her words, the rishis smiled and said: 'Tell us, who has ever listened to Narad's advice and continued to have a home? The man or woman who listens to Narad will assuredly abandon his home and become a beggar. Deceitful in mind, though in appearance a good man, he wishes to make every one like himself. You are putting faith in his word, and wish to marry as your husband a worthless, shameless, ragged mendicant, a wearer of skulls and snakes.'"
> Bal. 90 (88) 102.

It is impossible to refrain from passing an adverse criticism on an attitude which the poet, in common with others of his countrymen, has chosen to adopt. Despite the moral and spiritual heights to which Tulsidas often rises, we have to recognise that the poem is a strange medley. Defects such as have been mentioned are present everywhere throughout his work—defects which leave the Hindu disarmed and enfeebled when he would fight for righteousness. The Bhakti movement will never come to its own until India passes beyond the mythological stage and learns to believe in one God—a God who is worthy of her large-hearted devotion.

Two other matters of great importance call for consideration in this chapter: the poet's attitude with regard to caste, and his views on women. On both questions his opinions vary. We have seen the extraordinary kindness with which both Rama and Bharat treated the jungle tribes. Neither of them believed in the doctrine of untouchability. They ate the food these low-caste people brought, and both of them embraced Guha, the forest chieftain. As has been already remarked in an earlier chapter, there is no doubt that Tulsidas wished to make it perfectly clear that he rejoiced in such brotherly treatment. Nevertheless he recognises that it is unusual. He therefore brings the gods on the scene. They rain down flowers and express their wondering approval.

> "According to the world's ideas and the teaching of the Vedas this man is an outcaste in every way. If his shadow touches any one it is necessary to bathe. And yet Rama's young brother has embraced him and thrilled all over with joy at meeting him." Ayodh. (186) 194.

We have similar generosity expounded in the account of Rama's interviews with the dying vulture and the female hermit who was an outcaste. No doubt the poet's purpose here is partly theological. He wishes to make it plain that devotion can overleap all barriers. But coupled as these two other incidents are with the treatment of Guha, India has cause to be grateful for such emphatic and healthy counsel.

And yet here also we have to confess that the poet is not by any means consistent in his teaching, because throughout the poem he exalts Brahmins in the most extravagant fashion. And no more striking proof of that is to be found than in the fact that between his account of Rama's interviews with the dying vulture and the female outcaste, he places on the lips of Rama what seems a quite gratuitous observation :

> "I do not like those who oppress Brahmins. Those who, abandoning hypocrisy in thought, deed and word, serve these gods of the earth, bring under their control Brahma and Shiva with me and all the gods. A Brahmin, though he curse you and beat you, ought to be worshipped, so say the saints. A Brahmin should be worshipped though destitute of character and virtue, but not a Shudra, though possessed of every virtue and distinguished for his knowledge." Aranya, 56 (28) 42.

It is recognised as essential that the rules of caste should be adhered to, and among the many objectionable practices which prevailed in the Iron Age, the crow tells us that the laws of caste were ignored. Shudras dared to teach the twice-born, and maintained that they were as good as Brahmins. Nor does the poet recognise any other attitude. However liberal-minded he may be, confident as he is that God loves all, he believes that it will be a very disorderly world if men do not observe the rules of caste and adhere to the rank in which they were born. The Brahmins stand at the head of the social structure. They rank higher than kings. They are repeatedly spoken of as the gods of earth in contrast to the gods of heaven, and as such they ought to be treated. Only a few illustrations can be quoted. Not only kings but celestials bow before them. When Vishvamitra came to Dashrath's court, the king prostrated himself before the holy man and then caused him to sit on his own throne. Bal. 212 (218) 238. Rama and Lakshman humbled themselves in the presence of their religious teacher : "The two brothers pressed the guru's feet, they for love of whose lotus feet ascetics repeat many prayers and indulge in profound meditation." Bal. 231 (237) 258. Bharat, when he spoke to Brahmins, did so with joined hands and humble entreaty. He tells them to give their orders to everybody, whatever their rank and with reference to everything. He then went to the house of his guru and prostrating himself in his presence, asked permission to live the life of an ascetic. Ayodh. (310) 336. The god Shiva bowed his head in the presence of the Brahmins who came to his wedding. Bal. 109 (107) 123. While Vishnu, when Narad visited him in heaven, "got up with joy and went to receive him ; he caused him to sit beside him. The lord of all that moves and does not move said with a smile, 'It is a long time since you came to see me !'" Bal. 136 (134) 155. The honour they received is otherwise expressed when we read that Rama meditated on the feet of Shiva, his guru and Brahmins Bal. 357 (363) 391, and the hero's interest in them is equally manifest in the statements that Rama is "the well-wisher of gods, Brahmins and cows" Bal. 286 (292) 317, and "became incarnate for the sake of gods, Brahmins, cows and the earth." Kish. 31 (26) 29.

Extraordinary power is also attributed to them, and we are warned not to offend them.

"The fool who is envious of his religious teacher will fall into the *raurav* hell for an hundred Kalpas." Uttar, 156 (103) 170.

"The man who despises Hari and his guru will become a frog and will have that body for a thousand births. The man who despises a Brahmin, after enduring many hells will be born into the world as a crow." Uttar, 189 (117) 207.

"Listen to my true words" (says Shiva). "Vows and the service of Brahmins are pleasing to Hari. Never insult Brahmins. Reckon them as the equals of eternal Brahm. The bolt of Indra, my own great trident, the rod of Death and the terrible discus of Hari, those struck by them may not die. But the anger of a Brahmin is a fire that consumes." Uttar, 162 (105) 177.

"A Brahmin, by means of penance, is always powerful. No one is able to protect you from his anger. If you can get Brahmins into your power, then you have the Creator, Vishnu and Shiva in your power. I tell you true, with both hands upraised. In the presence of a Brahmin your greatness will avail you nothing." Bal. 170 (168) 194.

"If you reveal this, or if a Brahmin curse you, you will be destroyed. . . . A guru can save you from the anger of the Creator. But if the guru himself is hostile, there is nobody on earth who can save you." Bal. 171 (169) 195.[1]

In view of such beliefs it was natural that one of the signs that the Golden Age had come with Rama's return to Avadh, was the rendering of service to Brahmins by all men and women Uttar, 43 (22) 44, while the prince himself gave them gifts innumerable. Uttar, 45 (24) 46. It was not until the Brahmins gave the order that Rama sat down on his father's throne. Uttar, 20 (10) 21. No wonder Rama should say to Parashuram, "Such is the might of a Brahmin's descent that he who fears you is otherwise without fear" Bal. 284 (291) 316; or that the crow, speaking of his various transmigrations, should observe: "At last I obtained the form of a Brahmin, a rank difficult for a god to attain." Uttar, 166 (106) 181.

Very little is said as to what constitutes a Brahmin's duty. The poet is too anxious to insist on his privileges. But in the Uttar Kand 162 (105) 177 we read that Brahmins, who are of a forgiving disposition and desire to do good to others, are as dear to Shiva as Rama is; while Parashuram is told that a Brahmin's heart should be full of mercy Bal. 283 (289) 314, a quality in which he was very deficient. By way of contrast, however, we discover what Brahmins ought to be, by reading what they were really in the Age of Iron: unlettered, covetous, lustful, neglecting the rules of conduct, and marrying women from the Shudra caste.

It would be easy to find support for everything Tulsidas has claimed for his own caste in the earlier literature. But we shall search his pages in vain for teaching so broadminded as the *Mahabharata* and the *Laws of Manu* sometimes venture to assert.

[1] Rama says to Valmiki: To give satisfaction to a Brahmin is the root of happiness. The wrath of a Brahmin blazes for ten million generations. Bal. 231 (237) 258.

"Even in Shudras, truthfulness, charity, forgiveness, benevolence, mercy, kindness and knowledge of the Vedas . . . are to be found. The Shudra in whom these characteristics are present is no Shudra, and the Brahmin in whom they are wanting is not a Brahmin but a Shudra." *Maha.* iii. 180.

"Brahmins learned in the Vedas regard a (virtuous) Shudra as equal to Brahm himself." *Maha.* xii. 297.

"Let not a Brahmin, even though in pain, speak words cutting others to the quick; let him not injure others in thought or deed; let him not utter speeches which make others afraid of him, since that will prevent him from gaining heaven. A Brahmin should always fear homage as if it were poison, and constantly desire to suffer scorn as he would long for nectar. For he who is scorned may sleep with an easy mind, and with an easy mind walk here among men, but the scorner utterly perishes." *Manu,* ii. 161, 163.[1]

The passages which deal with women are particularly interesting. They help to give a clear picture of social conditions. When the kings came to Janak's capital to try and bend Shiva's bow, the arena was surrounded by tiers of seats, from which the people watched the contest with comfort. "Alongside, there was erected an extensive and handsome building, glistening in many colours, where the women of the city were seated, in accordance with their rank, and witnessed the affair in seemly fashion." Bal. 229 (235) 256. As Rama entered the town, the young women from the latticed windows of their houses saw his beauty and at once fell in love with him. Bal. 225 (231) 252. When Shiva and Brahma, with the other gods, came to witness Rama's wedding, they were surprised at the number of handsome men and women whom they saw.

[1] See M. N. Dutt's translation of *Mahabharata* (Calcutta), 3 vols.; and Buhler's translation of *The Laws of Manu* (Oxford).

Bal. 313 (319) 346. We read of lovely married women singing songs, while Brahmins recited texts from the Vedas. Bal. 312 (318) 345. And it was the same in Avadh. When Rama and Sita arrived there, we read that "crowds and crowds of beautiful women came to meet them . . . supplied with water pots and lamps, and singing songs as if they were embodied goddesses of speech." Bal. 343 (349) 377.

As for Sita, we read that she first saw her future husband in the royal garden. She had gone to worship at the shrine of Parvati and to ask the goddess for a handsome husband. She bathed in a pool near at hand, with her female companions. One of these attendants, who had gone to another part of the garden, came back with the news that she had seen two beautiful youths. Urged by her companions, Sita went to the place, and there she saw Rama. It was love at first sight. Seeing the beauty of Sita, he was filled with gladness. He was so overwhelmed that he could not speak. Sita was equally enthralled. She was possessed with longing. She was as glad as a man who recognises the treasure he has lost. Her eyes grew tired of looking at Rama and her eyelids forgot to wink.[1] Bal. 236 (241) 262.

Throughout the poem there is no suggestion of anything impure in the character of the poet's heroes. He is justified in his boast "here are no prurient and seductive stories."[2] And in that section which speaks of Rama and Sita as children, it is clear that their marriage was a marriage only in name.

[1] Rama afterwards said to Lakshman, "Vidhata knows the cause of everything. My lucky side is throbbing. It is a characteristic of the house of Raghu. None of them ever set their mind on an evil path. . . . I have never looked on the wife of another man even in a dream. . . . Those men are few who have never looked with longing at another's wife." Bal. 236 (242) 263.

[2] Growse's translation. Bal. 48 (46) 58.

When Sita went to the forest with her husband and brother-in-law, we get a pretty picture of her gracious treatment of the women in the villages through which they passed, and when they asked her who her two companions were, she told them how the younger was her brother-in-law, while the other was—here she paused, and, covering her face with the edge of her veil, remained silent. But with a coquettish glance she let them understand that the other was her husband. Ayodh. (112) 117. Rama's treatment of Sita in Avadh and in the forest is uniformly kind and loving. The ordeal of the fire has, as we have seen, been so altered for theological reasons, that it is robbed of its original cruelty. And once she was rescued from Lanka, the same loving thoughtfulness prevails.[1] In this respect, Tulsidas's picture is more generous than that of Valmiki's. And yet as a whole it is inferior to that of the earlier poet. Whether he realised it or not, Sita is the best-drawn character in the Sanskrit *Ramayana.* She expresses herself with fearless frankness and manifests all through her troubles, particularly when exposed to the ordeal of the burning fire, a strong and noble nature that scorns her husband's unworthy subterfuges.

Whatever a woman's life in practice may often happily have been, we are not allowed to forget what the theory was. A woman should always worship her husband's feet. " A woman's religion is to recognise her husband as

[1] This is on the assumption that we ignore the *Lav Kush Kand,* often added to the poem in popular editions, which tells of Sita being repudiated by Rama in obedience to the complaints of the citizens, that he should not keep in his zenana a woman who had been in Ravan's arms. There is reason for thinking that the corresponding book is a later addition to Valmiki's *Ramayana.* The *Lav Kush Kand* is a hopeless anti-climax. In the Bal Kand, 47 (45) 57, the poet himself speaks of his poem as containing seven books. The *Kashi Nagara Pracharini Sabha* edition of the text is purged of all interpolations, and without the eighth book, which it reckons as the crowning offence.

her only god." Bal. 111 (109) 125. It was Uma's mother who told her daughter that such should be her rule of life. But she added, " Why has the Creator made woman to be in subjection to others and not see happiness even in a dream ? " Sita herself addresses Parvati as the chief of women faithful to their husbands and reckoning them as gods. Bal. 241 (247) 268. While a rishi's wife, talking at length on what constitutes a woman's religion, says, " Mother, father, brothers and well-wishers are the source of moderate happiness, but a husband is a gift without limit. She is a vile woman who does not serve her husband" Aranya (2) 6, and she goes on to say that even when " he is old, ill, stupid, poverty-stricken, blind, deaf, passionate, if she treat him with dishonour, a woman will have to suffer many things in hell. Her one religious duty, her one fast and vow, is to love her husband's feet in deed, word and thought " ; not even in a dream must she think of another man. To deceive him, to love another, means that she will fall into hell for an hundred Kalpas, spending thus an hundred lives for the sake of a moment's pleasure. A woman can attain the highest state without any trouble by abandoning guile and by faithfulness to her lord. " Even a wicked woman, who serves her husband, obtains a blessed state, so say the four Vedas, and so too says to-day, Tulsi, the beloved of Hari." Aranya, (2) 6.

When Sita insisted on going to the forest with her husband, she said that life without him would make heaven a hell. " Without you, oh lord of my life, there is in the whole world nothing that can give me any kind of joy. Life without a body, a river without water, so is a woman without her lord." Ayodh. (63) 65.

Woman, when she is submissive and obedient, is happy. But she possesses a dangerous and destructive power. In particular a woman's guile is dealt with at length in the story of the hunchback and Kaikeyi.

> "A woman's character is like the sea, without a bottom." Ayodh. (26) 27.
>
> "The poets have spoken truly of the disposition of women in every respect incomprehensible, unfathomable, secretive. You may catch your shadow in a glass, but you cannot comprehend the ways of a woman. . . . What can fire not burn ? What can the sea not contain ? What is a weak woman not strong enough to do ?" Ayodh. (46) 47.

Illustration has already been given of the calamities that befel the Iron Age when husbands were in subjection to their wives. And that may be the reason why the poet says :

> "The man who can give up women has to be destitute of affection, an ascetic free from passion and strong-minded." Uttar, 179 (112) 194.

Tulsidas's own personal experience may have coloured his testimony. But it is, to say the least of it, unfortunate that he should have placed on the lips of Rama the excuses which his hero gives to Narad for preventing that holy man's marriage, and carrying off his phantom bride. It is recorded in the Forest book that Narad met Rama and said, "When you put forth your Maya and infatuated me, I was eager to arrange my marriage. Why did you not allow it ?" Aranya, 69 (37) 55. Rama explained that he was like a mother who would save her child from a snake or from fire, and then went on to declare :

> "Lust, anger, greed, pride and other passions form the mighty torrent of delusion (*moh*), but the most terrible of these, and the cause of greatest pain, is woman. She is the embodiment of illusion (*maya*). . . . Woman is the very root of wickedness, the cause of bitter pain, a mine of all suffering." Aranya, 71 (38) 56.

A little earlier he says to Lakshman :

"There are three very powerful evils. Lust, anger and greed. In a moment they will distress the minds of the wisest saints. The power of greed is in desire and pride, of lust nothing but a woman. The power of anger is in bitter words." Aranya, 64 (33) 48.

It has to be remembered that when he spoke in this fashion, Rama was searching anxiously for the lost Sita. He was not himself, and as if in excuse for his own extravagant speech, observes to his brother :

"The god of love, finding me in a maze due to separation (from Sita), devoid of strength and alone, has come near me. . . . Seeing me with my brother only, he has surrounded me with his army. Oh Lakshman, they who can see Love's army and remain steadfast, are worthy of remark. His one great strength is woman. The man who can escape from her is a very great warrior." Aranya, 64 (32) 46.

The word *kam*, which we have translated by sexual desire or lust, and which is also applied to *Kamdev*, the god of love, means just what we have rendered it. There is a higher and better word for love, *prem*. But here the poet is giving life as he himself had seen it, and yet with a mind devoid of prurience. Why he should have chosen this occasion for doing so, it is difficult to say. For the time being he was obsessed with the subject. And he closes the Aranya Kand with the warning :

"A young woman is like the flame of a candle. Do not let your soul be like the moth. Abandon sexual desire and intoxication. Worship Rama and always associate with good men." 75 (41) 60.

In concluding our study of these very inconsistent passages concerning women, reference must be made to

Rama's peculiar conduct when he feared his brother was going to die. In the greatness of his apprehension, he said :

> "If a stupid god (*daiv*) keep me alive, how can I go to Avadh and show my face after losing a beloved brother for the sake of a woman ? It would have been better to endure disgrace in the eyes of the world. The loss of a wife is no great loss." Lanka, 73 (58) 82.

XII.

THE POEM'S CONTRIBUTION TO THE RELIGIOUS THOUGHT AND LIFE OF INDIA.

REFERENCE has been made to the fact that Ramanuja did not stand alone when he attacked the doctrine of monism as expounded by Shankaracharya. There were others also who sought to confute the doctrine of Maya and establish the doctrine of *bhakti*, or love and devotion, on a secure basis. There was *Madhva*, whose system was frankly dualistic (*dvaita*), as he taught that there are five eternal distinctions between (*a*) God and the individual soul, (*b*) God and inanimate matter, (*c*) the individual soul and inanimate matter, (*d*) one individual soul and another, (*e*) one particle of matter and another; and there was *Nimbarka*, whose system was a dualistic monism (*dvait-advaita*), for he held that the inanimate world and the individual soul, while distinct from God, are as much one with Him as its coils are with a snake, or as waves are with water.[1] As has been said, these doctrines spread to Northern India, and by the time of the Middle Ages there were in existence, to use the arresting phrase of Sir George Grierson, *four Churches of the Reformation*, all of them more or less proclaiming the doctrine of *bhakti* and

[1] Bhandarkar, p. 57 and p. 62, on *Madhva* and *Nimbarka*. See also Grierson's article, " Bhakti-marga," *E.R.E.* There was a fourth system (*shuddh-advaita*), taught by *Vishnuswami*, whose views were developed by *Vallabha* on unhealthy lines, devotion being concentrated on *Radha*, the concubine of Krishna.

their belief in a personal God. Of these four Churches, far and away the most influential was that which inherited the teaching and traditions of Ramanuja. The inspirer of the movement has indeed become a somewhat legendary figure, for he has been declared to be an incarnation of the great serpent Shesh, and his image stands in many of the temples dedicated to Vishnu. To-day this sect, if it can be called a sect, bears the name of Shri Sampradaya,[1] or the system taught by Shri, the assumption being that the goddess Lakshmi communicated its tenets to the world. This system, however, looks to Ramanand and not to Ramanuja as its founder, and it is from the Ramavats or the Ramanandis, as they are more usually spoken of, that the most permeating and reforming influences have flowed, while their vigour has been revealed in the variety of other schools which have broken away from the parent stem and established themselves in various parts of the country.

Very little is known of the life and peculiar teaching of Ramanand. According to tradition, on one occasion when he returned to the headquarters of the Ramanuja sect from his wanderings somewhere in India, he was disciplined by his brethren on the ground that during his travels he could not have eaten his food with the privacy which their views demanded. Ramanand protested against such narrow opinions, and founded a sect of his own. He gave to his followers the name of *Avadhuta*, or the liberated ones; and liberated they must indeed have been, because his twelve disciples included a weaver, a leather worker, a barber, a woman and the revolutionary preacher Kabir.[2] Grierson quotes a saying of Ramanand's:

> "Let no one ask a man's caste, or with whom he eats.
> If a man show love to Hari, he is Hari's own."

[1] Sampradaya means *tradition*—something that has been given.

[2] See Wilson's *Religious Sects of the Hindus*, vol. i. p. 46.

But probably Ramanand's greatest service to India was his insistence on the worship of Rama and Sita. The other three Churches of the Reformation had a preference for Radha and Krishna—a preference which was destined to have an evil effect on the character of their worshippers. Tulsidas is usually spoken of as a Ramanandi, and certainly his sympathies were with them rather than with any other. But his quarrel with the Vishnava Vairagis at Ayodhya, and his transference to Benares, may have influenced his outlook. And it is with real passion that he writes in the Aranya Kand, 59 (30) 44:

> "Oh men, abandon all your various rites which are unrighteousness, and your many sects which create sorrow, and put your faith (*bishwas*) and love on Rama's feet."

Because whatever else Tulsidas may have been, he remains an orthodox Hindu. It is said that the early reformers were persecuted in Southern India by the followers of Shiva, while it is true that some of the Ramanandis at least have spoken disapprovingly of the worship of Shiva. But orthodox Hinduism cannot find fault with Tulsidas. He may proclaim more than some of his co-religionists relish, the need for repentance and faith in God. But he produces chapter and verse for everything he puts forward. He seeks to buttress all his doctrines by the very frequent assertion, "Thus do Ved and Puran declare." And as for everything else, he believes, as his countrymen believe, in all the gods, as well as in Brahma, Vishnu and Shiva. Vishnu, no doubt, is his *isht devta*, the god who is the object of his special worship; but he refuses adoration to none of the others, even when he is unable to refrain from saying what he thinks of some of them. It is true that he identifies Vishnu with the Supreme Soul of the universe, but when he does that, he does what others had been doing for centuries. In the sectarian Puranas it depended on the personal views of the writer whether Vishnu or Shiva would receive that honour. But in a compilation like the *Mahabharata*, both gods are recognised in turn, and for each of them supremacy is claimed. It is no exaggeration to say that Tulsidas accepts the whole mythology of Hinduism. He has no quarrel with any of its religious beliefs and practices. He believes in the myths and legends as to the creation of the world, the Sea of Milk, the churning of the Ocean, and the mind-born sons of Brahma. He writes with glee about the famous sacrifice of Daksh, the marriage of Shiva and the discomfiture of Parashuram, while a hundred other references, made sometimes in the briefest way, show that his memory was stored with the facts and fancies of his ancestral faith. He believes in the miraculous powers attached to certain holy places, such as Benares, and the benefits that accrue from bathing in the Ganges and other sacred rivers. He believes in Transmigration and in Karma. He believes in the wonderful results that can be achieved by the practice of penance, and he does his best to inspire in his readers a fearful reverence for Brahmins by dwelling over and over again on the amazing potency of a Brahmin's curse.

Tulsidas himself belonged to the Brahmin caste. But it has to be noted that he was a *Smarta* as well. All the authorities are at one in making that statement with regard to the poet. And whatever the name may have meant originally, it came to be applied to those who recognised and gave a combined worship to five particular gods. These are Vishnu, Shiva, Durga, Ganesh and the Sun.[1] The fact that special worship is directed to these five does not exclude the worship of the others. Should a man find any of them useful he is entitled to invoke their

[1] It will be remembered that Durga and Ganesh are the wife and son of Shiva.

assistance. And there is no reason why any of them should be excluded. Brahm may be the one Supreme Reality. He may be the only real, while all else is a dream. But gods, demons and men have, even in the system of Shankara, a provisional existence, and the followers of Shankara worship the gods as well as those who do not profess to be philosophers.[1]

As there are so many references to four of these five gods throughout the poem, and Shiva with his wife and son are so constantly worshipped at the present day by followers of Vishnu, it is desirable to inquire what led to these five being chosen to represent the whole pantheon.[2] A Brahmin pundit of the writer's acquaintance, standing before the little alcove in which they stood,[3] offered this explanation, which may be accepted as correct. Vishnu and Shiva represent the Triad, from which Brahma is excluded either because his reputation or his popularity suffered. Durga, the wife of Shiva, is chosen, because she represents *Maya* or, it may be, the *param shakti* of the gods. Ganesh has found a place because he has been associated pre-eminently with the granting of boons, and it is for boons that men pray ; while the Sun conveys the thought of the diffusiveness of deity and that God may be worshipped in any form.

[1] It is interesting to note what Farquhar tells us in this connection. He says that many Smartas believe that Shankara himself was the organising genius who imposed the rule, and he adds that many Smartas are followers of Shankara. *Outlines of Religious Literature of India*, p. 179.

[2] We read only once of prayer being addressed jointly to Vishnu, Shiva, Gauri, Ganesh and the Sun. Ayodh. 262 (262) 273.

[3] The five gods are usually represented by small idols placed on a tray in a recess in a Smarta's own house. Vishnu is represented by one or more salagram stones ; Shiva by one or more linga ; Durga, Ganesh and the Sun by images. Sometimes the Sun is not represented. Once I called attention to the Sun's absence. The worshipper took me out to the courtyard and pointing upward said, " It is not necessary. He is there."

It is sometimes suggested that the worship which Tulsidas accords to Brahma, Shiva and the lesser gods may be looked upon as akin to the adoration which is given to the saints of the Roman Catholic calendar. It is difficult to accept that interpretation, and even with regard to the lesser gods there is no reason why we should. In the Hindu scheme of things it is quite easy to define their position. They, as well as beasts and men, are ever revolving on the wheel of existence, waiting for release; the soul that has inhabited a man may in another transmigration be either a beast or a god. As for Brahma, Vishnu and Shiva, it is somewhat different. Their origin was otherwise; it is through them that the Supreme Spirit creates, preserves and destroys the world. But here also the explanation which the Hindu offers is not lacking in plausibility—at least so long as no one attempts to identify any of them with the Supreme God. That Tulsidas claims that rank for Vishnu is plain on every page of his poem. He goes, however, farther than that, and in his affection for Shiva and for his wife allows himself or some of his characters to use language in describing them which can belong to God alone :

"Oh god of all things, my lord Purari, the three worlds are full of thy glory. What moves and what does not move, serpents, men, gods, all worship thy lotus feet." Bal. 116 (114) 130.

"You, who are Maya and Shiva the adorable, are the father and mother of the whole universe." Bal. 93 (91) 105.

"Parvati is the mother of the world, the unborn, without beginning, the indestructible Shakti, the eternal half of Shiva ; she is the creator, the preserver and the destroyer of the world." Bal. 121 (105) 137.

"I worship Him who is endowed with superhuman

qualities, the embodiment of nirvana, the omnipresent, all-pervading Brahm, the manifestation of the Veda, the unborn Nirgun." Uttar, 157 (104) 172.

" He who does not love Shiva's lotus feet will not see Rama even in a dream. The mark by which to recognise a devotee of Rama is love unfeigned for the feet of the lord of all things." Bal. 113 (111) 127.

But the language which Rama himself uses with reference to Shiva is overwhelmingly convincing. It shows better than any other part of the poem what were the poet's own feelings. Rama is represented time after time as addressing his prayers to Shiva, but nowhere or with so much devotion as when he stood looking across to Lanka.

" When the All-merciful saw the very beautifully constructed bridge he smiled and said, ' This is a very fine and charming place. Its immeasurable glory no one can describe. Here I shall set up a Shiva. My heart desires it greatly.' Hearing this, the monkey king sent many messengers to summon and bring the great saints. Having set up the linga (the phallic emblem) according to the proper rites, he worshipped it, saying, ' There is no one I love like Shiva. If any one be called my servant and do violence to Shiva, that man even in a dream cannot be loved by me. If any one hostile to Shiva desires to be my devotee, he is a fool, with little intelligence, and hell is his portion. Lovers of Shiva who are enemies of mine, servants of mine who are enemies of Shiva, these men will dwell in a fearful hell for the period of a Kalpa.' " Lanka, 2 (2) 4.

It is almost impossible for the Western mind to comprehend such an attitude. Tulsidas, explain it how we will, has room for all the gods in his scheme of the universe. But, what is much more wonderful, he does not find it impossible to place Shiva and his wife side by side with

Rama and Sita in his worship and in his thoughts. We have here no real theism as the Western mind thinks of theism, and it is worth our while recalling the words of Bhandarkar who is acquainted with the outlook of his own people :

> "In the monotheistic religions of other countries the same god is feared and loved ; in India the god that is loved is Vishnu . . . while the god that is feared is Shiva."

Tulsidas then holds firmly to the whole system of Hinduism. He will not part even with Shiva in the interests of monotheism. If he was a reformer, he was a reformer from within. He enters no protest against idolatry, as Namdev and Kabir did. And he can have had no sympathy with the latter in his often quoted utterance :

> "The rosary is wood, the gods are stone :
> The Ganges and Jumna are water :
> Rama and Krishna are dead :
> The four Vedas are made-up stories."

Nor will it be denied that it was because Tulsidas remained within the fold of Hinduism, and did not even seek to form a sect, that he exercises so great an influence and remains so popular. He says nothing which can offend any of his hearers. He provokes no opposition. He calls forth no criticism, except from the apostles of monism, and they are so satisfied with the superiority of the path of knowledge by which they travel, that they can afford to ignore the advocates of *bhakti*. In any case, if *bhakti* is for the million, knowledge is for the choice, and the choice are always few.

While succeeding so wonderfully in conciliating opposition, and it is not suggested that Tulsidas at any time said what he did not believe, the poet has achieved his one great purpose. He has captured, in large measure, the common mind of Northern India and made it listen to his plea, that love for God is the chief end of man.

Another illustration of the way in which Tulsidas accommodates himself to the common mind of India is his attitude to the doctrine of Maya. It would be incorrect to say that either the poet or the average Hindu is an adherent of the school of monism. But the language of monism is often employed by both the poet and the ordinary man when they are impressed by the mystery of life and seek to solve its problems. The situation could not be better expressed than in the words of Farquhar, already quoted, with regard to Ramanand:

> "One of the characteristics of the whole movement that springs from him is a constant use of advaita phrases, a clinging to advaita concepts, while holding fast to the personality of Rama."

This statement can be applied with truth to Tulsidas—an opinion in which we are confirmed by Bhandarkar, who says that the poet's teaching is "based upon a dualistic philosophy, with a leaning towards the monism of the advaita system."

As the poet's teaching with regard to Maya is of the very greatest importance and colours his whole outlook, it will be necessary to examine afresh the references he makes to it throughout the poem. This procedure will involve a considerable amount of repetition. But no other course is possible, if we are to arrive at an impartial judgment.[1]

And first let us take those which speak of Maya as

[1] Sir George Grierson thinks that the references to Maya which hide Brahm from the soul are no part of the poet's real teaching. He holds that they are similes only, a use born of his association with the worship of Shiva, and that elsewhere Maya is merely magic used by the demons against Rama, or it represents a combination of the Gnostic Demiurge and the Christian Tempter. See his article in *E.R.E.* on "Tulsidas."

employed by the demons, a Maya which is akin to magic; though it must be noted that in all such cases Maya produces an illusory form which those who witness it imagine to be real. Of Ravan's son Megnad, we read that he entered his chariot made of Maya, and rose up into the air. Lanka, 84 (69) 94. The rocks and trees which the monkeys hurled at him were by the power of his Maya changed into wire cages.[1] Eventually he engaged in battle with Rama himself. On this occasion the arrows which the demon discharged at the hero changed into snakes, which wound themselves round the body of Rama, and brought him under their control. When they saw what had happened, the gods were filled with terror, but they need not have been alarmed.

> "He who is self-controlled, the eternal, the one, the unchangeable, who like an actor performs many kinds of deceit (*kapat*), it was to add glory to the field of battle that the Lord caused himself to be bound."

It is in connection with this mysterious incident that the poet indulges in one of his finest outbursts.

> "Can he, by the repetition of whose name holy men cut the bonds of existence, come into bondage to any one, the all-pervading Lord, the dwelling-place of all things?"
>
> "Human intelligence, strength and speech cannot expound the actions of Sagun-Ram. Realising this, those ascetics who are wise abandon all explanations and worship Rama."

The situation created, however, was so serious that it was necessary to send for Garud, the vehicle of Vishnu and the

[1] See also Bal. 187 (185) 211; Bal. 190 (196) 213, where the demons assumed many forms and knew all kinds of Maya; and Lanka, 69 (55) 77, where a demon erected a temple, garden and reservoir for himself by means of Maya.

great enemy of the snake race. Garud seized and ate up the serpents which had been fashioned by Maya, with the result that Maya disappeared. It will be remembered that Garud was so perplexed by this apparent defect in Rama that he sought for advice and comfort from both Brahma and Shiva. His doubts were only removed by the inspired crow.

Somewhat earlier in the battle, also, we read that Ravan's son exercised his Maya in the presence of him whose powerful Maya controls Shiva and Brahma, great and small. On this occasion the demon was able to pour down stones, ashes, filth, blood, bones and hair, while the air was filled with awful cries. The monkeys were terrified and said, " Every one of us will perish." But Rama was not deceived. He recognised that it was a play and nothing more, and " with one arrow he destroyed all the *maya*." Lanka, 64 (50) 72.

As for Ravan himself, when all his followers had been destroyed, he said :

> " I am alone, the monkeys and bears are many. I must exert unlimited Maya." Lanka, 104 (84) 113.

It was shown chiefly by the production of large numbers of Ramas and Lakshmans whose presence in every part of the field perplexed and confused the monkeys. Rama, of course, saw through the Maya, but every one else thought that it was real.

> " The lord of Koshal smiled to see his army in amazement. He fitted an arrow to his bow and in a moment he destroyed the Maya, and all the monkeys were glad."

The next deception in which Ravan indulged was to multiply not them but himself. And we are told that he made use of magic (*pakhand*).

> " In a moment he made himself invisible ; again the

> wretch revealed himself in countless forms. For every bear and monkey in Rama's army there was a Ravan manifested. Seeing these innumerable Ravans, the monkeys and bears fled in terror."

The gods also took refuge in flight, saying :

> " 'We may now abandon all hope of victory, brothers. A single Ravan conquered all the gods ; now there are many. Seek for caves in the mountains.' Only Brahma, Shiva and learned saints who know something of the Lord's glory remained." Lanka, 111 (92) 120.

Once more we are told that Rama smiled when he saw the gods in a panic.

> " In a moment the Lord destroyed all the Maya, even as darkness is dispelled at the rising of the sun."

In the long-drawn-out description of the battle with the demons, we read that Ravan a second time found it necessary to make himself invisible and then exert his Maya :

> " Seeing the great power of the monkeys, Ravan, after reflection, disappeared from view, and in a moment displayed Maya." Lanka, 116 (97) 125.

In the description which follows we are told that by means of this magic (*pakhand*) Ravan produced a great variety of evil spirits, goblins and witches, with bows and arrows, swords and skulls, the last filled with blood which the horrid creatures drank. Not content with these alarming portents which put the monkeys to flight, Ravan produced another form of magic, this time described as *kapat* or deceit, in which Hanuman was multiplied many times. These reduplicated Hanumans, with tails upraised, surrounded Rama, shouting, " Kill him, seize him, do not let him go." Once more we are told that Rama " destroyed the Maya with a single arrow."

In all these passages, whether we call the power which the demons exercised Maya or magic, it produces the same result. Something that is unreal is called into temporary existence, and assumes an appearance of reality. Is this not what the Vedantists say has happened on the grand scale, when Brahm and Maya, in association, are jointly responsible for the world around us ?[1]

There are a few illustrations of Maya being employed by men. Thus we read of a hermit, who had in former days been a king, using his Maya to bring destruction on an ancient enemy. Bal. 174 (172) 168. By means of his Maya he deprives his enemy's family priest of his intelligence ; and finally prepares a death-dealing dish that is formed of illusion (*maya*).

The lesser gods, also, were able to exercise Maya. We are told that Kaikeyi, being in the grip of the Maya of the gods, believed an enemy to be a friend, Ayodh. 17 ; and that the people of Ayodhya, tired out with sorrow and labour, fell asleep, the Maya of the gods deluding them somewhat. Ayodh. 82. Indra, as we should expect, uses this power in the most malignant fashion :

> " The king of the gods is the limit in deceitfulness and evil conduct. He loves to see another suffer and himself to prosper. His methods are like the methods of a crow. He is cunning and vile and believes in nobody. First he planned an evil thought and gathered deceptions (*kapat*) which he placed a sorrowful heap on the heads of all. Every one was deluded by the Maya of the god . . . with the exception of Bharat, Janak, the saints,

[1] In Aranya, 41 (22) 35, the demon changes himself into the form of a deer, which is called *Maya-mrig*, the " mimic deer." This was the deer that attracted Sita. In Uttar Kand, (66) 91, the Sita carried off by Ravan is called *Maya Sita*, because she was only a shadow of the real Sita. See also Bal. 187 (185) 211 ; Bal. 190 (196) 213 ; Lanka, 69 (55) 77 ; Sundar, 2.

> the ministers and those who were circumspect and wise. The Maya of the god affected all." Ayodh. 290 (290) 303.

It was at the instigation of Indra, jealous and afraid of Narad's ascetic power, that the god of Love tried to lead that holy man astray. While Narad was tempted by the voluptuous dances and songs of the heavenly nymphs, Love by means of his own Maya produced an unseasonable spring, with birds singing, bees humming and flowers in bloom. Bal. 134 (132) 153.

Narad's pride at being able to resist the efforts of Love led to his ultimate downfall. Because when he went to the Sea of Milk and boasted of what he had done in the presence of Vishnu, that greater deity resolved to exercise his own much greater Maya and tame his votary's pride.

> "The Maya of Raghupati is very powerful. Who is there alive whom it has not deluded (*moh*)?" Bal. 136 (134) 155.

Vishnu gave orders to his own Maya, with the result that there came into temporary existence a huge city, seven hundred miles in circumference, more beautiful than Vishnu's own capital, inhabited by very handsome men and women, with a king whose splendour exceeded that of an hundred Indras, and endowed with great power, glory and wisdom. Best of all, the king had a daughter of incomparable beauty, for whose hand Narad ventured to be a candidate. Of this princess it is said that she was a treasure-house of every good quality—thanks to the Maya of Hari. When Narad saw the princess he asked Vishnu to make him beautiful so that he might have some hope of winning her. As we know, the god gave him an ambiguous answer and the face of a monkey.

> "When the god who is compassionate to the humble saw the wide-spreading power of his Maya, he smiled

and said : ' Listen, Narad, I shall so act that your highest good will result." Bal. 138 (140) 158.

The saint had become so stupid, being in the power of Maya, that he did not understand the hidden meaning of Vishnu's words. When Narad found himself cruelly deceived, he was met by Vishnu, along with Lakshmi and the fictitious princess. And being in the power of Maya, he cursed the deity to be born as a man, to have monkeys for his companions and to lose his wife.

> " The Sea of Mercy then drew back the power of his Maya. When Hari removed his Maya neither Lakshmi nor the princess was there."

When Shiva had finished his account of this amazing incident which scarcely reflects credit on Vishnu, he said to Uma :

> " I have told you this story to show how Hari's Maya can delude men both holy and wise. . . . The Lord is playful, a well-wisher to those devoted to him ; easily reached by his servants ; the remover of all sorrow. There is not a god, or man or saint whom his powerful Maya has not deluded. Consider this in your mind and worship the mighty lord of Maya." Bal. 148 (146) 167.

When Vishnu became incarnate and was searching everywhere for Sita, Narad met him. Remembering how it was his curse that had really robbed the divine Rama of his wife, he ventured to ask :

> " When you gave commands to your Maya, and caused it to delude me, then I wished to arrange my marriage ; what was the reason why you did not let me do it ? "

To this question the prince replied :

> " Lust, anger, greed, pride and other passions form the mighty torrent of delusion (*moh*). Of these the most

terrifying and painful is woman, the embodiment of Maya." Aranya, 71 (38) 56.

The poet often used the word *moh* (delusion) in this connection. Time after time he tells us how Maya has deluded some one. Nor is there any doubt that Maya sometimes should be translated by infatuation, trickery or deceit, the purpose of the context being manifestly ethical, as in the following extracts :

"Oh Raghuraya, dwell in the hearts of those in whom there is no lust, anger, pride, arrogance, delusion (*moh*), greed, agitation, desire, violence, deceit, heresy, illusion (*maya*)." Ayodh. (124) 130.

"Anger, lust, greed, pride, Maya, they all disappear by the mercy of Rama." Aranya, 64 (33) 48.

"Abandon Maya and think of the other world." Kish. 27 (22) 25.

"The glamour of delusion (*moh*) is very powerful. The poets truly describe a woman's disposition. In their hearts there are always eight defects : Lack of foresight, falsehood, fickleness, Maya, fear, want of judgment, impurity and mercilessness." Lanka, 20 (16) 21.

When Tulsidas uses the word in this connection, he is thinking of the delusions, errors, blunders and follies to which men and women are subject, when, like people of other lands, they allow themselves to be blinded by the power of sin in any of its forms. But though he very often dwells on the infatuation of evil thoughts and desires, it is very remarkable that it is only in these four passages that he uses the word Maya with this signification in the first six books of the poem.[1]

[1] There are two other passages, however, which should not be forgotten : It is said of Narad that he had neither *moh* nor *maya* (Bal) 106 (104) 120), a statement difficult to accept in view of what happened

In the last book (Uttar Kand) we shall see how it is allied more closely with the poet's own special interpretation of life.

Before we deal with the many references to Maya in its relation to Rama, as the incarnation of the Supreme Spirit, reference must be made to the few occasions when Maya is associated with Brahma, Shiva and the Triad. Attention has already been called, at page 213, to the statement that the wife of Shiva is identified with Maya and Shakti, in language similar to what is used regarding Sita. As for Shiva, we read in the language of one of his worshippers :

> "In the grasp of thy Maya, foolish people continue to wander foolishly. Oh Lord Bhagwan, oh sea of mercy, be not angry with them." Uttar, 159 (105) 174.

There is one reference only to the Triad being associated with Maya :

> "The Maya of Vidhi, Hari and Hara is very powerful, but it cannot comprehend the mind of Bharat." Ayodhya, 283 (283) 295.

The statement about Brahma is quite incomprehensible, and cannot be reconciled with the rest of the poet's teaching:

> "Vidhi has created all things, both good and bad, pain and pleasure, sin and merit, day and night, demons and gods, high and low, amrit and life, poison and death, Maya and Brahm, the individual soul and the god of the world." Bal. 6 (6) 11.

Returning to Maya in its relation to Rama, the most exalted position it receives is when it is identified with Sita and the *param shakti* of the god. This is done on no less

when he was anxious to secure the hand of the princess. When Rama was asked to give an account of the virtues that marked a saint, he spoke of prayer, penance, religious observances, self-control, devotion to one's guru, Govind and Brahm, faith, forgiveness, friendship, mercy, a love for my feet and an absence of *maya*. Aranya, 73 (40) 58.

than three occasions. When the Supreme Spirit appeared to Manu and gave him the boon he craved, he said :

> "Assuming a form of my own accord, I shall be manifest in your house, . . . and this my Maya, the *primal energy* by which the world is created, will also descend." Bal. 157 (155) 179.

Valmiki, when he met Rama and Sita in the forest, said :

> "Rama, you are the guardian of the bridge of revelation, you are the lord of the world. And Sita is Maya who, in accordance with your will, creates, preserves and destroys the world. . . . Life is a play and you are its beholder. You make Brahma, Vishnu and Shiva to dance ; even they do not know your secret." Ayodh. 121 (121) 126.

Again we are told that when attending to the wants of her mothers-in-law, Sita assumed as many forms as she had mothers-in-law, and it is added :

> "Nobody noticed the mystery except Rama. All Maya is in Sita, who is Maya." Ayodh. 241 (241) 252.

These three statements use the very language of monism, and it is difficult to see how any one of them can be compared to a simile, though such similes do sometimes occur. Thus we read that as the three exiles walked along the forest paths, Rama went in front, Sita was in the middle and Lakshman brought up the rear :

> "Sita shone between the two, like Maya, linking Brahm and the individual soul." Ayodh. 118 (118) 123.

This comparison is repeated in practically the same words in the Aranyakand. (3) 10.[1]

[1] An illustration of the use of Maya as a simile and nothing more, will be found in Aranya, 65 (34) 50, where we read that the water of a lake could not be seen because it was covered so completely with lotuses, just as no one can see Brahm because He is overspread by

That Maya and, by implication, Sita is the Creator of all things is frequently asserted :

> " In obedience to his command, Maya creates a multitude of worlds in the twinkling of an eye." Bal. 230 (236) 257.
>
> " Air, wind, fire, water and earth, Maya has brought them into existence in obedience to thy command for the purposes of creation." Sundar, 62 (58) 61.
>
> " Life in all its varied forms, both what moves and what does not move " (says Rama), " is all created by my Maya. Uttar, 127 (85) 126.
>
> " By his power, Maya creates the multitude of worlds ; by his power Brahma, Vishnu and Shiva preserve, create and destroy them." Sundar, 20.
>
> " In every hair of Rama's body, there is a multitude of worlds, fashioned by Maya." Bal. 197 (203) 223.
>
> " Maya has brought all life, both what moves and what does not move, under its control." Bal. 205 (122) 231.

The poet, however, finds it necessary to insist that this *Maya* which is so powerful and brings everything under its control, is subordinate to Rama and afraid of him :

> " Maya is afraid of the Lord. He causes her to dance by the play of his eyebrows." Bal. 205 (211) 231.
>
> " Brahma, Vishnu, Shiva, the moon, the sun, the guardians of the spheres, Maya, life, Karma and this evil age, the great serpent, the kings of the earth, and what lordships there may be . . . consider it in your mind

Maya. Another simile occurs at Kish. 17 (13) 15 : " The water falling on the earth becomes dirty, like the soul when involved in Maya." Note also the interesting passage where the body of Rama is described in the terminology of the Sankhya philosophy : " *His smile is Maya.*" Lanka, 18 (15) 20. See, too, the statement about the creeper at p. 154. The creeper is Maya.

and reflect well upon it, the will of Rama is on the heads of all." Ayodh. (243) 254.

"The all-pervading Brahm, the supreme God, is beyond the influence of Moh and Maya." Uttar, 80 (58) 81.

"I worship under his name Rama, the god Hari, in the power of whose Maya is the whole creation, Brahma, gods and demons." Bal. invocation.

It was necessary to insist on this, because in his incarnation Rama seemed so often to act like an ordinary man. He is therefore declared to be beyond the influence of Maya, while he is repeatedly addressed as the lord of Maya.

"Hail! Hail to him who cannot be destroyed, who dwells in all hearts, the all-pervading highest joy, exempt from Maya . . . who created the three worlds, without the assistance of any other." Bal. 191 (197) 217.

"With joined hands Rama's mother said: 'How shall I sing thy praise, eternal one? Vedas, Puranas declare thee to be incomprehensible, beyond Maya, the three qualities and knowledge.'" Bal. 197 (203) 223.

"For the sake of Brahmins, cows, gods and saints you descended in human form in a body fashioned according to your own pleasure beyond the influence of Maya, the qualities and the perception of the senses." Bal. 198 (204) 224.

"I worship Rama, the storehouse of the qualities, the unconquered, Nirgun, the unchangeable, free from Maya, the god of gods." Lanka invocation.

"He who is Sachchidanand, beyond knowledge, speech and perception, the unborn, beyond the influence of Maya, the mind and the qualities, manifested his unrivalled deeds." Uttar, 47 (26) 48.

"Hari's Maya has deluded saints and sages. The

Lord is playful, helpful to his devotees, easy of access to his servants, the remover of all sorrow. Gods, men, saints, there is not one of them whom powerful Maya has not deluded. Reflect upon this in your mind and worship the great lord of Maya." Bal. 148 (146) 167.

"If you practise Maya on a servant of the lord of Maya, it will recoil upon yourself." Ayodh. 209 (209) 218.

"Seeing that gods and saints were afraid, He who is the lord of Maya performed a mighty diversion." Aranya, 31 (15) 25.

"So saying, the demon went and by means of Maya made by the wayside a temple, a lake and a garden. When he saw the beautiful place, the Wind god's son thought, 'I shall ask the sage's permission, drink of the water and take rest': because the demon had assumed a false dress. He wished to delude the servant of the lord of Maya." Lanka, 69 (55) 77.

"There again I saw Rama, the wise, the merciful Bhagwan, the lord of Maya. I reflected on the matter time after time. My mind was enveloped with delusion (*moh*) and confusion." Uttar, 119 (81) 122.

Illustrations have already been given of how Rama exercised his Maya against the demons, and of his intervention in the case of Narad, prior to his incarnation. There are several examples of how he treated Uma, his own mother and others, which cannot be ignored. It will be remembered how Shiva and Uma met Rama searching for his lost wife. Shiva at once began a hymn of praise, in which he spoke of Rama as the Supreme God. This, Uma could not understand. If He was the Supreme God, how could He have lost his wife ?

"Recognising the strength of Hari's Maya, Shiva said, 'Since there is so much doubt in your mind, go and put him to the test.'" Bal. 63 (61) 74.

The test she applied was to assume the form of Sita and stand before him. But it was not possible to deceive Rama.

> " The master of the gods saw through the deceit, he who sees all things and knows the heart, the remembrance of whom dispels ignorance, the all-knowing Rama, Bhagwan, even him Uma sought to deceive—thus you can judge the pertinacity of a woman's nature. But recognising the power of his Maya, Rama smiled and said : Where is Mahadev ? " Bal. 64 (62) 75.

Rama graciously revealed his divine form and removed Uma's doubts. But when she went back to her husband, she had not the courage to confess that she had assumed Sita's form. Indeed she told a lie and said she had applied no test at all.

> " Then Shankar saw by means of profound contemplation what Uma had done. He bowed his head to Hari's Maya which had been sent to make Uma tell a lie." Bal. 67 (65) 78.

The same idea of being misled by Rama is repeated by Shiva a few stanzas farther on. When speaking of heretics, he says :

> " They cannot distinguish between Agun and Sagun Brahm. They babble a variety of meaningless words, and in the grip of Hari's Maya go astray in the world." Bal. 124 (122) 138.

This Maya may also be playfully and lovingly exerted. And of this we have a most interesting illustration in the way Rama as a little child bewildered his mother. A full account of that incident has been given in the relevant chapter at page 100. Here it is enough to note that when Rama had shown to his mother his entire marvellous form, with hundreds of millions of worlds in every single hair:

> "As she looked at this Maya, very incomprehensible in every way, she stood with joined hands and very afraid. She saw that which causes life to dance, she saw the devotion which sets it free." Ayodh. (212) 221.

Rama told his mother not to mention what he had done to any one. But she replied:

> "And do you, oh Lord, never again pervade me with your Maya."

On the first occasion that Hanuman met Rama, he thought he was a man like other men, and apologised for his blunder by saying:

> "In the grip of your Maya, I wandered astray, and for that reason did not recognise the Lord." Kish. (1) 3.

And then he added:

> "The soul (*jiv*) is deluded by your Maya, but afterwards by your affection it obtains freedom."[1]

The passages which have been already quoted show how strong a hold the doctrine of Maya had secured over the poet's mind. Numerous and convincing as they are they must, however, yield in importance to those which have yet to be examined. Because one feels that Tulsidas from time to time realises, and with varying degrees of intensity, that a belief in Maya endangers not only the personality of Rama, but the whole doctrine of *bhakti*. Indeed, it is apparent, as the poem approaches a close, that he realises that fact increasingly, and in the last book gives a direction and an emphasis to his teaching difficult to reconcile with

[1] **For other similar references to Maya, see Kish. 9 (6) 8; 15 (10) 12; and 25 (20) 23, quoted at pp. 136 and 138; also Sundar, 12, where Sita says, "Who can conquer the unconquerable Rama? Such a ring cannot be fashioned by Maya."**

what he has often elsewhere said. Yet even there he makes no attempt to confute the doctrine of Maya. He can only tell us how to evade its power. Maya exists. He does not attempt to deny its existence. But Rama also exists, and he is more powerful than Maya. The world may be a dream, but Rama is real. There is no illusion so far as he is concerned. The poet even dares to speak scoffingly sometimes of Maya's power. The man who puts his faith in Rama will find the ocean of existence no broader than a cow's step. Maya is a dancing girl, but Bhakti is Rama's bride. There were some, however, who had failed to appreciate Rama's greatness, "enemies of Hari, who did not know the difference between truth and falsehood." Of this we have an early and vigorous warning in the Bal Kand. When his wife wondered how Rama could possibly be God, Shiva replied :

> "Ignorant people do not recognise their own error : stupid souls attribute delusion (*moh*) to the Lord ; just as persons of no discernment, when they see clouds in the sky, say that the sun has become dim : or who look at the moon through their fingers, and two moons show themselves. Delusion affects Rama in the same degree that smoke and dust darken the sky. The objects of sense, the organs of sense, the gods, the individual soul, all more or less are possessed of intelligence. But the supreme enlightener of all is the eternal Rama, the Lord of Avadh. Whatever in the world is capable of being enlightened, Rama enlightens it. *He is the lord of Maya,* the dwelling-place of knowledge and virtue ; by his truth and with the help of delusion, *stupid Maya* appears as true. Just as in a shell there is a false appearance of silver, and through the rays of the sun a mirage appears, although these manifestations are false for all time, nevertheless no one can get free from the delusion

(*bhram*). In the same way the world is associated with Hari. The world is false (unreal); nevertheless it can cause pain, like a man whose head is cut off in a dream; until he awakes, the pain is there." Bal. 125 (123) 140.

Such an utterance does not take us very far, and it may be that the poet himself felt so. He is still dallying with the doctrine of Maya and the unreality of the world. So he takes refuge in the language of faith where he is more at home, and thus proceeds without a break, Shiva being still his mouthpiece:

" 'He by whose mercy such error is wiped out, is the merciful Raghurai, whose beginning and end no one can fathom, though the Vedas have hymned it to the best of their ability. Without feet he walks; he hears without ears; without hands he works in many ways. Without a mouth he can enjoy all tastes; without a voice he speaks with great power; without a body he touches; without eyes he sees; without a nose he smells. Thus his doings of every description are not of this world. His glory cannot be told. He, whom the Vedas and the enlightened sing, and on whom the saints meditate, is the son of Dashrath, the well-wisher of those devoted to him, the lord of Kosal, Bhagwan. By the power of his name I deliver from sorrow those whom I see dying at Kashi. He is my Lord; the master of all that moves and that does not move; Raghubir, who dwells within all hearts. By repeating his name a helpless man burns up the sins he committed in his various births, while those who repeat it with honour cross the sea of existence as if it were a cow's step. *Rama is the Supreme Spirit* (*Paramatma*). Your errors and the words you employed, Bhavani, were very improper. When such doubts come into the heart, knowledge, self-control, and virtue depart.' Listening to Shiva's error-destroying address, the whole fabric of her evil heresy disappeared; love and belief (*priti pratiti*) in Rama's feet arose; her grievous want of faith (*asambhavna*) passed away."

In the Aranya Kand we have a still more interesting passage, all the more interesting because it is manifestly intended as a specially serious attempt to show how *bhakti* rises superior to the practice of religious rites, asceticism and knowledge. Nevertheless it begins, more than any of the utterances we have examined, with the language of monism, and asserts the identity of the individual soul with God. Its value is still further enhanced by the fact that Rama himself is the speaker. It was the perplexity of Lakshman which afforded his brother the opportunity. One day when they were in the forest, Lakshman said:

"Explain to me knowledge (*gyan*), asceticism (*vairagya*) and *maya*. Show me what is that *bhakti* (devotion) to which you manifest your mercy. Tell me, Lord, and explain it all, the difference between God (*ishwar*) and the soul, by means of which arises love for your feet, and grief and error vanish." Aranya, 20 (10) 18.

This appeal may have been prompted by the declaration made a short time before by the rishi, Agastya:

"Listen, Bhagwan. Your Maya is a widespreading fig tree. The many multitudes of worlds are its fruit, while all things that have life are like the insects that dwell within the fruit." Aranya, 19 (9) 17.

In response to his brother's request, Rama made a long reply, which is given in full at page 126. Here it is sufficient to repeat the references to Maya:

"I and mine, thou and thine, are the product of Maya. Maya has brought the multiplicity of souls under its control. The senses and the objects of sense, as far as the mind can travel, are all Maya; understand that, brother. Soul is that which because of Maya does not know itself to be God (*ish*), the giver of bondage and liberation, who is over all, the sender forth of Maya, the goal." Aranya, 21 (11) 19.

Having spoken in this fashion, Rama, without any warning, turns his back on what he has said about knowledge, ignorance and Maya, and making a scale of values, religious practices, asceticism, knowledge and devotion, awards the palm to devotion.

"From the practice of religious rites, asceticism springs; from meditation (*yog*), knowledge; and knowledge, so the Vedas say, is the giver of salvation. But that by which I am quickly moved is devotion to me. It yields happiness to my devotees. . . . Both knowledge and ignorance are subordinate to it. *Devotion*, brother, *there is nothing to be compared to it, as a source of happiness*."

In the last book of the poem, which, as has been suggested, presents us with new features of the doctrine of Maya, Rama once more speaks at length. And the passage is peculiarly important because, though he continues to recognise the influence of Maya, he so tilts the balance, not only against Maya, but against knowledge, religious observances, fasts, vows, prayers and penance, that the path of devotion, *bhakti marg*, is seen to be by far the easiest and most pleasant road. Shortly before, when in converse with his brothers, he had spoken of Maya in the conventional way:

"Men in the grip of delusion (*moh*) commit many kinds of sin. In their selfishness they destroy (their chances in) the next world. In the form of Time I give to them the fruit of their deeds, good and bad. Those who are very wise, thus reflecting, worship me, recognising the pain of mundane existence. They abandon action (*karm*) which yields results, good and bad, and worship me, the lord of gods, men and saints. I have described the qualities of the good and the wicked. Those who remember will not fall into the ocean of existence. Listen, brothers, virtue and vice in their various forms are fashioned by Maya. The right thing to do is not to pay attention to either of them. To pay attention shows want of discernment." Uttar, 62 (41) 63.

But when addressing a meeting of Brahmins, religious teachers and the people of Avadh soon after, Rama makes a lengthy speech [1] in which the new attitude we have referred to is still more emphatically apparent, and men are justified by faith and sanctified by grace :

"The sacred books say it is great good fortune to be born in the form of a man. That is a condition which the gods find it difficult to reach. It is in that condition that one can realise oneself. It is the gateway of salvation. . . . A human body is not obtained in order that we may enjoy the fruits of sense. These fruits yield heaven for a very little while. But the result in the end is pain. No one ever speaks well of such a person. He gathers peppercorns and loses the best of precious stones. His life, which cannot be destroyed, continues to wander in the womb of the 8,400,000 births, revolving for ever at the will of Maya, surrounded by Time, Karma, his natural disposition and the three qualities. But some time or other God (*ish*) takes mercy on him and, without any reason except affection, gives him a man's body. And this human body is the boat by which he may cross the ocean of existence. With my grace as the favouring wind . . . he finds easily the means of

[1] See pp. 158–160, where the speech is given in full. Here we give quotations only.

transport which otherwise would be difficult to obtain. The man, then, who finds the means of transport in this fashion and fails to cross life's ocean is an ungrateful fool. . . . It is an easy and pleasant path, the path of devotion to me. . . . The path of knowledge is very difficult to traverse. The obstacles are numerous. The means of accomplishment are severe. And when a man has endured many afflictions, what does he obtain ? The man who is without *devotion* is not loved by me. The path of devotion is free. It is a mine of every happiness. . . . Tell me, what are the hardships that are connected with the path of devotion ? Profound meditation, sacrifices, the repetition of prayers, asceticism, fasting, none of them are necessary. What is required is a sincere disposition, a mind devoid of guile, always content with whatever happens. In love with my name, which is a home of all the virtues, free from selfishness, arrogance and delusion (*moh*), the happiness of such a man as I have described is the sum of supreme felicity." Uttar, 64 (43) 65.

Here there is not only the linking up of morals and religion, which is so frequent and beautiful a trait in the teaching of the poem, but such an enhancing of the power of faith in God, such an enlarging on the easiness of travel by the *bhakti marg*, that those who have trodden either the *path of knowledge* or the *path of works*—religious observances, fasting and prayer—may well hide their diminished heads. They are not required. And if we go back a few pages we shall find the same idea expressed in the hymn which the Vedas sing in praise of Rama. Like others, they are impressed by the power of Rama's fearful Maya. But far beyond the power of his Maya is the power of *bhakti.*

"Hail, merciful Lord, we worship you along with your Shakti. Gods, demons, serpents, men and every living thing are all in the grip of your fearful *maya*.[1] Night and day they wander exhausted in the path of existence, sated with Time, karma, and the three qualities. . . . Oh Rama, able to destroy fear and sorrow, protect us, we pray. Those who, intoxicated with pride of knowledge, treat with dishonour your world-conquering devotion, may obtain a rank greater than that which the gods find it difficult to secure ; nevertheless we have seen them fail. On the other hand, those who repeat your name cross the ocean of existence without any difficulty. . . . Those who meditate on Brahm, the unborn, the one without a second (*advaita*), accessible only by inference, beyond understanding, let them talk of what they know, oh Lord ; but we shall always sing the glory of your incarnation." [2] Uttar, 28 (13) 27.

There now remain to be considered those references to Maya which are to be found in the second half of the Uttar Kand. As has been said in the tenth chapter, the poet makes the inspired crow his mouthpiece and addresses himself in a very real and sometimes a very novel fashion to a comparison and a reconciliation, if that be possible, of the rival conceptions of Maya and *bhakti*.[3] There are three passages in particular which claim our attention. Two of these have been already given at length in the chapter referred to. But following our practice, the references to Maya are set forth once more.

[1] The word *vishan*, which is translated as fearful, may also mean uneven, bad, wicked, hard to be comprehended. It is with a definite object, no doubt, that Tulsidas makes the *Vedas* disparage knowledge (*gyan*) in the interest of devotion (*bhakti*) ; the *gyan marg* as against *bhakti marg*. The third path is *karm marg*—the way of works or religious observances.

[2] See the passage in greater fullness at pp. 153–155.

[3] The word Maya appears at least 150 times throughout the poem. In the latter half of the Uttar Kand it appears almost 50 times.

(1) The first deals with the bewilderment which took possession of Garud when he saw Rama made captive in the demon's bonds, and describes his subsequent interview with the crow. In his perplexity Garud said :

> "I have heard that the all-pervading, passionless Brahm, beyond the influence of Maya and delusion (*moh*), has descended to the earth, but I see nothing of his glory. By the repeating of his name, men escape from the bonds of existence. Can this Rama be he, when a base-born demon binds him in serpent coils ?" Uttar, 80 (58) 81.[1]

Garud first appealed to Narad, Brahma and Shiva, and they observed in turn :

> "Rama's Maya is very powerful. That which time after time has made me dance, has spread itself over you. The great delusion (*moh*) has sprung up in your mind."[2] Uttar, 81 (59) 82.
>
> "Poets and learned pandits come under Maya's power. The power of Hari's Maya cannot be measured. It has often made me dance." Uttar, 82 (60) 83.
>
> "The Lord's Maya is very powerful. Who is so full of knowledge that delusion (*moh*) does not touch him ? The vehicle of Vishnu, for him Maya was too strong. No wonder sinners are deluded. It deludes Shiva and the Creator. What then are others ? Helpless and weak ! Knowing that this is so, seers worship Bhagwan, who is the Lord of Maya." Uttar, 85 (62) 85.

But when Garud, the vehicle of Vishnu, arrived at the crow's dwelling-place :

> "his Maya, delusion (*moh*) and anxiety all disappeared." Uttar, 86 (63) 87.

[1] See p. 163.

[2] "Time after time, he who is supremely wise (Narad), declared the power of Hari's Maya." Uttar 82 (60) 83.

This statement accords with what we read earlier :

> " The virtues and vices, in their various forms fashioned by Maya, along with delusion, love and other errors of judgment which envelop the whole world, never go near that mountain." Uttar, 79 (57) 80.

As for the crow, he refused to believe that Garud had been really bewildered :

> " You had no doubt, delusion, Maya. In sending you under the pretence of being deluded, Raghupati did me a kindness." Uttar, 96 (69) 98.

But despite this statement, he proceeds to declare that Maya has blinded every one, including Brahma and Shiva, and asks :

> " Who is there in the world whom Maya has not pervaded ? There is no one so strong but desire lays hold of him, even as the weevil worm does with wood. The desire for a son, for wealth, for a woman, whose understanding have not these three soiled ? They are all Maya's followers. Her power is unmeasured. Who can describe it ? When Shiva and Brahma see it, they are afraid. What need to take account of others ? The mighty army of Maya pervades the world. Her generals are lust and other kindred evils. Her warriors are pride, hypocrisy and heresy. She is the servant of Raghubir, and though we recognise her to be false, yet there is no escape without the mercy of Rama. Maya causes all the world to dance. Her doings none can comprehend. By the play of the Lord's eyebrows she dances like an actress with all her company." Uttar, 97 (70) 100.

This is the utterance to which Sir George Grierson particularly refers when he finds so close a parallel to the Christian Tempter in the language of Tulsidas. And it is certainly not unreasonable to imagine that in the course of his wanderings, the poet may have forgathered with some Mohammedan Maulvi or Jesuit priest, and learned from them to identify Maya and her mighty army with the Devil and his angels. But whatever the influence of Christianity on the Bhakti movement as a whole may have been, we can find a closer parallel, not only to the Christian Tempter but also to the Gnostic Demiurge, much nearer home in the *Bijak* of Kabir.[1] According to Kabir, the Supreme God is not the Creator of the universe. It was the handiwork of Niranjan, whom God brought into existence and provided with a wife, whose name was Maya. Of Maya and her evil influence, Kabir has more to say than even Tulsidas. She is the old witch, the temptress, the great bandit, who has taken the whole world captive. She has decked herself with delusion.

> " She drew after her Shiva and Brahma, and lures away all others with her. On one side stand gods, men and saints ; on the other side she alone. Her glance fell on them, she spared none. She set one seal on all and in her veil enmeshed them." [2]

Whether he was indebted to Kabir or not for this new attitude to Maya, it is unquestionable that in the extract we have given Tulsidas looks at Maya from a fresh point of view. He sets her apart. She is no longer Rama's primal energy who accompanies him from heaven, his Maya, his *param shakti*, who becomes incarnate at the same time as he does. We have seen how she was often thought of as a more or less magical force which he was

[1] It will be remembered that Kabir was one of Ramanand's disciples and lived one hundred years before Tulsidas.

[2] See Kabir's *Bijak*, p. 175, translated by Rev. Ahmad Shah (Hamirpur, 1917), who says, " Maya leads the whole world astray in error, and salvation from the ocean of existence, the endless cycle of birth and rebirth, is impossible, except by the knowledge of the One and devotion to Him alone " (p. 36).

able to exercise and to withdraw at will. We have seen, too, that gods, demons and men possessed similar powers, which are spoken of as Maya. But here, as we say, is something new. Maya is spoken of as a mysterious and awful instrument of evil. She stands at the head of an army of vices who wage war on the souls of men. And yet it must not be forgotten that there is the other element also—the element which, even when he is carried away with his new idea, the poet will not allow himself to forget. Because however great and evil her influence may be, Maya continues to be recognised as the agent and servant of Raghubir.

On the face of it, this looks very inconsistent. But it is not so inconsistent as it seems. We have to remember the poet's cardinal doctrine. It was that the world, with everything it contains, both what moves and what does not move, is an expression of the Divine power and purpose. He will allow nothing to exist that is beyond their grasp. And because he believed that, it was inevitable he should say that Rama was Maya's lord. Nevertheless he was anxious in the interests of morality to bring home the fact that sin and vice were not only abhorrent and real, but that God was not to blame if they hampered and stained the soul. And when he does so, he is shedding his pantheistic conceptions for the time at least, and refuses to think that both virtue and vice are to be traced back to God. Rama himself is made to say :

> " And yet when men do not secure salvation and go to the other world and there suffer torment, beating their heads, they falsely lay the blame on Time, Karma and God (*ishwar*)." [1] Uttar, 64 (43) 65.

[1] The chapter on " Kal, Karma, Vidhi " must not, however, be forgotten, and the way in which Rama himself there put the blame on them.

An opinion with which the crow agrees when he tells the king of birds :

> " Stupid and unlucky persons in the power of Maya and with a curtain over their minds, in their foolish obstinacy raise doubts and attribute their own ignorance to Rama." Uttar, 103 (73) 107.

Sin, then, is something which ought not to be. It is contrary to the will of God. Had Tulsidas been a pantheist really at heart, he would not have worried about sin. But he believes in the personality of God.

> " The religion of Nirgun Brahm was not agreeable to me. Love for Sagun Brahm had a greater hold on my heart." Uttar, 170 (107) 185.

And though with certain aspects of his mind he sometimes approaches perilously near the same opinion, he neverthless refuses to accept the statement of the rishi :

> " Between Him and you there is no difference, like water and the wave." Uttar, 170 (107) 185.

And asks :

> " How can a soul in the grip of Maya be the same as God (*ish*) ? " Uttar, 172 (108) 186.

One would therefore be inclined to hold that in this great passage Tulsidas is doing something more than using language that suggests comparison with a Gnostic Demiurge and the Christian Tempter. His belief in a personal God and his love for righteousness have brought him face to face with the problem of evil. He has not given us a solution. Nobody has. But he knows that the problem would be darker if he lost his faith in God and in the beauty of holiness.

(2) The second passage is the crow's account of his experiences with Rama during his childhood in Avadh. Some of the statements regarding Maya are in the conventional

style. Others proclaim the need and the power of Devotion :

> "Maya enveloped me by the contrivance of Raghupati. But the Maya caused me no pain. Souls of every kind are in the grip of Maya. If all were of the same degree of knowledge, what would be the difference between God (*ishwar*) and the soul ? The soul in his pride is in the grip of Maya ; Maya, the storehouse of the qualities, is in the grip of God (*ish*). The soul is in the power of another. Bhagwan is free. Souls are manifold. The husband of Lakshmi is one. Though the distinctions made by Maya are unreal, without Hari's help your countless efforts will not avail." Uttar, 110 (77) 114.

When he jumped down Rama's throat the crow saw everywhere

> "the merciful Bhagwan, the lord of Maya." 119 (81) 122.

And when he came out of it again,

> "Rama, seeing his perplexity, restrained the power of his Maya."

But when the crow asked as a boon that his heart might be filled with devotion to Rama, he was promised that he would obtain not that boon alone. It would be followed by others, because Devotion is the mine of every happiness :

> "Sages cannot secure it, though they make a million attempts, repeating prayers, practising asceticism and giving their bodies to be burned. Every good quality will dwell in your heart—devotion, knowledge, wisdom, self-control. You will know every secret. And in the accomplishment of it, by my grace there will be no pain. The errors produced by Maya will not pervade you." Uttar, 125 (84) 128.

In a subsequent exposition of his doctrine (*siddhant*), Rama said :

> " My Maya is the cause of the world, living creatures of every kind, both what moves and what does not move. They are all dear to me ; they are all created by me."

But he has a special place in his heart for those who are devoted to him :

> " It is the truth. No one is so dear to me as my own servants. If the Creator were lacking in devotion, of all creatures he would be unloved by me ; whereas the very lowest soul, if he have *bhakti*, is very much loved indeed." Uttar, 127 (85) 130.

This statement is confirmed by the crow's summing up of his own religious experience, very beautifully expressed :

> " Maya has never enveloped me since Rama made me his own.[1] And I tell you, oh king of birds, from my own experience, without the worship of Hari your trouble will not depart. Without Rama's grace, you will not understand his power ; without understanding his power, there will be no faith (*pratiti*). Without faith, there is no love (*priti*). Without love, devotion (*bhakti*) is not steadfast. It is like oil in water." Uttar, 129 (87) 132.

(3) The third and final passage to which reference must be made did not find a place in the chapter dealing with the crow's philosophy. It is of peculiar interest and forms a suitable close to our discussion of the poet's teaching. And for the reason that it brings together not only *Maya* and *Bhakti*, but introduces *Gyan* (knowledge) also, and when it does so, it gives the most elaborate assertion which Tulsidas makes throughout his poem of the superiority

[1] In Uttar 127 (85) 129, the promise was also given—" The errors produced by Maya will not pervade you."

of Devotion to Knowledge: *bhakti-marg* as against *gyan-marg*. It is his final and, as he must have felt, his most convincing proof. And yet by his recognition of knowledge as a valuable discipline, he probably seeks to conciliate opponents. Indeed, at times he makes concessions to the doctrine of monism, not easy to reconcile with the retort which the crow gave to the rishi when he somewhat contemptuously asked:

> "How can a soul in the grip of Maya, cut off from others and stupid, be the same as God?" Uttar, 172 (108) 186.

Indeed, it was the crow's account of his argument with the rishi which provoked the curiosity of Garud and led to the important announcement which we shall now quote:

> "'There is one thing I wish to ask, oh sea of compassion, my lord, tell me and explain. Saints, sages, Vedas and Puranas say nothing is so difficult to attain as *gyan* (knowledge). So the sage told you.[1] But you did not honour it as you honour devotion. Between knowledge and devotion, what is the distinction?' The well-disposed crow was pleased to hear this question of the king of birds and graciously replied: 'Between devotion and knowledge there is no difference. Both dispel the pains which spring from existence. Sages say there is some distinction. But listen with attention to what I say. Knowledge, asceticism, profound meditation and discernment, these are all masculine. The male in every way possesses dignity and strength. The female is naturally weak and stupid. It is only a man

[1] At first the rishi, being a follower of *advaita*, spoke in praise of Knowledge. Eventually he is represented as changing his attitude and singing the praises of Hari and faith.

free from passion and strong-minded who is able to give up women, not a sensualist in the power of worldly objects and hostile to the feet of Raghubir. Even sages, learned and treasure-houses of wisdom, become agitated when they see a woman's fawn-like eyes and moon-like face. Woman's Maya is manifest to all. I am not here expressing any biased opinion. I merely declare the teaching of the Vedas, Puranas and saints. A woman is not infatuated (*moh*) by a woman's form; this never happens. But listen. Maya and Bhakti are both feminine, as every one knows. Again Bhakti is beloved by Raghubir, while he looks on Maya as only a dancing girl. Raghuraya is favourable to Bhakti, and in consequence Maya fears her greatly. Rama's Bhakti! There is no one like her. She is without limit. He in whose heart she dwells is blessed for ever. Seeing her, Maya is stricken with awe and can do nothing of her own power. Those sages who are specially wise, as they reflect on this, recognise that Bhakti is the treasure-house of all happiness. This mystery of Raghunath no one will quickly comprehend. He who by Raghupati's mercy does understand it will never, even in a dream, be the victim of delusion (*moh*). Listen now to the difference between *gyan* and *bhakti*. For those who listen, the result is an unbroken love for Rama's feet. Listen, my son, to this untellable story. It may be conceived but it cannot be told. The soul is a part of God (*ishwar ansh*), indestructible, intelligent, pure, by nature an accumulation of joy. But it comes under the power of Maya and is caught like a parrot or a monkey. The foolish soul is tied with a knot, and though it is an unreal knot, release is difficult. Since the soul has become involved in worldly objects, the knot is not loosened and there is no happiness. The Vedas and Puranas have proposed many expedients, but

> there is no escape. It becomes more and more entangled. The soul is filled with the darkness of delusion (*moh*), and it cannot see in what way the knot is to be unloosed. When God (*ish*) causes such a combination, it is likely there will be no release.' " Uttar, 177 (111) 192.

The poet then proceeds in parabolic language to picture the efforts of the soul to secure release :

> " If, by the mercy of Hari, sincere piety comes like a cow and dwells in the heart, then the prayers, penances, fasts and the innumerable religious rites and observances which the Vedas prescribe as the correct rule of conduct are the green grass on which the cow grazes." 181 (113) 197.

With the help of her calf which is love, the heel-rope which is abstinence, the milk bowl which is faith (*bishwas*) and the cowherd who is a mind without guile, the milk of true religion is at last obtained. It is set to boil on the fire of continence, then the air of patience cools it, while the rennet of steadfastness turns it into curds. Contentment is the maid who churns it. Discernment is the vessel in which it is churned. Self-restraint is the churning pole. Truth and good works the string. As a result there is procured the pure, spotless, excellent butter of asceticism.

The poet, so far, has spoken of the heart or *hriday*, in which the cow of piety comes to graze. He now refers to it as intelligence or *buddhi*, and tells us how, after lighting the fire of abstract meditation (*yog*) and bringing the coals of good and evil actions, Intelligence allows the butter of Knowledge (*gyan*) to cool, while the dirt of self-seeking (*mamta*) is burned. Having thus secured a perfectly clean butter, Intelligence pours it into the lamp of the soul (*chit*) and places the lamp on the stand of equanimity. From the cotton plant (*kapas*) of the three conditions and the three qualities, it produces the cotton of the fourth condition (*turiya*) and from this prepares a wick.[1] 182 (114) 198.

"In this way there is lighted a lamp full of splendour replete with knowledge (*gyan*), in which, when they approach it, all the grasshoppers of pride and other vices are consumed. (The conviction that) *I am He*; existence, indivisible, that is the lamp's intensely burning flame. The joy which springs from this experience of the spirit (*atma*) is manifest. The distinctions and errors, rooted in existence, are destroyed. Delusion (*moh*) and the other unnumbered hosts of darkness are wiped out. It is thus that Intelligence finds a light, and sitting in the house of the heart (*ur*) seeks to disentangle the knot. Should any one discover how to untie the knot, then that soul has achieved his purpose. But when Maya sees the soul loosening the knot, it causes many difficulties and gives orders to many and varied agents. They come and expose Intelligence to greedy desire. By force, by fraud, by scheming, they get near the lamp and blow it out. But if Intelligence is very wise, he knows they are not friendly and does not give them a glance even. If no harm result to Intelligence from these impediments, then the gods (*sur*) tyrannise over him. The Senses are so many doors and windows. At each there sits a god, keeping watch. When they see a sensual breeze beginning to blow, in sheer perversity they open the doors. Should the breeze get into the house of the heart, the candle of *gyan* (knowledge) is extinguished. With the light extinguished,

[1] We are already acquainted with the three qualities, *sattva, rajas, tamas*. But the three conditions are new. According to the Vedanta philosophy they are the three conditions of the soul; waking, dreaming, and profound, dreamless sleep. The fourth condition (*turiya*) is, says Monier Williams, that state in which the soul has become one with Brahm, the universal spirit.

the knot cannot be untied. Intelligence has been confounded by the wind of sensuality. The senses and the gods do not approve of Knowledge. They are always fond of sensual pleasure. The wind of sensuality having made Intelligence a fool, who can again light the lamp? The soul has once more to endure the many and varied pains of transmigration. Oh, Garud, Hari's Maya is very difficult to traverse. It cannot be crossed. Knowledge is difficult to describe, difficult to understand, difficult to acquire. If by a happy chance true knowledge is acquired, many hindrances still remain. The path of knowledge is like the edge of a sword. For those who fall upon it, there is no salvation. On the other hand, they who do achieve their purpose and for whom the path is freed from obstruction, obtain the highest state, release from transmigration. But release from transmigration (*kaiwalya*), the highest state, is very difficult to obtain, as saints, Puranas, Vedas and other Scriptures declare." 184 (114) 201.

And now comes the contrast, about which the poet wishes there shall be no mistake :

"But by the worship of Rama, salvation (*mukti*) comes without asking for it, as it were by chance. As water cannot rest without support, however numerous your efforts, so the happiness of salvation (*moksh*) cannot be got apart from devotion to Hari. Wise devotees of Hari, as they thus reflect, speak disrespectfully of release from the body (*mukti*) and are desirous of *bhakti*. By the practice of *bhakti* without effort and toil, Ignorance (*avidya*), which is the cause of mundane existence, is destroyed.[1] You eat for the sake of filling the stomach,

[1] *Sansar,* often rendered *world,* means a passing through a succession of states, the circuit of mundane existence, transmigration. See Monier Williams's *Sanskrit Dictionary,* p. 1040.

and the heat of the stomach digests the food. Likewise devotion to Hari is easy and gives satisfaction. Who will be such a fool as not to rejoice in it? Without the feeling, *I am the servant and Rama is worthy of devotion*, the sea of existence cannot be crossed. Reckon this to be the established truth (*siddhant*) [1] and worship Rama's lotus feet. He can make the wise foolish and the foolish wise. Such power belongs to Raghubir. The soul that worships him is blessed." Uttar, 183 (115) 202.

The poet's attitude to Maya is one more illustration of the fact that he is an orthodox Hindu, profoundly influenced by the thoughts of those around him and by the literature of his country. Beginning with the *Rig-Veda* where "Indra by his magic powers (*maya*) goes about in many forms," [2] to the comparatively modern *Vishnu Purana* which tells of how Vishnu produced from his body an illusory form (*maya moh*), and speaks of Maya as the mother of the world,[3] that literature was accustomed to the use of *moh* and *maya*. Take, for instance, the *Bhagavadgita*, which contains the beginnings of the *bhakti* movement. It is true there are only five references to Maya. But on page after page of that short work we read how the soul suffers from delusion, how it is bewildered and beguiled. And the word that is employed is always *moh* or some of its compounds. With such precedents before him, and surrounded as he was by Shiva-worshipping Vedantins, it is not surprising that Tulsidas should have yielded to the prevailing atmosphere and made such a constant use of *advaita* phrases. It is not suggested that he accepted the

[1] *Siddhant*: the established line of reasoning or view of any question, the true logical conclusion, proved fact, established truth, axiom, dogma. Monier Williams, p. 1114.

[2] Griffith, *Hymns of Rig-Veda*, vi. 47, 18; and Hume, p. 105, quoted in *Brihad Aranyaka Upanishad*.

[3] See Wilson's translation of *Vishnu Purana*, vol. iii. p. 206; vol. v. p. 95.

interpretation which Shankara put upon those phrases. He believed too strongly in a God endowed "with all imaginable auspicious qualities," and in the personality of Rama, for such an inference to be possible. Nevertheless the tendency is there, and we cannot minimise it. The effort which Ramanuja made to show that the Upanishads could not be used to prove the theory of illusion, had apparently no influence on Tulsidas.[1] He has none of the zeal which the earlier advocates of *bhakti* displayed in confuting the doctrine of Maya. And as we have seen, he is to a large extent unconscious of the problem by which they were faced or of the danger to which their movement was exposed.

Nevertheless, one certain fact remains, and it is a fact which we must emphasise. However great Maya's influence may be, account for her origin as we please, she is, in the long run, compelled to yield to something greater, and that is *bhakti*. We may exalt her and say that she is Rama's *primal energy*, by means of which he creates, preserves and destroys the world. She may be his instrument for deceiving gods and men, or she may be identified with Sin. We may forget that she is Sita, Rama's bride, and reduce her to the status of a dancing girl. But whatever the part she plays, we are never allowed to forget that Rama is her lord. The poet's language is full of contradictions. Of one thing, however, he is never in any doubt. Rama is real, if all else is a dream. And that is Tulsidas's message to the world. It may be that he was wise in his generation. To the Western student, the philosophy of Ramanuja makes a stronger appeal. It seems to us that only on such

[1] That modern scholars also differ in their interpretation of the Upanishads is shown by the following: "Gough maintains, in my judgment, an erroneous position, *viz.*, that the Upanishads teach the pure Vedantism of Shankara." Hume, *The Thirteen Principal Upanishads*, p. 38.

a foundation is there room for the exercise of love and piety in a world of reality.[1] But though the poet has surrendered much that his predecessors had gained by trying to achieve a compromise between theism and monism, the very fact that he does so, has enabled him to win and keep the ear of India. With one aspect of his mind he thinks and speaks in terms of the *advaita*; with the other he thinks and speaks of a personal God, who loves him and whom he loves.

And it is on that note we would wish to close our examination of the poet's contribution to the religious thought and life of India. He believes with all his heart and soul that God became incarnate to render a service to the world. Such a belief must inevitably produce feelings of gratitude in those for whose sake the service is rendered. This is a conviction which took possession of India at an early stage in its religious history. The earlier incarnations, the fish, the boar, the tortoise, were of a cosmological character. The appeal to the individual was largely in abeyance. The personal element first showed itself in the manifestation of the man-lion, when Vishnu appeared to save his devotee Prahlad, and again, though in destructive fashion, in Rama of the Axe and Buddha. But Vishnu's incarnations as Krishna and Rama introduced a new element. In both these cases we find the god not only taking human form, but living among men, sharing their sorrows and their joys, inviting their love and rewarding their devotion. This is a necessary element in all true religion. Present in Hinduism from the time of the *Bhagavadgita*, it has grown and flourished in congenial soil. It has found its highest and most spiritual expression in the work of Tulsidas. His hero is the worthiest figure in all Indian literature.

Some reference should be made to the claim that has been put forward that for much that is valuable in its teaching, the *bhakti* movement is indebted to Christianity.

[1] Bhandarkar, *op. cit.* p. 51.

It is impossible not to be impressed by passages such as the one which appears in the *Mahabharata*, describing Narad's visit to the white island, where he saw men possessing the lustre of the moon, and was told that the great being worshipped there could only be seen by those devoted to him.[1] Nor can we ignore the fact that it was in South India, where the Nestorians had planted a vigorous church in the early centuries of the Christian Era, the doctrine of *bhakti* first secured a philosophic defence and was established on a secure basis.

It is true that there are many ideas common to both Christianity and *bhakti*. They are at one in making much of God's grace and minimising the value of works. They both tell us that love is the fulfilling of the law. They both proclaim that a pure heart is where God delights to dwell. And they both promise immortal life, not in God but with God. But while we recognise such similarities, that does not necessarily mean that these similarities are due to borrowing from Christian sources. Inspiration there very probably was, but it is difficult to deny that India had the beginnings of a *bhakti* movement of her own and believed in *avatars* before the dawn of the Christian Era.[2]

[1] See the Shanti Parva., chaps. cccxxxvii., cccxl. of the *Mahabharata*. Bhandarkar (Vaishnavism, etc.) quotes the passage, pp. 4–8. See also my *Summary of the Mahabharata*, pp. 177–180. For an interesting account of the *bhakti marg* and the influence of Christianity, see Grierson's article in *E.R.E.*, vol. ii. p. 539. Bhandarkar recognises that the Krishna birth stories were borrowed. Hopkins's chapter, "Christ in India," in *India, Old and New*, should also be referred to, especially the parallels he finds between the Gospel of John and the *Bhagavadgita*. But see Monier Williams's *Indian Wisdom*, Muir's *Metrical Translations from Sanskrit Writers*, and Barth's *Religions of India*.

[2] This is on the assumption that those portions of the *Bhagavadgita*, which teach devotion to a personal God in the form of an *avatar*, were written before the influence of Christianity could spread to India. For the conflict of opinion as to the date and structure of the poem, consult Garbe on the "Bhagavadgita" in *E.R.E.*, and his reference to the contrary views of Holtzmann.

When that is so, may we not hold, despite the many startling coincidences, that God has spoken to both East and West in language that is akin. The hearts of men are everywhere very much the same, and it is natural, when they believe in an incarnate God towards whom they entertain feelings of love and devotion, that these feelings should be expressed in words and acts that will remind us of what was said and done in other lands.

INDEX

Note on the Pronunciation of Hindi Words.

In Hindi, short *ă* has the sound of *a* in *rural*; long *ā* has the sound of *a* in *father*; short *ă* at the end of a word is not sounded; short *ĭ* has the sound of *i* in *fill*; long *ī* has the sound of *i* in *police*; short *ŭ* has the sound of *u* in *pull*; long *ū* has the sound of *oo* in *tool*; the vowel *o* corresponds to *o* in *go*, it never has the sound of the English *o* in *top*.